WINDOWS® 8
QuickSteps®

Marty Matthews

New York Chicago San Francisco
Lisbon London Madrid Mexico City
Milan New Delhi San Juan
Seoul Singapore Sydney Toronto

*The **McGraw·Hill** Companies*

Cataloging-in-Publication Data is on file with the
Library of Congress

Windows® 8 QuickSteps®

1234567890   QVR QVR   1098765432

ISBN   978-0-07-179846-3
MHID   0-07-179846-4

SPONSORING EDITOR / Roger Stewart

EDITORIAL SUPERVISOR / Jody McKenzie

PROJECT MANAGER / Vastavikta Sharma, Cenveo Publisher Services

ACQUISITIONS COORDINATOR / Ryan Willard

TECHNICAL EDITOR / John Cronan

COPY EDITOR / Lisa McCoy

PROOFREADER / Paul Tyler

INDEXER / Valerie Haynes Perry

PRODUCTION SUPERVISOR / Jean Bodeaux

COMPOSITION / Cenveo Publisher Services

ILLUSTRATION / Cenveo Publisher Services and Erin Johnson

ART DIRECTOR, COVER / Jeff Weeks

COVER DESIGNER / Pattie Lee

SERIES CREATORS / Marty and Carole Matthews

SERIES DESIGN / Mary McKeon

*To **Carole** and **Michael**,*
Thanks for being there, I love you, and appreciate your being in my life.

About the Author

Marty Matthews' experience with computers extends from some of the early mainframe computers to the most recent personal computers, tablets, and smartphones. He has been a programmer, systems analyst, computer service company vice president, and software company president. He has firsthand knowledge of how to program and use a computer, as well as how to use what a computer can do.

Marty also has a knack for explaining how to use computers in such a way that makes it easy to understand. For 28 years Marty and his wife Carole have authored, co-authored, or been responsible for the production of more than 100 computing-related books, including ones on desktop publishing, web publishing, Microsoft Office, and Microsoft operating systems—from MS-DOS through Windows 8. Recent books published by McGraw-Hill include *Windows 7 QuickSteps, Windows 7 for Seniors QuickSteps,* and *Computing for Seniors QuickSteps.*

Marty and Carole live on an island in Puget Sound in Washington state.

About the Technical Editor

John Cronan has more than 30 years of computer experience and has been writing and editing computer-related books for 18 years. His recent books include *eBay QuickSteps Second Edition, Dynamic Web Programming: A Beginner's Guide, Microsoft Office Excel 2010 QuickSteps,* and *Microsoft Office Access 2010 QuickSteps.* John and Faye (and cat Little Buddy) reside in Everett, Washington.

Contents at a Glance

Contents

1

2

5

6

10

Acknowledgments

This book is a team effort of truly talented people who I have worked with for many years and in the process we have become good friends. This team includes: **John Cronan**, technical editor; **Lisa McCoy**, copy editor; **Paul Tyler**, proofreader, **Valerie Perry**, indexer; **Ryan Willard**, acquisitions coordinator; **Vastavikta Sharma**, project manager; **Jody McKenzie**, editorial supervisor; and **Roger Stewart**, editorial director. A lot of effort and a part of themselves have gone into this book. It wouldn't be the book it is without all of them. Thanks, John, Lisa, Paul, Valerie, Ryan, Vastavikta, Jody, and Roger!

Introduction

QuickSteps books are recipe books for computer users. They answer the question "How do I…" by providing a quick set of steps to accomplish the most common tasks with a particular operating system or application.

The sets of steps ("QuickSteps") are the central focus of the book and show how to quickly perform the many functions and tasks needed to use Windows 8. Notes, Tips, and Cautions augment the steps, and are presented next to the text they relate to. The introductions are minimal, and other narrative is kept brief. Numerous full-color illustrations and figures, many with callouts, support the steps.

QuickSteps books are organized by function and the tasks needed to perform that function. Each major function is a chapter. Each task contains the steps needed to accomplish it, along with the relevant Notes, Tips, Cautions, and screenshots. You can easily find the tasks you want to perform through

- The table of contents, which lists the functional areas (chapters) and tasks in the order they are presented

- A QuickSteps list of tasks on the opening page of each chapter

- The index, which provides an alphabetical list of the terms that are used to describe the functions and tasks

- Color-coded tabs for each chapter or functional area, with an index to the tabs in the Contents at a Glance (just before the table of contents)

Conventions Used in This Book

Windows 8 QuickSteps uses several conventions designed to make the book easier for you to follow. Among these are

- **Bold type** is used for words or objects on the screen that you are to do something with, like "…select **File Explorer**, and open **Charms**."

- *Italic type* is used for a word or phrase that is being defined or otherwise deserves special emphasis.

- <u>Underlined type</u> is used for text that you are to type from the keyboard.

- SMALL CAPITAL LETTERS are used for keys on the keyboard, such as ENTER and SHIFT.

- When you are expected to enter a command, you are told to press the key(s). If you are to enter text or numbers, you are told to type them.

With the advent of touch and the remaining heavy dependence on the mouse and keyboard, it is important to understand how we have elected to describe the commands that use these three tools. Chapter 1, with its illustrations and tables, spends much of the chapter explaining this. Several of the tables are repeated at the end of the book for a quick reference.

Chapter 1

Stepping into Windows 8

Windows 8 is the latest version of the Windows operating system from Microsoft and represents a dramatic change from earlier versions. An *operating system* performs *the* central role in managing what a computer does and how it is done. An operating system provides the interface between you and the computer hardware: It lets you open and save a file, print a document, connect to the Internet, or transfer information over a local area network (LAN) and a great many other tasks without you knowing anything about how the hardware works.

This chapter explains how to start Windows 8; how to use the screen, including a touch screen, a mouse, windows, menus, and dialog boxes; and how to shut it down and get help.

In this chapter you may feel like you are trying to get a drink from a fire hose. There is a lot of detailed information that is required to cover the three methods of using Windows 8: with touch, with a mouse, and with a keyboard. Absorb what you can, but don't worry about remembering every keyboard shortcut or every possible way to move your fingers on a touch screen. Even after 20 years of using Windows and a year of using Windows 8, I can't remember it all. For that reason I have created three tables later in this chapter (Tables 1-2, 1-3, and 1-4). These have been repeated at the end of the book and can be removed. They are also available for download from our website QuickStepBooks.com/Windows8Cheats. Refer to these tables often as you are reading this book and using Windows 8 on your own.

START AND USE WINDOWS

Windows 8 can be used in three ways:

- **Touch** If you have a multi-touch display screen, you can use one or more fingers on the screen. See "Use Touch" later in this chapter.
- **Mouse** If you have a mouse, you can use it. See "Use a Mouse" later in this chapter.
- **Keyboard** If you have a keyboard, it can be used. See "Use the Keyboard" later in this chapter.

In many cases you will have a choice of two or more of these methods. In this chapter we'll explain each of the methods in depth and define words (*italicized*) that will be used throughout the rest of the book, which allows you to choose the method you want to use in a particular case. In this chapter and the beginning page of the next couple of chapters we'll reinforce this by further describing the options that are available.

Getting into and using Windows 8 is not that different from previous versions of Windows, except that there is now a separate Lock screen and you may be able to use touch.

▷▷ Start and Log On to Windows 8

To start Windows, simply turn on the computer. Press its power button or push the on/off switch.

When you turn on the computer you should see the opening Lock screen similar to the one shown next, although it may be customized by the computer manufacturer and have a different background.

From the Lock screen you need to display the Log On screen where you can enter a password. To do that:

1. Display the Log On screen with:

   - **Touch** Move your finger (*swipe*) up from the bottom of the screen.
   - **Mouse** Point on the bottom border of the screen, and press and hold the left mouse button while moving the mouse up toward the top (*drag*).
   - **Keyboard** Press SHIFT or SPACE or almost any other key.

2. If you see two or more users on the screen:

   - **Touch** Touch or *tap* your name, picture, or icon, or that of the default user.
   - **Mouse** Point at and press the left mouse button or *click* the name, picture, or icon you want.
   - **Keyboard** Press TAB one or more times to *select* the name, picture, or icon you want, and press ENTER.

3. Enter your password:

   - **Touch** Tap the text box where a password needs to be entered to bring up the touch keyboard, tap the keys needed for your password, and tap ENTER.
   - **Keyboard** Type your password and press ENTER.
   - **Mouse** Click the **Ease Of Access** icon in the lower-left corner of the screen, click **On-Screen Keyboard**, and click the keys needed for the password. (The on-screen keyboard is different from the touch keyboard, but you can also use the mouse with the touch keyboard after you bring it up with touch. See "Use the Touch Keyboard" later in this chapter.)

Windows will log you on to the system and open the Start screen, like this:

If someone else, such as a system administrator, installed Windows 8 on your computer, he or she should have given you a password. If you purchased a computer with Windows 8 installed on it or you upgraded to Windows 8, you will be asked to enter a new user name and password. As you will see in Chapter 8, you can change passwords and add users if you wish.

Note If you are logging on to a domain (see Chapter 9), you will be asked to press **CTRL+ALT+DEL** at the same time. Do so; then enter your user name and password, and press **ENTER** if needed.

📭 Use a Mouse

A *mouse* is any pointing device—including a trackball, stylus or digitizer pen, or a mouse—with two or more buttons. I assume you are using a two-button mouse. Moving the mouse moves the pointer on the screen.

You can control the mouse with either your left or right hand, in which case, the purpose of the buttons may be switched. (See Chapter 2 to switch the buttons.) This book assumes you are using your right hand to control the mouse and that the left mouse button is also called "*the* mouse button." The right button is always called the "right mouse button." If you switch the buttons, you must change your interpretation of these phrases.

> **Tip** As is generally true in the computing community, I will use the word "*app*" whenever I am talking about an application or program that can run on a computer. Also, when I use the word "*computer,*" I'm talking about any device, including desktop, laptop, notebook, netbook, tablet, or slate, that can run Windows 8. (Smartphones might eventually be included in this statement, but in the near term I don't see them running Windows 8 as described here. Apps do apply to the programs that run on smartphones.)

The actions of the mouse allow you to:

- **Highlight** an *object* (a button, an icon, a border, etc.) on the screen by pointing to it. *Point* at an object on the screen by moving the mouse until the tip of the pointer is on top of the object.

- **Select** an object on the desktop or start an app on the Start screen by clicking it. *Click* means to point at an object you want to select and quickly press and release the left mouse button.

- **Open** an object such as a folder, or start an app on the desktop by double-clicking it. *Double-click* means to point at an object you

want to open and press and release the mouse button twice in rapid succession.

- **Open** an object's *context menu*, which allows you to do things specific to the object, by right-clicking it. *Right-click* means to point at an object you want to open and quickly press and release the right mouse button.

- **Move** an object on the screen by dragging it. *Drag* means to point at an object you want to move, and then press and hold the mouse button while moving the mouse. You will drag the object as you move the mouse. When the object is where you want it, release the mouse button.

Mirror Touch

Windows 8 has added several new mouse moves to mirror what can be done with touch.

- **Switch to the Start screen** by moving the mouse to the lower-left corner of the screen while in the desktop or a Windows 8 style application (see discussions of both of these later in this chapter) and clicking the Start Screen icon, which will appear.

- **Switch to a recently opened window** by moving the mouse to the upper-left corner of the screen to display a thumbnail of the most recently opened window, given that one was recently opened, and clicking it to open that window.

- **Switch to other open windows** by moving the mouse to either the upper- or lower-left corners of the screen and then moving the mouse down or up to display all of the open windows, any of which can be clicked to be opened.

- **Open Charms** by moving the mouse to the lower-right or upper-right corner of the screen and then moving the mouse up or down to open the *Charms* pane; any of the Charms themselves can then be clicked to open windows or perform functions. See "Use Charms" later in this chapter.

> **Note** If you move the mouse to the upper- or lower-right corners without then moving it up or down and just point to the corners, you briefly get a "ghost" image of the Charms. After moving the pointer up or down, the "full" Charm pane appears, as well as the enlarged time and date box, similar to what is shown later in Figure 1-1.

Use Touch

Touch screens have been around for a number of years and supported by previous versions of Windows, but before Windows 8 there were relatively few users of them. Modern tablets and touch screens for desktop and laptop computers are changing that. Windows 8 and the most recent devices support *multi-touch* where five or more fingers can be sensed at

Table 1-1: Finger Movements for a Touch Screen

Description	Motion
Select an object on the screen or start an app on the Start screen by touching or *tapping* it once with a single finger, similar to clicking with a mouse.	
Open an object or start an app on the desktop by tapping it twice with a single finger, similar to double-clicking with a mouse.	
Move an object on the screen by holding a finger on an object while moving it in any direction, similar to dragging with the mouse.	
Open an object's context menu, which allows you to do things specific to the object in one of two ways, both having the same effect as right-clicking with the mouse: By holding a finger on the object (pressing down and holding a single finger on the object for a moment, waiting for a box to appear, and then releasing the finger), which works best on the desktop By swiping down (very briefly rest a finger on the object and then quickly move it down while maintaining contact with the object), which works best on the Start screen	
Scroll the screen, a window, or a pane by moving a finger up or down or left or right on the screen; a mouse needs to use a scroll bar or a wheel (see "Use a Window" later in this chapter).	
Zoom in (enlarge what is shown on the screen) by placing two fingers on the screen and spreading them apart; a mouse requires zoom controls that are not always present. (Think of this as spreading a tear in a piece of paper apart so you can see what is underneath.)	
Zoom out (reduce in size what is shown on the screen) by bringing two fingers together. (Think of this as gathering together an area so you can see more of what surrounds it.)	
Turn a page by flicking one finger in either direction.	
Open Windows and controls by swiping a finger from the frame around the screen on to the screen: From the right edge, this action opens the Charms pane (see "Use Charms" later in this chapter). From the left edge, this action opens other apps that have been previously started. From the bottom and top in Windows 8 style applications, this action opens controls and other features. See "Use Windows 8 style Windows" later in this chapter.	

one time. For the most part touch replaces what you can do with a mouse. The touch motions for the related mouse actions are shown in Table 1-1.

CAUTION! Do not use anything on a touch screen except a finger or possibly a stylus, if it came with the screen. Especially do not use a pencil or ballpoint pen.

Use the Keyboard

While a keyboard can obviously be used to enter text into the computer, it can also be used for many control purposes as an option to using touch or the mouse. This applies to the physical set of keys in a laptop or notebook computer, or the separate device used with a desktop computer. While there is a keyboard that can be displayed on a touch screen, it is primarily for entering text and has limited use in control for the obvious reason that other touch options are available for that. (See "Use the Touch Keyboard" next.)

The general control functions that can be performed with a physical keyboard include:

- **Select** an object on the desktop by repeatedly pressing **TAB** or one of the **ARROW** keys until the object is selected.
- **Open** a selected object or start an app by pressing **ENTER**.
- **Open** a selected object's context menu by pressing the CONTEXT MENU key on the lower right of the main section of most keyboards.

Some keys on a physical keyboard perform special control functions as shown in Table 1-2.

The **WINDOWS** key on the lower left of most keyboards, between **CTRL** and **ALT**, has taken on greater significance in Windows 8. Table 1-3 shows the **WINDOWS** key assignments.

Use the Touch Keyboard

If you are using a computer with a touch screen, you can bring a keyboard up on the screen that you can use with touch, as shown next.

There are three ways to bring up the touch keyboard:

- Tap in a text box or text area, such as the text box for entering a password.
- Tap the keyboard icon in the notification area in the lower right of the desktop.

Table 1-2: Special Control Keys

Key(s)	Description
ALT+F4	Close a window or an app
ALT+SHIFT+ARROW KEYS	Move the selected object on the screen in the direction of the arrow keys
CTRL+plus sign key (+)	Zoom in
CTRL+minus sign key (–)	Zoom out
CTRL+ALT+DEL	Open system options, including ones for shutting down

- Swipe in from the right of the screen to open Charms, tap **Settings**, tap **Keyboard**, and tap **Touch Keyboard And Handwriting Panel**.

The default keyboard that opens is primarily for typing alphabetic letters. If you need to type numbers or special characters, tap the **&123** key in the lower-left corner to bring up this keyboard.

You can get additional special characters by touching the brighter, right-pointing arrow in a circle. The above keyboards are normal or standard keyboards. If you touch the keyboard icon in the lower-right corner of the keyboard, you can select an alternative split keyboard or a handwriting tablet if you have a stylus available. The split keyboard has a key in the lower left, similar to the standard keyboard, to display special characters. The split keyboard also has a unique key, a vertical column of dots that allows you to select the size of the keys.

Table 1-3: Actions Taken with Various WINDOWS Key Combinations

Key(s)	Description
WINDOWS	Switches to the Start screen from the desktop and to the desktop from the Start screen once the desktop has been otherwise opened.
WINDOWS+ 1, 2...	Switches to the desktop and opens the first, second, etc., application on the taskbar.
WINDOWS+B	Switches to the desktop and selects the notification area.
WINDOWS+C	Opens Charms.
WINDOWS+D	Shows the desktop, hiding open windows.
WINDOWS+E	Switches to the desktop and opens File Explorer.
WINDOWS+F	Searches files.
WINDOWS+H	Opens the Share pane.
WINDOWS+I	Opens the Settings pane.
WINDOWS+K	Opens the Devices pane.
WINDOWS+L	Locks the computer and displays the Lock screen.
WINDOWS+M	Switches to the desktop and minimizes the current window.
WINDOWS+O	Turns a tablet's autorotate between portrait and landscape on or off.
WINDOWS+P	Opens the settings for a projector.
WINDOWS+Q	Searches apps.
WINDOWS+R	Switches to the desktop and opens Run.
WINDOWS+U	Switches to the desktop and opens the Ease of Access Center.
WINDOWS+W	Searches settings.
WINDOWS+X	Opens the System menu.
WINDOWS+Z	In a Windows 8 style window, displays the App bar.
WINDOWS+.	Snaps an app first to the right side of the screen and then to the left.
WINDOWS+TAB	Switches among apps.
WINDOWS+ HOME	Closes all but the selected window on the desktop. When pressed a second time it reopens all windows originally open.
WINDOWS+F1	Opens Windows Help.
WINDOWS+ PRT SCN	Saves an image of the screen to the Clipboard; **+ALT** saves just the open window.
WINDOWS+ UP ARROW	Maximizes the selected window. If this is followed by **WINDOWS+ DOWN ARROW** the window is restored to its original size.
WINDOWS+ DOWN ARROW	Minimizes the selected window, unless the window was originally maximized, in which case the window is restored to its original size.
WINDOWS+ LEFT ARROW	The selected window fills the left 50 percent of the desktop. If this is followed by **WINDOWS+RIGHT ARROW** the window is restored to its original size.
WINDOWS+ RIGHT ARROW	The selected window fills the right 50 percent of the desktop. If this is followed by **WINDOWS+LEFT ARROW** the window is restored to its original size.
WINDOWS+ SHIFT+ UP ARROW	The selected window fills the desktop vertically, but maintains its previous width. If this is followed by **WINDOWS+SHIFT+DOWN ARROW** the window is restored to its original size.

There is actually a second keyboard that can be displayed on the screen, called the On-Screen Keyboard, that is for use with a stylus or a mouse. You can open this keyboard by tapping or clicking the **Ease Of Access** icon in the lower left of the login screen and tapping or clicking **On-Screen Keyboard**.

 Tip The split keyboard can be helpful when holding a tablet, allowing you to use both thumbs to type, like texting on a cell phone.

Review Terms and Conventions

This book is meant for all Windows 8 users, including those who have touch, as well as those who have a mouse and keyboard. As a result, I will often use terminology that is not specific, allowing you to choose from among the three techniques. Table 1-4 shows the action terms I will use along with their context and how these terms should be implemented with a mouse, touch, or a keyboard. If you have the options, you can choose which you want to use.

Table 1-4: Implementing Common Terms with a Mouse, Touch, and a Keyboard

Action Term	With a Mouse	With Touch	With a Keyboard
Select an object on the desktop, in a window or dialog box, or on a menu	**Click** the object	**Tap** the object	Use **TAB** or the **ARROW KEYS** to highlight the object
Start an app in the Start screen	**Click** the tile	**Tap** the tile	Select the object and press **ENTER**
Open an object on the desktop such as a window or folder	**Double-click** the object	**Double-tap** the object	Select the object and press **ENTER**
Start an app on the desktop	**Double-click** the app	**Double-tap** the app	Select the object and press **ENTER**
Open an object's context menu	**Right-click** the object	**Touch** and hold for a moment, then release	Select the object and press the **CONTEXT-MENU** key
Open the app bar for an app	**Right-click** the app	**Swipe down** the app	Select the object and press the **CONTEXT-MENU** key
Move an object on the screen	**Drag** the object with the mouse	**Drag** the object with your finger	Select the object and press **ALT+SHIFT+ARROW KEYS**
Point on an object such as a title bar or border	Move the mouse so it is on the object	Move your finger so it is over the object but not touching it	Use **TAB** and **ARROW KEYS** to select the object
Switch to the desktop from the Start screen	**Click** the desktop tile	**Tap** the desktop tile	Press **WINDOWS+D**
Switch to the Start screen	**Point** to the lower-left corner of the screen and click	**Swipe** from the right edge and tap the **Start** icon	Press **WINDOWS**
Switch to another running app	**Point** to the upper-left corner, move down, and click the app	**Swipe** from the left edge until the app opens	Press **WINDOWS+TAB**
Open Charms	**Point** to the lower-right corner and move up	**Swipe** from the right	Press **WINDOWS+C**

Often in a list of steps there will be a number of them in succession. For example, to display the Ancestry document in the Ancestry folder on my computer, I could use (see Figures 1-5, 1-10, and 1-12 later in this chapter):

> "From the Start screen, switch to the desktop, start File Explorer, open **Libraries**, open **Documents**, open **My Documents**, open the **Ancestry** folder, and open the **Ancestry** document."

Using the mouse, this would be:

> "From the Start screen, click the desktop tile, click the **File Explorer** icon in the taskbar, click **Libraries**, double-click **Documents**, double-click **My Documents**, double-click the **Ancestry** folder, and double-click the **Ancestry** document."

Using touch this would be:

> "From the Start screen, tap the desktop tile, tap the **File Explorer** icon in the taskbar, tap **Libraries**, double-tap **Documents**, double-tap **My Documents**, double-tap the **Ancestry** folder, and double-tap the **Ancestry** document."

To remove the repetitive words and shorten this, I will use the vertical line, or "pipe," character to represent in this case a succession of "open." (The pipe character will mean repeat the last action term spelled out.)

> "From the Start screen, switch to the desktop, start **File Explorer**, open **Libraries** | **Documents** | **My Documents** | **Ancestry** folder | **Ancestry** document."

This assumes you know when "open" means "click" or "tap," and when it means "double-click" or "double-tap." This will become second nature after a while, but if you are unsure, click or tap once and if that doesn't work, double-click or double-tap.

 Tip Starting an app on the desktop itself requires a double-click or double-tap, unless the app is on the taskbar at the bottom of the screen, in which case, starting the app requires only a single click or tap.

Select a Windows View

There are two primary views in Windows 8, the *Windows 8 style* interface, which is new to Windows 8, and the *desktop,* which is similar to the desktop in previous versions of Windows and is used with all legacy applications and other functions.

Explore the Windows 8 Style Interface

The Windows 8 style interface uses the entire screen and hides all Windows controls behind the edges of the screen. The Windows 8 style interface is used with applications written for Windows 8 and with the Start screen that opens upon starting Windows 8. The concept behind the Windows 8 style is to give the maximum exposure and simplicity to what is being displayed on the screen and not have it crowded and confused with controls. Figure 1-1 shows this with the Start screen, first by itself (Figure 1-1a), as you see it when you first start Windows 8, and then in Figure 1-1b with the *screen edge controls* (or Charms) that

Figure 1-1a: The Windows 8 style interface is demonstrated here with the Start screen, first, by itself, as shown here.

can be brought in from the right side of the screen, as explained in "Use a Mouse" and "Use Touch" earlier in this chapter. See "Use Windows 8 Style Windows" later in this chapter.

Use the Start Screen

The Start screen, shown in Figure 1-1, which is new to Windows 8, replaces the Start menu in previous versions of Windows and provides the primary means of starting apps and opening system features. The Start screen displays *tiles* that represent apps or features that can be started or opened. The tiles, which are laid out horizontally over several screens, can be customized, as you will see in Chapter 2. To locate and start or open a tile:

- **Touch** Move your finger across the screen from right to left to display the tile you want to open/start and then tap the tile. The speed at which you move your finger will determine how far the tiles move.

- **Mouse** Move the mouse pointer to the bottom of the screen and use the horizontal scroll bar that is displayed, as described in "Use Classic Windows" later in this chapter, and then click the tile.

- **Keyboard** Use the scroll keys on the keyboard (**UP**, **DOWN**, **LEFT**, **RIGHT**, **PAGE UP**, **PAGE DOWN**, **HOME**, and **END**) to move a selection box to the tile you want to start and then press **ENTER**.

*Figure 1-1b: **The Windows 8 style interface is demonstrated here with the Start screen, with the Charms that can be brought in from the right edge of the screen.***

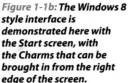

Use the Desktop

The Windows 8 desktop, shown in Figure 1-2, can hold windows and run apps within it. In its simplest form you see a background scene, a bar at the bottom with buttons on the left, and the time and date and other icons on the right. There may also be one or two icons in the upper-left area.

The desktop is, in a sense, a special app that you start from the Start screen and can switch between it and other Windows 8 apps that are open. At the same time it's different from Windows 8 style apps in that it has its own controls and acts much like the desktop in older versions of Windows.

To open the desktop from the Start screen:

Start the desktop (tap or click its tile or press **WINDOWS+D**) to display a minimal desktop, as you see in Figure 1-2.

The desktop is used for windows, dialog boxes, and icons

The Recycle Bin icon opens a folder of deleted files

Desktop icon for an app you can run, or a file or folder you can open

The taskbar shows apps that are running and other apps that are "pinned" to it

The mouse pointer shows where the mouse is pointing

The notification area holds icons of running system programs

Figure 1-2: **The Windows 8 desktop provides a workspace to hold windows of running apps and open folders similar to prior versions of Windows.**

To return to the Start screen from the desktop:

Switch to the Start screen (point to the lower-left corner of the screen and click, or swipe from the right edge and tap the **Start** icon, or press **WINDOWS**).

Explore the Desktop

The desktop provides a place to display and run legacy (Windows 7 and prior) apps or new apps written for the legacy environment.

- The **desktop** itself is the entire screen, except for the taskbar at the bottom. Windows, dialog boxes, and icons, such as the Recycle Bin, are displayed on the desktop. You can store *shortcuts,* which are icons for your favorite apps, on the desktop (see Chapter 2). You can drag windows, dialog boxes, files, and icons around the desktop. Double-click or double-tap an icon on the desktop to open it.

- The **taskbar** across the bottom of the screen contains the active *tasks,* which are icons and titles of the apps that are running on the computer, folders that are open, or apps or folders that are "pinned" to it. The taskbar also holds the notification area and Show Desktop button on the right. Click or tap an app on the taskbar to open it.

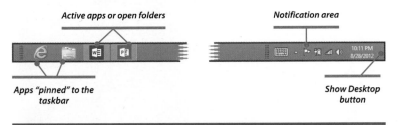

Active apps or open folders   Notification area

Apps "pinned" to the taskbar   Show Desktop button

 Note Your taskbar may have more or fewer objects than those shown here.

- **Desktop icons**, which can be in any number and anywhere on the desktop, are in the upper-left corner of Figure 1-2. Desktop icons

represent apps or folders that can be started or opened and moved about the screen. The Recycle Bin is a desktop icon for a folder that contains all of the files that have been deleted since the Recycle Bin was last emptied. Double-click or double-tap a desktop icon to open or start what it refers to.

- The **mouse pointer**, or simply the *pointer* or *mouse,* shows where the mouse is pointing. Move the mouse to move the pointer.

Use the Notification Area

The *notification area* on the right of the taskbar contains the icons of special programs and system features, as well as the time and date:

- **Show hidden icons**   Click or tap the up arrow to see the icons of hidden programs, and then click any you wish to open.

- **Open a system feature**   Click or tap one of the icons in the middle to open a system feature.

- **Set the time and date**   Click or tap the time and date area to see a calendar and an analog clock, and then click or tap **Change Date And Time Settings** (see related Note).

- **Show the desktop**   On the far right of the taskbar is an unmarked rectangular area, which, if you click or tap it, will minimize all open windows and dialog boxes and display the desktop. Clicking or tapping it again restores all open windows and dialog boxes. Simply moving the mouse over (also known as *mouse over*) this button temporarily makes all open windows and dialog boxes transparent until you move the mouse away.

> **Note** If you are connected to the Internet, you should never need to set your time and date, even when changing to or from daylight saving time, because Windows automatically synchronizes your computer's time with a local time server.

> **Note** The icons you have in the notification area will depend on the apps and processes you have running and the system features you have available. The icons shown here include Keyboard ⌨, which opens the touch keyboard; System Messages ⚑, which accesses the Action Center; Power 🔋 and Wireless ▰, which appear on a tablet or notebook computer; and Speakers, which allows you to control the sound from your computer ◀). You may have Network 🖳, which opens the Network and Sharing Center in place of Wireless, and no Power icon if you are using a desktop computer.

▷▷ Use Charms

There are several controls available on both the Start screen and the desktop, called "Charms," that are initially hidden.

Open Charms

To open the Charms:

- **Touch**   Move your finger from *off* the screen on the far right, on to it (*swipe* from the right edge). The Charms will open as shown on the right. Tap a charm, such as **Settings**, to open it.

- **Mouse**   Move the mouse into the lower-right or upper-right corner of the screen and then move it up or down the right edge. The Charms will open as shown on the right. Click a charm, such as **Settings**, to open it.

- **Keyboard**   Press **WINDOWS+C**. The Charms will open as you see on the right. Use the arrow keys to highlight a charm, such as **Settings**, and press **ENTER** to open it.

Explore Charms

Five Charms are displayed in the pane that opens on the right of the screen:

- **Settings**   Provides a number of primary controls related to the current screen (see Figure 1-3):

  - **Power**   Allows you to shut down the computer, restart it to refresh Windows and/or applications, or put the computer to "sleep" in a very low-power mode where it can be quickly restarted. See "End Your Windows Session" later in this chapter.

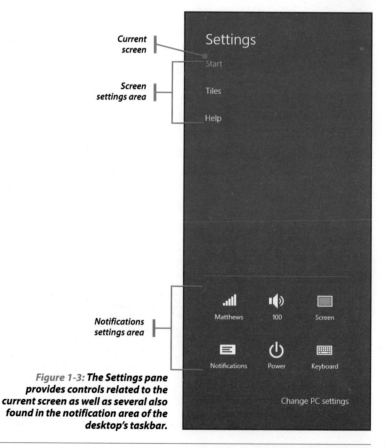

Figure 1-3: **The Settings pane provides controls related to the current screen as well as several also found in the notification area of the desktop's taskbar.**

- **Notifications**   Allows you to select how long you want to hide system messages that you receive, such as a security notice.

- **Network**   Displays the status of the network and/or wireless connections you are using.

- **Sound**   Allows you to adjust the level of sound being produced, or mute it completely.

- **Screen**   Allows you to adjust the brightness of your screen, if possible, and turn on or off the ability of a tablet to rotate the screen.

- **Keyboard**   Opens the on-screen keyboard if a touch screen is available.

- **Settings**   Allows you to adjust controls for the current screen.

- **Help**   Opens Windows Help; see "Get Help," later in this chapter.

- **Change PC Settings**   Opens PC Settings; see Chapter 2.

- **Devices**   Controls the devices connected to your computer.

- **Start**   Switches between the Start screen and the desktop.

- **Share**   Shares apps and their data.

- **Search**   Searches files, applications, and settings.

Use Start Screen Tiles

The Start screen, shown in Figure 1-1, contains tiles for starting apps and displaying information. As you will see in Chapter 2 you can change the order of the tiles and size, as well as add and remove tiles to reflect the apps and functions you use most frequently, as I have done in Figure 1-4

Figure 1-4: *The Start screen can be rearranged and changed as you wish so that it is most easy for you to use.*

(compare this to Figure 1-1). The tiles on the Start screen are semi-permanently "pinned" there, but that is something you can control (see Chapter 2).

Open Folders and Files

The lower two tiles on the left in Figure 1-4, which aren't displayed by default (see Chapter 2 to for these changes), File Explorer and Computer, open containers, called *folders,* used for storing information in *files* on the computer. The File Explorer app is used with both tiles to display the information in the different folders. Clicking or tapping:

- **File Explorer** opens a folder containing the user's libraries (with four subsidiary folders) and other features.

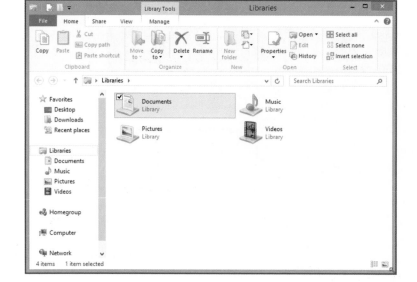

- **Computer** opens and displays the disk drives on your computer. By double-clicking or double-tapping a disk drive, you can open the disk drive to display the folders within it.

In either folder, by double-clicking or double-tapping a folder (or selecting one and pressing **ENTER** on the keyboard) you can open it to display the folders and files within it, as shown in Figure 1-5.

> **Tip** In Chapter 3 you will see how to search for and start an app not on the Start screen.

File Explorer and the handling of files and folders will be discussed further in this chapter and again in Chapter 3.

Start an App

Most of the tiles displayed on the Start screen are apps, such as Calendar, Weather, Word, Excel, and Mail. These need to be started in order to use them. The method for starting an app depends on where the app icon is located:

- **On the Start screen** Click or tap the app tile.
- **On the desktop** Double-click or double-tap the app icon, or "shortcut."
- **Pinned on the desktop's taskbar** Click or tap the app icon.
- **In the notification area** Click or tap the app icon.

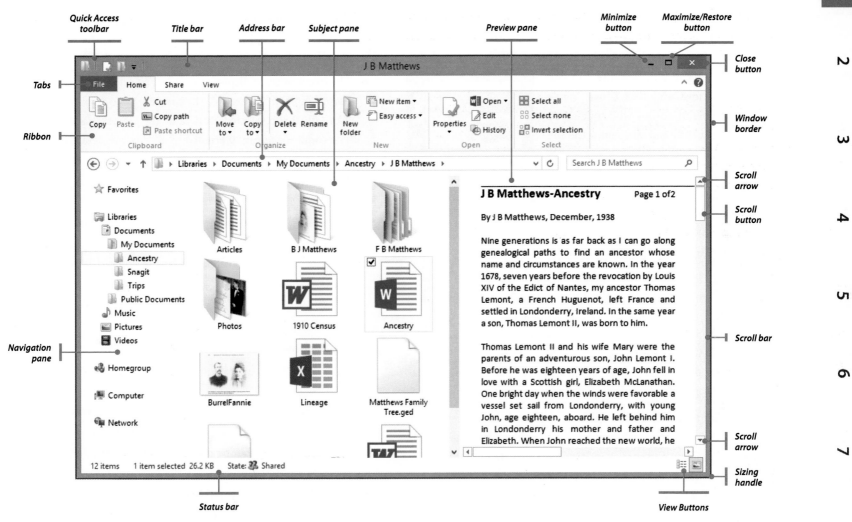

Figure 1-5: *From the Computer folder you can open any disk, folder, and file on your computer.*

Close an App

When you are done using an app, you may simply go on to other apps, leaving the original "running." Actually, it uses very little of the system's resources when you leave it in this way. Eventually Windows will see that it is not being used and shut it down. If for security or other reasons you want to close or shut down an app, you may do it in several ways:

- An open Windows 8 style app can be closed by dragging the top of the app with a mouse or a finger to the bottom of the screen.

- A Windows 8 style app that is hidden by the desktop can be closed by pointing at the **Start** icon in the lower-left corner of the screen and dragging up the left edge of the screen to display the apps that are running. Right-click the app you want to close, and click **Close**. While it's possible to do this with touch, you most frequently end up opening the app instead of closing it.

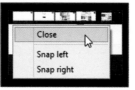

- An app opened on the desktop can be closed by clicking or tapping the **Close** button in the upper-right corner of the window (see Figure 1-5 earlier in this chapter).

Use an App Image

In Windows 8 apps are displayed in two ways, the classic window similar to those in Windows 7 and earlier versions that use the desktop, and Windows 8 style screens that are new to Windows 8.

Use Classic Windows

Many of the apps that you will use with Windows 8 open a classic window on your desktop, as shown with the File Explorer window in Figure 1-5.

The window in Figure 1-5 has a number of features that are referred to in the remainder of this book. Not all windows have all of the features shown in the figure, and some windows have features unique to them. Also, some of the details in this window, not described here, are described elsewhere in the book.

- The **Quick Access toolbar** hold tools you often use, such as New Folder for creating a new folder.
- The **title bar** is used to drag the window around the screen, and may contain the name of the app or folder in the window.
- The **address bar** displays the address of what is being displayed in the subject pane. In Figure 1-5, this is the J B Matthews folder, in the Ancestry, My Documents, and Documents parent folders in Libraries.

- The **subject pane** displays the principal objects in the window, such as files, folders, apps, documents, and images. The subject pane is always displayed.
- The **preview pane** displays the object selected in the subject pane. For example, in Figure 1-5, the preview pane displays a particular Word file that is selected. By default, the preview pane is turned off. The same space can alternatively display the details pane, which provides information about the selected object in the subject pane.
- The **Minimize button** decreases the size of the window so that you see it only as a task on the taskbar.
- The **Maximize/Restore button** increases the size of the window so that it fills the screen. When the screen is maximized, this button becomes the **Restore button**, which, when clicked, returns the screen to its previous size.
- The **Close button** shuts down and/or closes the app, folder, or file in the window.
- The **window border** separates the window from the desktop, and can be used to size the window horizontally or vertically by dragging a border.
- **Scroll arrows**, when clicked or tapped, move the window contents in small increments in the direction of the arrow.
- The **scroll button** can be dragged in either direction to move the contents accordingly.
- The **scroll bar** allows you to move the contents of the pane within the window so that you can see information that is not displayed. Clicking or tapping the scroll bar itself moves the contents in larger increments. The scroll bar only appears when there is more content than what can be displayed.
- The **sizing handle** in each corner of the window allows it to be sized diagonally, increasing or decreasing the window's height and width together when you drag a handle.

- The **navigation pane** provides links to the most commonly used folders related to the user who is logged on, as well as an optional hierarchical list of disks and folders on the computer. The navigation pane is turned on by default.

- The **ribbon** contains tools related to the contents of the window. Click or tap a tool to use it. The ribbon may not be displayed until one of the tabs is clicked or tapped.

- **Tabs** allow you to select from several different groups of ribbon tools.

Tip Double-clicking a window's title bar toggles between maximizing and restoring a window to its previous size.

Use Windows 8 Style Screens

Windows 8's Windows 8 style screens, shown with the Calendar app in Figure 1-6, initially fill the entire screen, and their controls are only available when you want them. To display the *App bar* with the controls, as shown in Figure 1-7:

- **Touch** Swipe from outside the display up from the bottom

- **Mouse** Right-click an inactive area (not a link) of the display

- **Keyboard** Press WINDOWS+Z

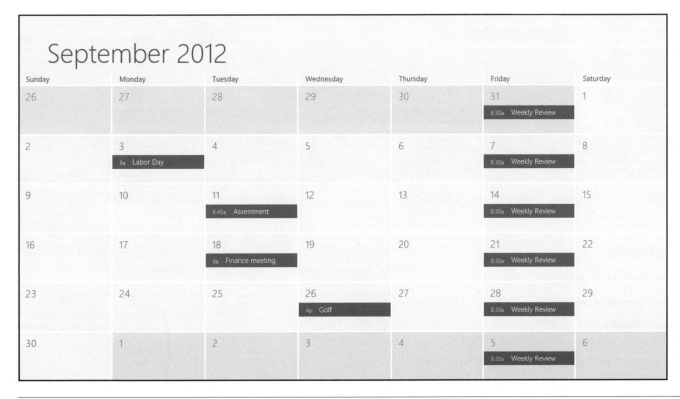

September 2012

Sunday	Monday	Tuesday	Wednesday	Thursday	Friday	Saturday
26	27	28	29	30	31 8:30a Weekly Review	1
2	3 9a Labor Day	4	5	6	7 8:30a Weekly Review	8
9	10	11 8:45a Assessment	12	13	14 8:30a Weekly Review	15
16	17	18 9a Finance meeting	19	20	21 8:30a Weekly Review	22
23	24	25	26 4p Golf	27	28 8:30a Weekly Review	29
30	1	2	3	4	5 8:30a Weekly Review	6

Figure 1-6: **Windows 8 style applications fill the entire screen with their information, and do not initially display controls.**

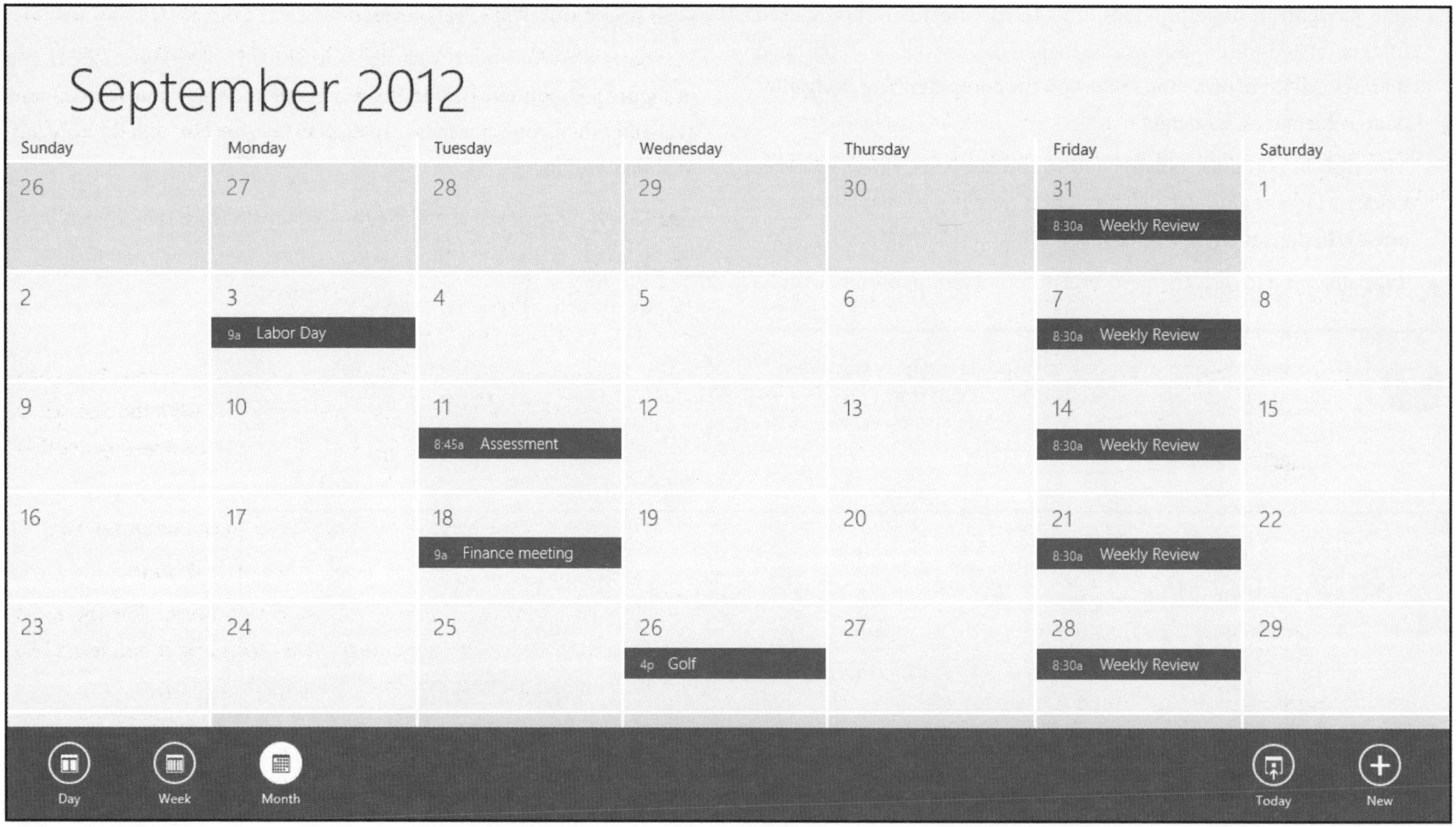

September 2012

Sunday	Monday	Tuesday	Wednesday	Thursday	Friday	Saturday
26	27	28	29	30	31 **8:30a** Weekly Review	1
2	3 **9a** Labor Day	4	5	6	7 **8:30a** Weekly Review	8
9	10	11 **8:45a** Assessment	12	13	14 **8:30a** Weekly Review	15
16	17	18 **9a** Finance meeting	19	20	21 **8:30a** Weekly Review	22
23	24	25	26 **4p** Golf	27	28 **8:30a** Weekly Review	29

Day Week Month   Today New

*Figure 1-7: **When a Windows 8 style application displays controls, it uses an App bar at the bottom of the screen, and sometimes an options bar at the top.***

To hide the App bar and its controls:

- **Touch**   Tap in an inactive area of the app
- **Mouse**   Click an inactive area of the app
- **Keyboard**   Press **WINDOWS+Z**

The controls on the App bar are unique to the app being run. The controls for Internet Explorer are described in Chapter 4.

> **Tip** The Settings pane on the right, opened from Charms, provides additional controls and options for an open Windows 8 style app.

Use a Dialog Box

Dialog boxes gather information, although they are now less commonly used than in previous versions of Windows. A *dialog box* uses a common set of controls to accomplish its purpose. Figure 1-8 shows a frequently used dialog box with many of the controls often seen.

The common controls in dialog boxes are used in the following ways:

- The **title bar** contains the name of the dialog box and is used to drag the box around the desktop.
- **Tabs** let you select from among several pages in a dialog box.

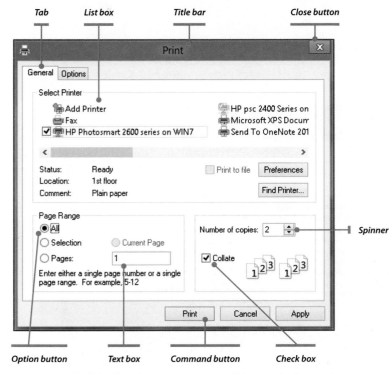

Figure 1-8: **This dialog box demonstrates some of the standard controls you'll find in dialog boxes.**

- A **list box** lets you select one or more items from a list; it may include a scroll bar, as is the case with a horizontal scroll bar in Figure 1-8.
- A **drop-down list box** (not shown), when opened, displays a list from which you can choose one item that will be displayed when the list is closed.
- **Option buttons**, also called radio buttons, let you select one among mutually exclusive options.
- **Check boxes** let you turn features on or off.
- A **text box** lets you enter and edit text.
- **Command buttons** perform functions such as closing the dialog box and accepting any changes (the Print button), closing the dialog box and ignoring the changes (the Cancel button), or opening another dialog box (the Preferences button).
- A **spinner** lets you select from a sequential series of numbers.
- A **slider** (not shown) lets you select from several values.

You will have many opportunities to use dialog boxes. For the most part, you can try dialog boxes and see what happens; if you don't like the outcome, you can come back and change the setting.

 Note The line between windows and dialog boxes is not always clear. The purpose of a window is to display information, while the purpose of a dialog box is to gather information. Most windows have a title bar with the Minimize, Maximize/Restore, and Close buttons, and the app name in the middle of the title bar. All windows also have a border and sizing handles, both of which can be used to change the size of the window.

Use a Menu

A *menu* provides a way of selecting an action, such as selecting toolbars, as shown in Figure 1-9. Menus are not frequently used on many programs written for Windows 8, but are generally in older programs. To use a menu in an open window:

1. Select (click or tap) the menu name on the menu bar.

2. Select the option you want.

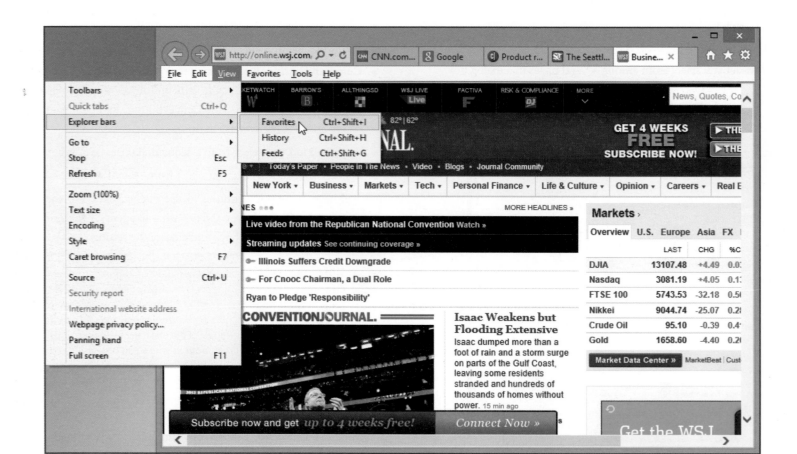

Figure 1-9: **By default, menus are not shown in either version of Internet Explorer, but in the desktop version you can display them by pressing ALT.**

Navigate the Windows Desktop

When multiple windows are open in the desktop, and possibly a dialog box or two, navigating among them and displaying the one(s) you want can be difficult. Figure 1-10, for example, shows such a situation. Windows 8 has a number of features to handle this:

- **Aero Peek** To see what's hidden on the screen
- **Aero Shake** To minimize other open windows
- **Aero Snap** To resize and position windows
- **Jump lists** To see recent files and app options
- **Taskbar previews** To see what is open in an app

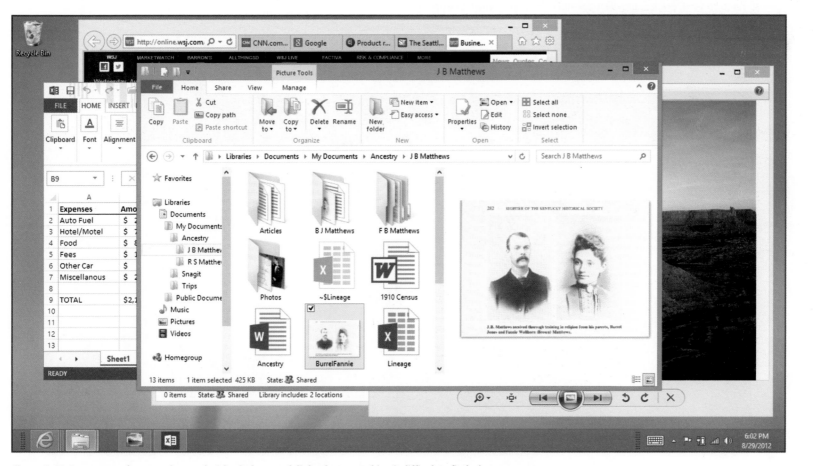

Figure 1-10: A screen can become cluttered with windows and dialog boxes, making it difficult to find what you want.

Aero Peek

Aero Peek allows you to see what's hidden on the desktop behind all the open windows. You can do this on a temporary (or "peek") basis or a more long-lasting one.

> **Note** If your Aero Peek is off by default, turn it on from the desktop by opening the taskbar's Properties menu (right-clicking or pressing and holding for a moment on the taskbar) and then selecting (clicking or tapping) **Properties**. In the Taskbar Properties dialog box that opens, on the Taskbar tab, select **Use Peek To Preview The Desktop** so it has a check mark, and then select **OK**.

- **Temporarily peek** at the desktop:

  Move the mouse pointer to ("mouse over") the **Show Desktop** area on the far right of the taskbar (must be done with the mouse). All the open windows will become transparent ("glass") frames, as you can see in Figure 1-11, and you can then see what was hidden on the desktop, such as the items in Figure 1-11.

- **Return** to the original desktop after a temporary peek:

  Move the mouse pointer away from the Show Desktop area. All the open windows will reappear, as shown in Figure 1-10.

Figure 1-11: **With Aero Peek, all open windows become transparent.**

- **Hide** all open windows so you can see and work on the desktop:

  Select (click or tap) the **Show Desktop** area on the far right of the taskbar. All the open windows will be hidden, and you can move the mouse around the entire desktop.

- **Unhide** all open windows and return to the original desktop:

  Select (click or tap) the **Show Desktop** area on the far right of the taskbar. All the open windows will be returned to their original position.

Aero Shake

Aero Shake allows you to minimize all open windows except for the one you are "shaking." To "shake" a window:

- Point to the title bar of the window you want to remain open with either the mouse or your finger. Press and hold the mouse button or your finger on the title bar while moving your hand rapidly to the left and then to the right, as if you were shaking it.

  –Or–

- Select the window you want to keep displayed. Press and hold **WINDOWS** while pressing **HOME**.

To return the minimized windows to their original size and position, repeat the same steps.

Aero Snaps

Aero Snaps "snaps" a window to various parts of the screen, a function similar to the Maximize/Restore button (which can still be used) on the title bar of a selected, floating (not already maximized) window, with some useful additions:

- **Maximize** a floating window:

  Point within the title bar of a window, not on its edge, and drag it to the top of the screen. The window will be maximized to fill the screen.

–Or–

Press and hold **WINDOWS** while pressing the **UP ARROW**.

- **Restore** a maximized window (independent of how it was maximized):

  Double-click or double-tap the title bar.

  –Or–

  Select the window you want to be restored. Press and hold **WINDOWS** while pressing the **DOWN ARROW**.

- **Vertically maximize** a floating window while not spreading it out horizontally:

Point to the top or bottom *edge* of a window, and drag it to the corresponding edge of the screen. The window will be vertically maximized.

–Or–

Select the window you want to be maximized. Press and hold **WINDOWS** while pressing **SHIFT+UP ARROW**.

- **Restore** a vertically maximized window:

Point to the top or bottom *edge* of a window, and drag it toward the center of the screen. The window will be resized as you drag it down.

–Or–

Select the window you want to be maximized. Press and hold **WINDOWS** while pressing **SHIFT+DOWN ARROW**.

- **Left-align** a floating window and have it occupy 50 percent of the screen:

Point to the title bar of a window, and drag it to the corresponding edge of the screen. When the mouse pointer (not the window's edge) reaches the edge of the screen, the window will fill the left 50 percent of the screen.

–Or–

Select the window you want to be aligned. Press and hold **WINDOWS** while pressing the **LEFT ARROW**.

- **Right-align** a floating window and have it occupy 50 percent of the screen:

Point at the title bar of a window, and drag it to the corresponding edge of the screen. When the mouse pointer reaches the edge of the screen, the window will fill the right 50 percent of the screen.

–Or–

Select the window you want to be aligned. Press and hold **WINDOWS** while pressing the **RIGHT ARROW**.

- **Restore** a window that is filling 50 percent of the screen:

Double-click or double-tap the title bar *twice*.

–Or–

Select the window you want to be restored. Press and hold **WINDOWS** while pressing the key opposite to the one used to enlarge it.

–Or–

Point at the title bar of a window, and drag it away from the window edge it was aligned to.

Jump Lists

Jump lists are a context or pop-up menu for application icons on the taskbar. When you right-click or hold your finger on an app icon on the taskbar, a menu will appear above it containing a list of recent files or webpages, as well as options to close the app, pin or unpin it from the taskbar, and open the app with a blank file or web page.

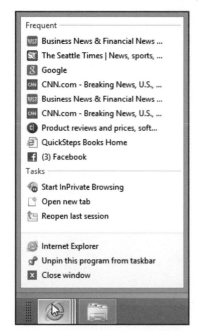

Taskbar Previews

Taskbar previews are a miniature image, or thumbnail, of an open window attached to a taskbar icon. When you mouse over an icon on the taskbar (there is not a consistent way to do this with touch, but a stylus held a small fraction of an inch off the screen will do it), a thumbnail of the open window or windows related to that icon will temporarily appear, as shown here. If you then move the mouse to the thumbnail, a temporary full-sized image will appear (see Figure 1-12). When you move the mouse off the thumbnail or the icon, the corresponding image will disappear. Open a window by clicking its thumbnail. Close a window by clicking the **Close** button on the thumbnail.

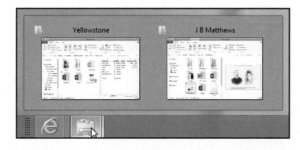

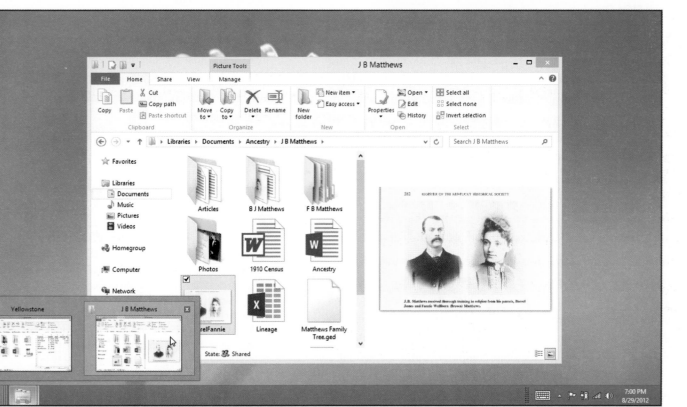

Figure 1-12: **The natural instinct is to move the mouse from the thumbnail to the temporary larger window to open it, but that causes both images to disappear. You must click the thumbnail.**

Tip Look at the icons on the taskbar in Figure 1-12. It is obvious by its bright highlight that the File Explorer icon is selected and the one displaying the thumbnails.

End Your Windows Session

You can end your Windows session in several ways, depending on what you want to do. All of these can be found on the Settings pane.

1. Open **Charms** and select **Settings | Power**.

2. Select **Shut Down**.

The meanings of the various options are as follows:

- **Shut Down** Closes all active apps and network connections and logs off all users so that no information is lost, and then turns off the computer (if it is done automatically) or tells you when it is safe for you to turn it off. When you start up the computer, you must reload your apps and data and reestablish your network connection (done by Windows) to get back to where you were when you shut down.

- **Restart** Closes all active apps and network connections and logs off all users so that no information is lost. Windows is then shut down and restarted. This is usually done when there is a problem that restarting Windows will fix or to complete setting up some apps.

- **Sleep** Leaves all active apps, network connections, and your user account active and in memory, but also saves the state of everything on disk. Your computer is then put into a low-power state that allows you to quickly resume working exactly where you were when you left. In a desktop computer, it is left running in this low-power state for as long as you wish. In a mobile computer (laptops, notebooks, netbooks, tablets, and slates), after three hours or if the battery is low, your session is again saved to disk and the computer is turned off.

Resume from Sleep

There are several ways to resume operation after a computer has been put into Sleep mode, which depend on your type of computer, how it was put to sleep, and how long it has been sleeping. A computer can be put into Sleep mode either by your action or as the result of the computer not being used for a time, which is controlled in the Power Options (see Chapter 5). The ways to resume include the following:

- Press any key on your keyboard, move the mouse, or touch the screen (if you have a touch screen). This works with most desktop computers and mobile computers that have only been asleep a short time.

- Quickly press and release the power button on your computer. This works with most recent computers of all types. Holding down the computer's power button for very long will, in most cases, either fully turn off the computer or cause it to restart (shut fully down and then restart).

- Open the top. This works with most mobile computers that have a flip top.

Tip There are two distinct schools of thought on whether you should use Sleep or Shut Down when you leave the computer for any length of time. The primary considerations are security and power usage. Older computers used less power running in Sleep mode than the power consumed during shutting down and starting up. New computers have reduced the power consumed during these events, so it is now a toss-up. From a security standpoint, there is no security like having your computer completely turned off. A computer is also fairly secure in Sleep mode, but it is theoretically possible for a hacker to awaken it. The choice becomes a matter of preference. I turn my computers off; my wife leaves hers on.

Get Help

Windows 8 Help provides both built-in documentation and online assistance that you can use to learn how to work with Windows 8. For example, to use Help:

1. From the Start screen, open **Charms** and select **Settings | Help**. Help options will appear at the top of the Settings pane that will be different depending on what was on the screen when you opened Charms, like what is shown in Figure 1-13 that was opened from the Start screen.

2. Select the option that is correct for you.

Note If you follow the steps in the "Get Help" section starting from the desktop you will open the Windows Help and Support shown next.

← Help

Adding apps, websites, and more to Start

Finding things with Search

Rearranging tiles on Start

Need more help?

Learn the basics:
Get started with Windows 8 and Start

Get support:
Visit the Windows website

*Figure 1-13: **The Windows 8 Help pane provides options for working with what else is on the screen.***

Chapter 2

Customizing Windows 8

Windows 8 has many features that can be customized. You can keep the default setup, or you can change the look and feel of the Start screen and desktop, including rearranging, adding, and removing objects, as well as how apps and system features, such as sound, operate. This chapter will explore all of that.

CHANGE THE LOOK OF WINDOWS 8

An important aspect of Windows that leads to your enjoyment and efficient use of it is how it looks. Windows 8 provides significant flexibility in this area. You can change how the screen looks, including the Start screen, the desktop, and the Windows apps such as File Explorer.

▶▶ Customize the Start Screen

The Start screen is the focal point of Windows 8. It contains *tiles* that represent *apps*, programs or applications such as Internet Explorer and Microsoft Word that you can run on your computer. The Start screen is the primary place where apps are started and control functions are accessed. Because of its central focus, it is very important that it be customized to your needs, both for efficiency and to reduce possible irritation. The changes you can make to the Start screen are many and include the following:

- Rearrange the tiles so the ones you use are most readily available.
- Add tiles that aren't already shown on the Start screen.
- Remove tiles that you don't often use.
- Change the shape and content of a tile.

- Group tiles that relate to each other.
- Change the Start screen's background.

Rearrange Tiles

Rearranging the tiles is easy—just move them (drag with either the mouse or your finger) where you want them. The tiles on the left should be the ones you use most often, and so you should move the tiles around to facilitate that. Figure 2-1 shows an arrangement that works for me.

 Tip Have patience while rearranging tiles. They tend to jump into particular spots, not always the one you want them in. Keep trying and they will eventually go where you want them.

Add Tiles

The tiles that you initially see on the Start screen have been *pinned* there much as you would put a "sticky note" on some surface or tack something

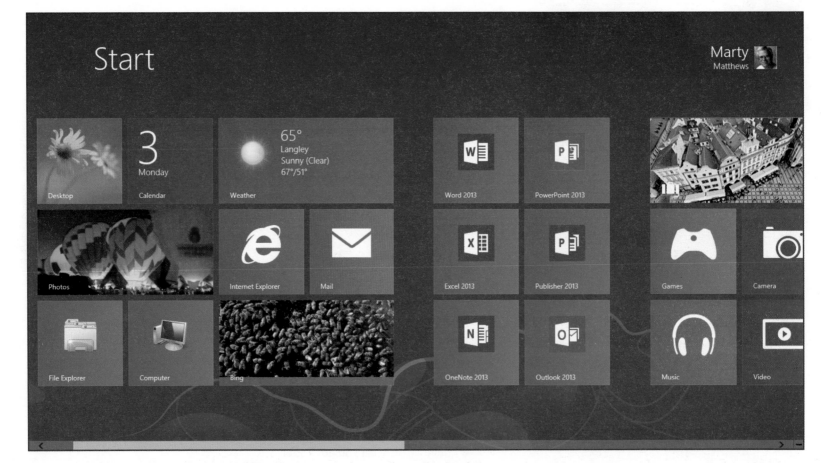

Figure 2-1: The tiles on the Start screen should reflect what you use on the computer, as this does for me.

to a corkboard. You can add tiles to the Start screen from the list of apps that are installed on your computer, and you can install new apps.

- To pin an app already installed:

  1. Open the App bar:

     Mouse Right-click a blank area of the Start screen.

     Touch Swipe up from the bottom of the screen.

     Keyboard Press **WINDOWS+Z**.

2. Select (click, tap, or press **ENTER**) **All Apps** in the App bar to open a list of all the apps installed on the computer, as you can see in Figure 2-2.

3. Open the App bar for the app you want to pin to the Start screen:

   Mouse Right-click the app.

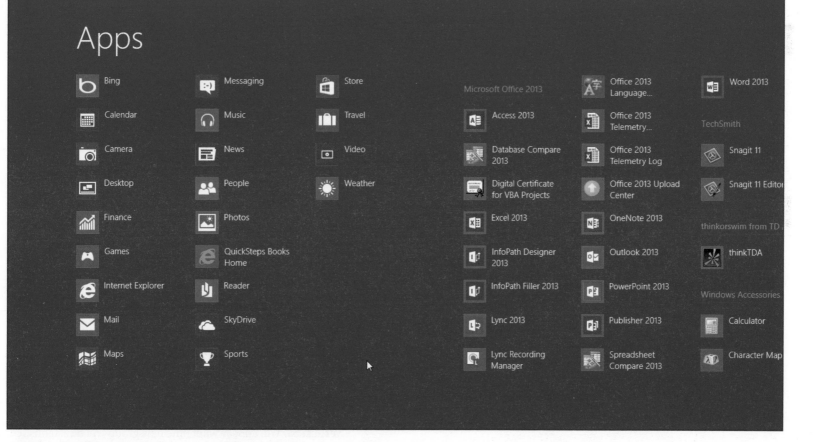

*Figure 2-2: **The All Apps screen will show you all the apps installed on your computer.***

Touch Swipe down the app by very briefly resting your finger on it and then quickly moving your hand down while maintaining contact with the app.

Keyboard Use the arrow keys to select the app and press the context key.

The App bar again opens, now with new options, including Pin To Start.

4. Select **Pin To Start**. The app will now appear on the Start screen until you remove it.

- To pin a new app to the Start screen:

  Install the new app as you are directed. It will be added automatically to the Start screen, and in some cases with ancillary apps that you may or may not want to leave on the Start screen.

Remove Tiles

To remove tiles from the Start screen, open the App bar for the app you want to remove and select **Unpin From Start**. To remove several apps at one time, select them all (by right-clicking each of them) and then select **Unpin From Start**.

 Tip App tiles that you remove from the Start screen with Unpin are still installed on the computer and are available in All Apps. It might make sense to remove all tiles that you don't see an immediate need for and then, as you find you are using some you removed, add them back.

Change Tiles

The tiles on the Start screen can *sometimes* be changed in size (made larger or smaller) and made to be live to display real-time information in the tile. For example, the options available for the Weather app allow you to make the tile smaller and to make it live. To change a tile, open the App bar and select the options that you want, as you can see in the Weather tile with live data.

Group Tiles

The Start screen, by default, displays the app tiles in several random groupings. You can change the contents of these groupings by rearranging, adding, and removing tiles, as described earlier in this chapter. You can also create new groups, reorder groups, and name groups, as you can see in Figure 2-3.

- To create a new group:

  1. Add and remove the apps on the Start screen so that you are left with only the apps that you will primarily use.

  2. Move (drag) a tile that you want in the new group either to the blank area between groups or to the far right of all groups to establish a new group in that location, as shown next. A gray vertical bar will appear where the new group will be established.

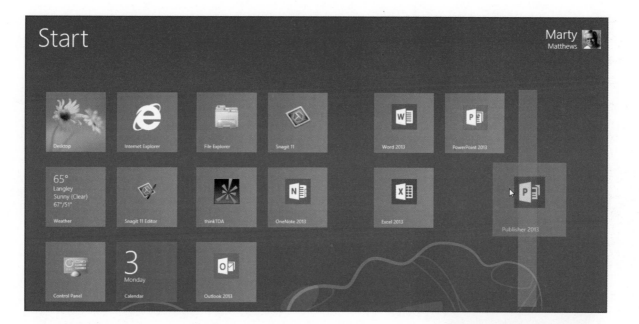

3. Move the remaining tiles that are to be in the new group above, below, or in between existing tiles.

- To reorder groups:

  1. When you have created the groups with the tiles you want in each, you can change the left-to-right order of the groups by first zooming out or shrinking the Start screen groups:

     Mouse By clicking the minimize icon in the far lower-right corner.

     Touch By bringing two fingers together on the screen.

     Keyboard By pressing **CTRL**+minus sign key (–).

  2. Move one or more groups on the screen so they are in the order you want them.

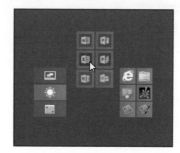

- To name groups:

  1. While the Start screen is still zoomed out, open the App bar for the group you want to name.

  2. Select **Name Group** on the left of the App bar, type the name you want, and select **Name**.

 Tip When using touch, drag the group to be moved toward the top of the screen, and then drag it where you want it.

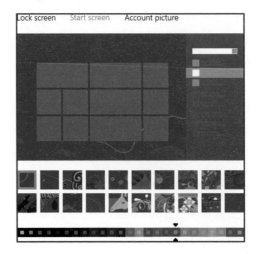

Figure 2-3: *Grouping and naming tiles on the Start screen will help you find related apps.*

Change the Start Screen Background

The Start screen can be changed to incorporate one of several patterns and one of a number of color pairs.

1. Open **Charms** and select **Settings | Change PC Settings** at the bottom right of the Settings pane. The PC Settings Windows 8 window will open as you can see in Figure 2-4.

2. With Personalize selected on the left, select **Start Screen** at the top on the right. A preview of the Start screen will appear at the top of the right pane with pattern and color pair selection bars beneath it.

Figure 2-4: *PC Settings provides access to the controls for a number of features in Windows 8.*

3. Select each of the pattern choices and then each of the color pairs and observe the effect in the preview at the top.

4. Based on what you have seen, select the pattern and color pair you want to use in the Start screen.

▷▷ Customize the Desktop

Much of the desktop is controlled by the Personalization window. Open it to make many of the changes in this section. (Several of the features controlled in the Personalization window, such as sounds and the mouse pointer, are discussed on their own later in this chapter.)

1. From the Start screen, select the **Desktop** tile to display it. Open the desktop's context menu (right-click or press, hold, and release an area of the desktop without an icon).

View	▶
Sort by	▶
Refresh	
Paste	
Paste shortcut	
Undo Delete	Ctrl+Z
New	▶
🖥 Screen resolution	
🖥 Personalize	

2. Select **Personalize**. The Personalization window opens, as shown in Figure 2-5.

Change the Desktop Themes and Colors

You can use any picture, color, or pattern you want for your desktop background. Windows 8 comes with several alternatives, and you can download many more. From the Personalization window:

 Tip You can control many facets of Windows 8 just by changing the theme.

1. Review the themes that are available with Windows 8 (or select **Get More Themes Online** to view Microsoft's online library). Select the theme you want to use. With each theme you can select a desktop background and a window color, as well as the sounds used and a screen saver.

2. Select **Desktop Background**. Select the **Picture Location** down arrow, and select a source of pictures (see Figure 2-6), or select **Browse** and navigate to a location on your computer where you have a picture you want to use (Chapter 3 explains how to navigate on your computer). Select **OK**, and select the picture or pictures desired.

3. Select **Save Changes** to close the Desktop Background window.

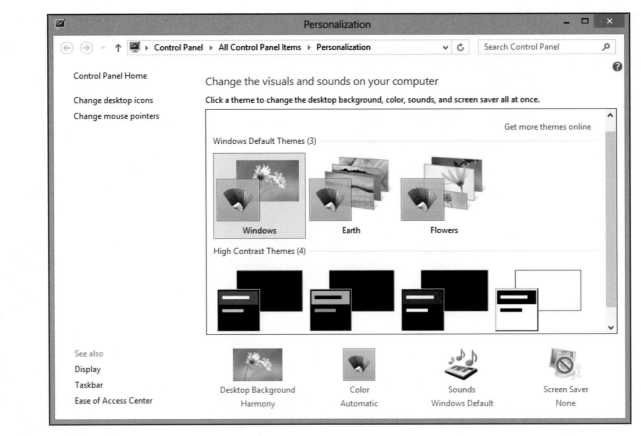

Figure 2-5: The Personalization window lets you change the appearance of the desktop in Windows 8.

4. At the top of the themes list, select **Save Theme** to save any changes to a current theme or to save a new theme.

5. In the Save Theme As dialog box, name the theme, and select **Save**.

Note You can select a new theme and almost immediately see the changes on the desktop. If you don't like the changes, select a different theme.

Change the Resolution and Text Size

Depending on your computer and monitor, you can display Windows 8 with various resolutions and text sizes. You can select the text and object size or only specific areas of text in the Display window and then go on to adjust the resolution. From the Personalization window:

1. Select **Display** in the lower left. The Display window will appear, as shown in Figure 2-7.

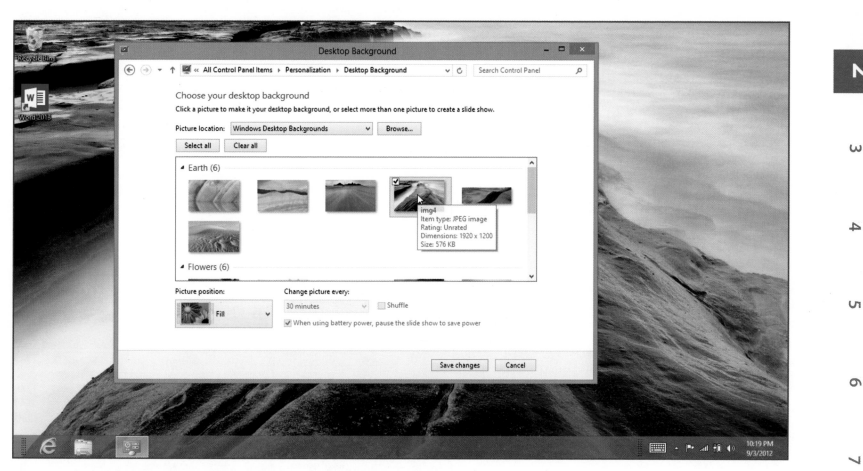

Figure 2-6: Selecting a background picture causes it to be displayed instantly as your background.

2. Select the size of all items by clicking one of the three sizes and/or select the text area down arrow, and select the size you want and whether you want it bold. When you are ready, select **Apply**.

3. Select **Adjust Resolution** in the upper left. If you have more than one display device, select **Identify**. The display's number appears on each screen. In the Display drop-down list, select the display whose resolution you want to change.

4. Select the **Resolution** drop-down arrow. Move the slider up or down to adjust the resolution. (You can try this and if you don't like it, come back and change it.)

 Tip Each resolution is tuned to a particular screen style; for example, widescreen (16 × 9) as dynamically previewed in the upper part of the window.

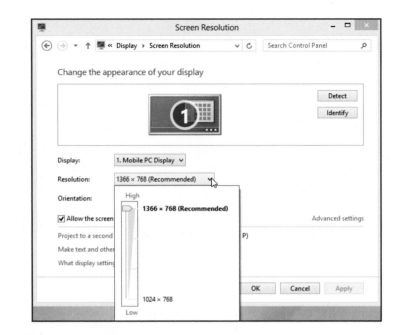

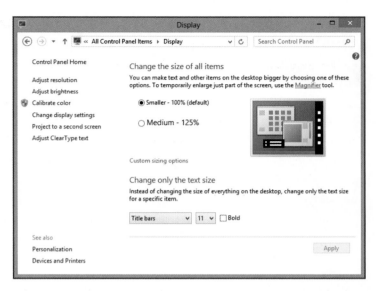

Figure 2-7: Increasing the text and object size lets you see less of what's on the screen, but what you see is larger and possibly easier to read.

5. Select **Apply** to save the settings, and then select the **Back** arrow in the upper-left area until you are back to the Personalization window.

 Note The Advanced Settings link at the right of the Screen Resolution window provides access to settings that are specific to your display hardware.

Alter the Appearance of Objects

You can alter the appearance of windows, icons, and dialog boxes, changing their shapes and colors, as well as the font used in those objects. From the Personalization window:

1. Select **Color** at the bottom center of the window. The Color And Appearance window will open.

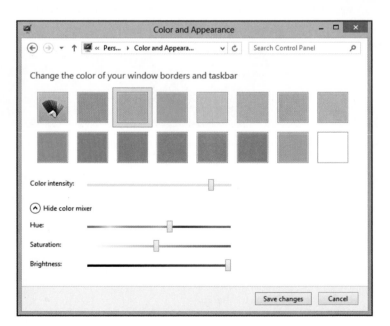

2. Select a different color scheme, if desired; change the color intensity; or mix your own color.

3. Select **Save Changes** to return to the Personalization window and select **Close** to close it.

Add App Icons to the Desktop

When you first use Windows 8, you will only have a couple of icons on the desktop, including the Recycle Bin, which is the only one Windows puts there by default. Some computer manufacturers may include additional icons. The purpose of having app icons on the desktop, called *shortcuts*, is to be able to easily start the apps by double-selecting their icons. You can have Windows app icons as well as other app icons on the desktop.

Add Windows App Icons

To add Windows app icons, such as for User Files, to the desktop and customize them:

1. Open the desktop's context menu, and select **Personalize** to open the Personalization window.

2. Select **Change Desktop Icons** on the upper left to open the Desktop Icon Settings dialog box.

3. Select up to five icons that you want to have on the desktop. For example, you might add User's Files. The others you probably use less often, and they can be accessed quickly from the Start screen.

4. To customize a Windows app icon, select the icon and select **Change Icon**. A dialog box will appear displaying alternate icons.

5. Select the alternative you want, and select **OK**.

6. When you are satisfied with the Windows app icons you have selected and/or changed, select **OK**. Your new icon will appear on the desktop.

7. Select **Close** to close the Personalization window.

Add Other App Icons

To add other app icons to the desktop:

1. Select the **Start** screen, open the Apps bar, and select **All Apps**.

2. Open the Apps bar for the app and its icon you want on the desktop, and select **Open File Location**.

3. Open the context menu for the file and select **Send To | Desktop (Create Shortcut)**. The app's icon will appear on the desktop.

Change Desktop Icons

When you have the icons that you want on the desktop, you can change the size of the icons, their order, and their alignment through the desktop context menu.

Open the desktop's context menu, and select **View** to open the View submenu.

Resize Icons

Windows 8 gives you the choice of three different sizes of icons. The size you choose is a function of both the resolution you are using on your display and your personal preference. By default (the way Windows is set up when first used), your icons will be medium size. From the **View** submenu:

Select each of the sizes to see which is best for you.

Align Icons

You can move desktop icons where you want them; by default, Windows 8 will align your icons to an invisible grid. If you don't like that, from the View submenu:

Select **Align Icons To Grid** to clear the check mark and allow any arrangement on the desktop that you want.

If you should move your icons around and then change your mind, reopen the View submenu and:

Select **Align Icons To Grid** to reselect it. Your icons will jump to the invisible grid and be aligned.

Arrange Icons

By default, there is no particular order to the icons on the desktop, and you can move them into the order that suits you. However, you can have Windows arrange and sort the icons in several ways. From the View submenu:

Select **Auto Arrange Icons**. By default, the icons will be placed in a column alphabetically by name, except that the system icons (Computer, Recycle Bin, Internet Explorer, User's Files, Control Panel, and Network) will be at the top.

If you want to change the order in which Windows 8 arranges desktop icons:

1. Open the desktop's context menu, and select **Sort By** to open that submenu.

2. Select one of the options to have the icons sorted in that manner.

Rename Desktop Icons

When you add app icons to the desktop, they may have the word "Shortcut" in their names, or they may have names that are not meaningful to you. To rename desktop icons:

1. Open the app's context menu, and select **Rename**.

2. Type the new name that you want to use, and press **ENTER**.

⊳⊳ Change the Taskbar

The taskbar at the bottom of the Windows 8 screen has four standard areas: pinned apps on the left, running apps in the middle, and the notification area and the Show Desktop button on the right. You can change the taskbar by moving and sizing it and by changing its properties.

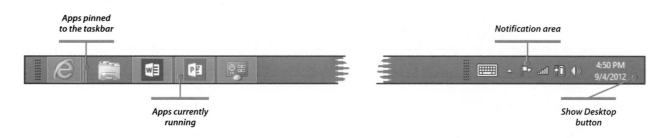

Apps pinned to the taskbar

Apps currently running

Notification area

Show Desktop button

Move and Size the Taskbar

You can move the taskbar to any of the four sides of the screen. Do this by moving any empty area of the taskbar to another edge. For example, Figure 2-8 shows the taskbar moved to the right edge of the screen.

You can size the taskbar by moving the inner edge (top edge when the taskbar is on the bottom) in or out. Here is a taskbar at double its normal size.

In either case, you must first unlock the taskbar. See "Change Taskbar Properties," next, to do this.

Change Taskbar Properties

A number of taskbar features can be changed through the Taskbar Properties dialog box (see Figure 2-9).

Open Taskbar Properties

Open the taskbar context menu, and select **Properties**. The Taskbar Properties dialog box appears with the Taskbar tab selected. (Select **Apply** to test a change without closing the dialog box.)

Unlock the Taskbar

Your taskbar may be locked, which will prevent it from being moved or resized. If yours is locked, you should unlock it for the work in this chapter.

Select **Lock The Taskbar** to remove the check mark and unlock the taskbar.

Hide the Taskbar

Hiding the taskbar means that it is not displayed unless you move the mouse to the edge of the screen containing the taskbar. By default, it is displayed.

Select the **Auto-Hide The Taskbar** check box and hide the taskbar.

Use Small Buttons

If you want to conserve desktop space and you have good eyesight, you can make the taskbar buttons smaller.

Select the **Use Small Taskbar Buttons** check box and make the icons smaller.

*Figure 2-8: **A taskbar can be moved to any of the four sides of the screen.***

Customize Taskbar Buttons

There are three choices for customizing taskbar buttons:

- Always combine similar items and hide the labels, such as app names.

- Combine similar items when the taskbar is full, but display the labels.

- Never combine similar items under any circumstances and display the labels.

Combining similar items, for example, puts all Microsoft Word documents in one icon or all Internet pages in one icon so that they take up less room on the taskbar. By default, similar items are combined.

Select the **Taskbar Buttons** down arrow, and make your choice.

Use Aero Peek

As you saw in Chapter 1, Aero Peek allows you to see the desktop and what is under the open windows on the screen when you move the mouse

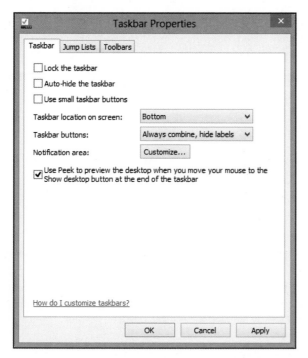

*Figure 2-9: **You will use the taskbar often, so it should look and behave the way you want.***

to the Show Desktop button on the far right of the taskbar. If yours is turned off (not checked):

Select **Use Peek** to add the check mark and turn on this capability.

Close Taskbar Properties

After you've made any of these changes to the taskbar, select **OK** to enable them and close the Taskbar Properties dialog box.

▷▷ Change the Notification Area

The notification area on the right of the taskbar can also be changed through the Taskbar Properties dialog box (see "Change Taskbar

Properties" for instructions on displaying the dialog box). The notification area, which can get crowded at times, contains app icons put there by Windows and other apps. You can control which icons are displayed along with their notifications, which icons are hidden while their notifications are displayed, or which icons are not there at all. To change the notification area:

Select **Customize** opposite Notification Area. The Notification Area Icons window will appear, as shown in Figure 2-10.

Customize Notification Icons

To customize the behavior of icons in the notification area:

Select the drop-down list opposite the icon you want to change, and select the behavior you want.

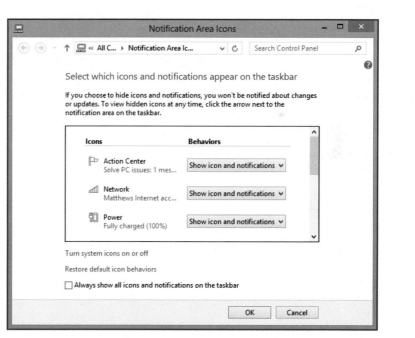

*Figure 2-10: **Turn off the notification area icons that are not useful to you.***

Display System Icons

Up to six system icons—Keyboard (on computers with touch), Action Center, Network, Volume, Power (on mobile computers), and Clock—are shown in the notification area by default. You can turn them off if you wish.

1. Select **Turn System Icons On Or Off**.

2. Select the drop-down list opposite an icon name, and select **Off** to not display it.

3. When you have made the changes you want, select **OK**.

Close Taskbar Properties

After you've made any of these changes to the notification area, select **OK** to enable them and close the Notification Area Icons window. Select **OK** again to close the Taskbar Properties dialog box.

▷▷ Permanently Pin Icons to the Taskbar

Windows 8 provides the ability to permanently "pin," or attach, frequently used app icons to the taskbar starting from the left. Once there, the icons are visible (unless you hide the taskbar), and the related app can be started by selecting it (with a single click or tap) until you unpin it. By default, Windows 8 has two icons pinned to the taskbar: Internet Explorer and File Explorer. You can pin additional icons, you can remove those that are currently pinned, and you can rearrange the current icons.

Pin an Icon to the Taskbar

After you have used Windows 8 for a while you may find that you use an app more often than others and would like to have it more immediately available in the desktop. This is what pinning to the taskbar is for. You can do that by either:

> Locating the app icon in File Explorer, the Start screen, or on the desktop; opening its context menu; and selecting **Pin To Taskbar**.

–Or–

Starting a desktop app in any of the ways described in Chapter 1. When it has started, open its icon on the taskbar's context menu, and select **Pin This Program To Taskbar**.

> **Note** You can pin a file or folder to the File Explorer icon on the taskbar by opening File Explorer, navigating to the file or folder, and moving it to the File Explorer icon on the taskbar. Access the pinned file or folder by opening the File Explorer icon's context menu and selecting it.

Remove an Icon Pinned to the Taskbar

To remove an app icon pinned to the taskbar:

> Open the icon's context menu and select **Unpin This Program From Taskbar**.

Rearrange Icons Pinned to the Taskbar

The icons that are pinned to the taskbar can be moved around and placed in any order.

> Move icons pinned to the taskbar to where you want them.

▷▷ Change the File Explorer Layout

File Explorer is used to locate and access files stored on your computer. The discussion about using File Explorer is the main focus of Chapter 3. Here, where we're talking about customizing the look and feel of Windows 8, we'll briefly talk about customizing File Explorer. The File Explorer window shown in Figure 2-11 (as well as the image in Chapter 1) has a full set of panes turned on. By default, the preview pane is not visible. You can turn these panes on and turn other panes off using the File Explorer ribbon.

The ribbon has five tabs (four of which are shown in Figure 2-11). The File, Home, and Share tabs will be discussed in Chapter 3. Here we'll talk about changing the app's layout using the View tab.

Open File Explorer

File Explorer can be opened in either the Start screen or the desktop, both of which take you to File Explorer on the desktop. By default, though, File Explorer is not pinned to the Start screen, so you must use All Apps.

From the Start screen, open the Apps bar, select **All Apps**, move the screen contents until you see File Explorer, and then select it.

–Or–

On the left of the taskbar on the desktop, select the **File Explorer** icon.

File Explorer

Change Panes

File Explorer can display up to three panes containing up to four sets of information. The left pane can only be the navigation pane displaying disk drives and folders, but you can turn it on or off. The center pane is the subject pane and is always present. The right pane can be turned off, and when it is on it can display either the preview of a document or detailed information about the document.

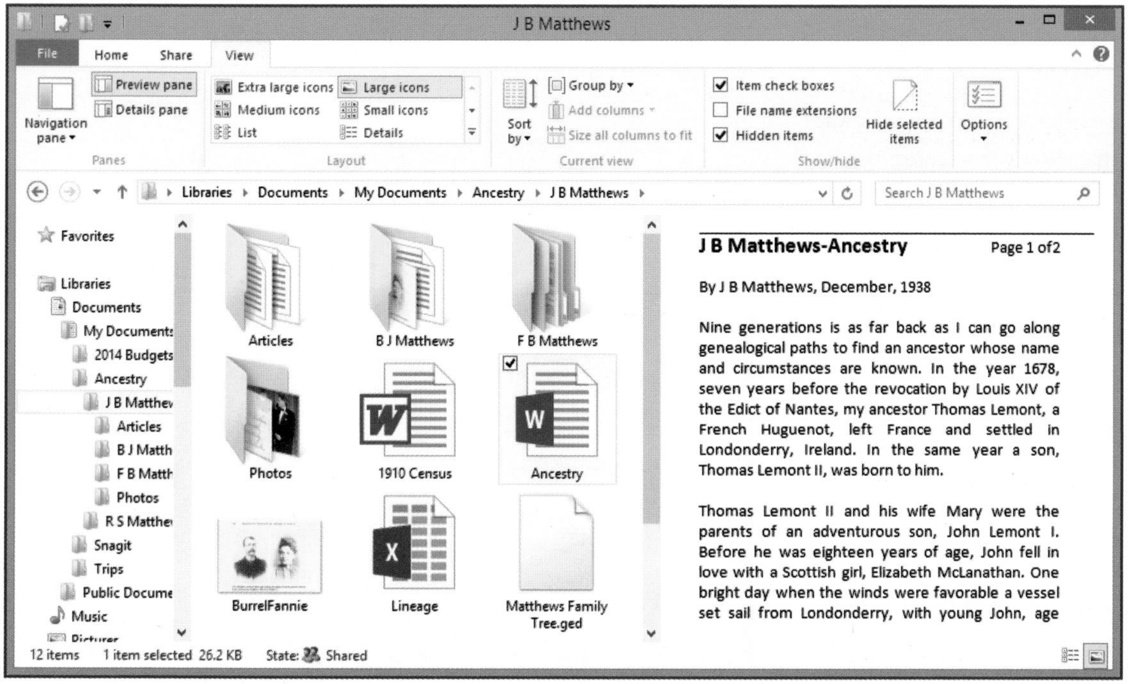

1. Select the **View** tab at the top of File Explorer.

2. Select **Navigation Pane** on the left of the View ribbon to open its menu.

3. If there is a check mark next to Navigation Pane in the menu, select it to close the pane. If there is no check mark, select it to display the pane.

*Figure 2-11: **Windows 8 added a ribbon to File Explorer, giving it a new ease of customization.***

4. If the preview pane is not displayed (not highlighted in the ribbon), select **Preview Pane** to display it, or if it is displayed, select **Preview Pane** to close the pane.

5. If the details pane is not displayed (not highlighted in the ribbon), select **Details Pane** to display it, or if it is displayed, select **Details Pane** to close the pane.

Change Icons

The manner that File Explorer uses to represent files and folders has a number of options, including lists, tiles, and icons, and the icons can take several sizes, as you can see in the Layout area of the ribbon.

Point on each of the options in the layout area of the File Explorer's ribbon to see what it looks like, and then select the one you want to use.

CONTROL HOW WINDOWS 8 OPERATES

How Windows 8 operates is probably at least as important to you as how it looks. Windows 8 has a number of controls that allow you to customize its operation. The primary container, actually a folder, that provides access to these controls is the Control Panel, which has been in the last several versions of Windows. Windows 8 has two other sets of controls, some of which are the same, the Windows 8 PC Settings app, and the system menu, opened by right-clicking the lower-left corner of the screen or pressing **WINDOWS+X** (at the time this was written, it cannot be opened with touch). We'll begin by looking at the Control Panel and some of its controls, and then take a look at PC Settings and the system menu.

▷▷ Use the Control Panel

The Control Panel is a facility for customizing many of the functions in Windows. The individual components of the Control Panel are discussed throughout this book (several in this chapter); this section is an introduction to the Control Panel itself.

Open the Control Panel

To open the Control Panel:

1. In the Start screen, begin typing <u>Control Panel</u>. The Apps search window will open displaying the Control Panel app.

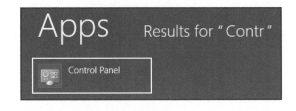

–Or–

In the Start screen open the App bar, select **All Apps**, and move the screen contents until you see **Control Panel**.

2. Select **Control Panel**. The Control Panel is displayed. By default, it will be as shown in Figure 2-12.

*Figure 2-12: **Category view provides a hierarchy of windows that leads you to the settings you want to change.***

–Or–

From either the Start Screen or the desktop, right-click the far bottom-left corner or press **WINDOWS+X** to open the System menu and select **Control Panel**.

Switch the Control Panel View

The Control Panel has three views: the default Category view, shown in Figure 2-12, which groups Control Panel functions; and Large and Small Icons views (Figure 2-13 shows Large Icons view), which shows all the Control Panel components in one window. (Mobile computers will show additional hardware devices unique to them.)

When in Category view, select the **View By** down arrow on the right, and select either **Large Icons** or **Small Icons**.

When in Large or Small Icons view, select the **View By** down arrow on the right, and select **Category** to switch back to that view.

Open a Control Panel Category

Category view groups components into categories that must be opened to see the individual components, although some subcategories are listed.

Select a category to open a window for it, where you can either select a task you want to do or open a Control Panel component represented by an icon, as you can see in Figure 2-14 for the Hardware And Sound category on a tablet PC.

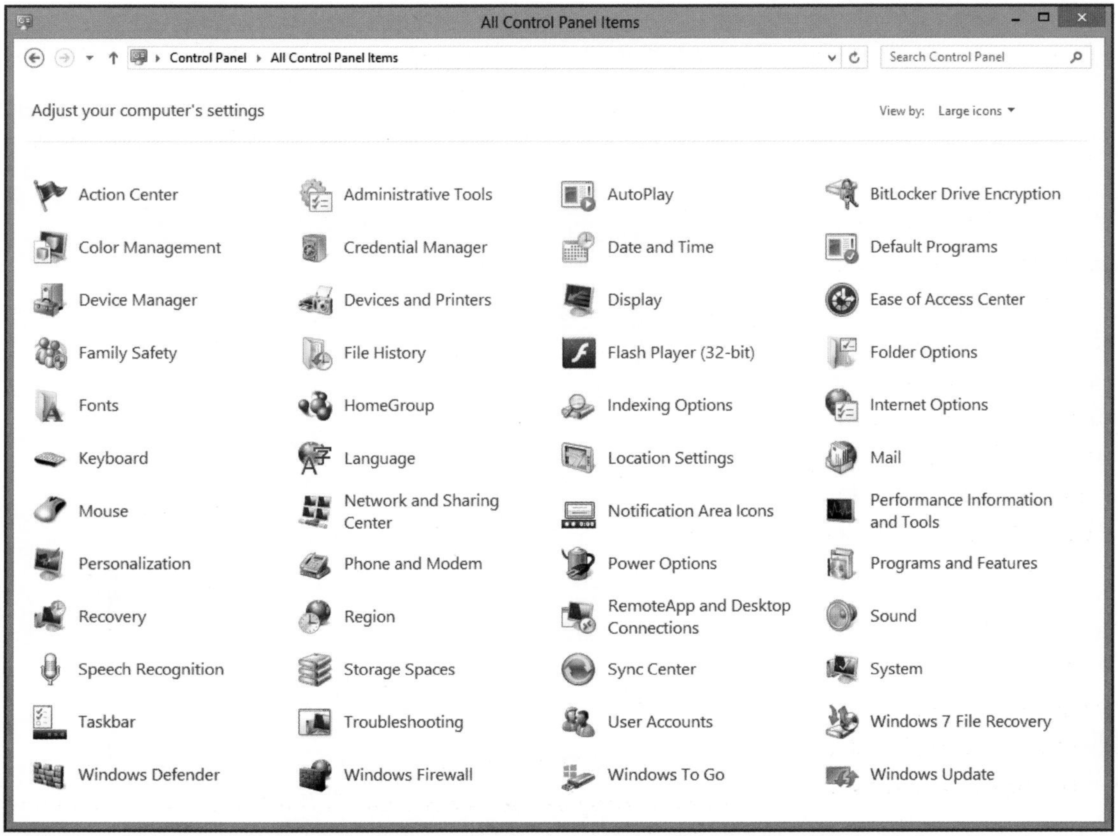

All Control Panel Items

Control Panel ▸ All Control Panel Items

Search Control Panel

Adjust your computer's settings

View by: Large icons ▾

- Action Center
- Administrative Tools
- AutoPlay
- BitLocker Drive Encryption
- Color Management
- Credential Manager
- Date and Time
- Default Programs
- Device Manager
- Devices and Printers
- Display
- Ease of Access Center
- Family Safety
- File History
- Flash Player (32-bit)
- Folder Options
- Fonts
- HomeGroup
- Indexing Options
- Internet Options
- Keyboard
- Language
- Location Settings
- Mail
- Mouse
- Network and Sharing Center
- Notification Area Icons
- Performance Information and Tools
- Personalization
- Phone and Modem
- Power Options
- Programs and Features
- Recovery
- Region
- RemoteApp and Desktop Connections
- Sound
- Speech Recognition
- Storage Spaces
- Sync Center
- System
- Taskbar
- Troubleshooting
- User Accounts
- Windows 7 File Recovery
- Windows Defender
- Windows Firewall
- Windows To Go
- Windows Update

Open a Control Panel Component

When Category view's secondary windows are opened, as in the previous step, the icons for individual Control Panel components are displayed. In either Large or Small Icons view, these component icons are directly displayed. To open a component:

Select the component's icon.

*Figure 2-13: **The Control Panel's Large Icons view shows all of the components in the Control Panel.***

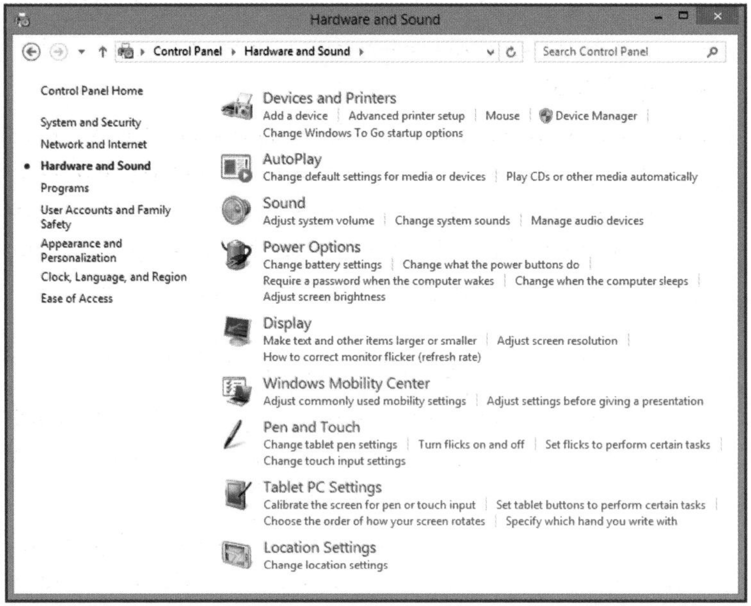

Figure 2-14: *The beauty of the Control Panel's Category view is that components spread around in an icon view are grouped together.*

🠶 Set and Use the Date and Time

Many Control Panel components are also available from other locations. For example, the Control Panel's Date And Time component opens the same dialog box that appears when you select the time and date in the lower-right corner of the screen and then select **Change Date/Time**. The time and date may seem simple enough, but significant capability lies behind these basic numbers.

1. Move the mouse until your cursor is on the time in the notification area. The current day and date will appear.

2. Select the time or date. The full calendar and clock appear.

3. Select **Change Date And Time Settings**. The Date And Time dialog box will appear, as shown in Figure 2-15.

4. With the Date And Time tab selected, select **Change Date And Time**. The Date And Time Settings dialog box appears.

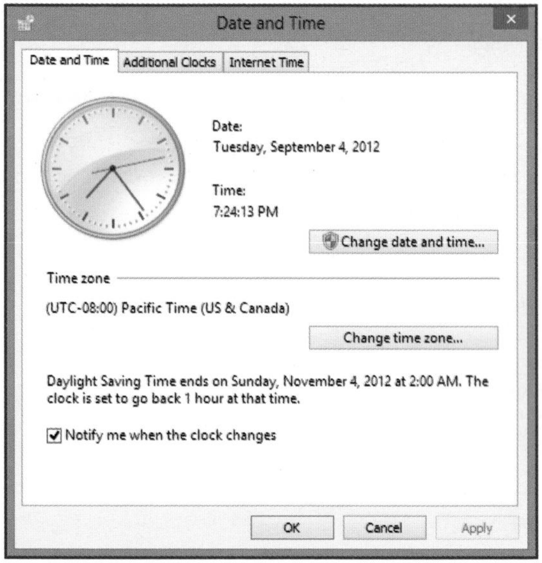

Figure 2-15: *Setting the date and time is normally automated using an Internet time server.*

Note The blue and yellow shield on the Change Date And Time button tells you that the function being selected requires administrator permission. You must be signed on as an administrator, or have a password for an administrator, to change the date and time.

5. Use the arrows on the calendar to change the month. Or, select the month to display the year, use the arrows to change the year, select the month, and then select a day.

6. Double-click or double-tap an element of time (hour, minute, second, A.M./P.M.), and use the spinner to change the selected time element. Select **OK** to close the Date And Time Settings dialog box.

7. Select **Change Time Zone**, select the **Time Zone** down arrow, and select your time zone.

8. Where applicable, select **Automatically Adjust Clock For Daylight Saving Time** if it isn't already selected and you want Windows 8 to do that. Select **OK** to close the Time Zone Settings dialog box.

9. Select the **Additional Clocks** tab to add one or two clocks with different time zones. Select the first **Show This Clock** check box, open the drop-down list box, and select a time zone. Enter a display name, and repeat for a second additional clock, if desired. (The additional times will appear when you point to the time in the notification area.) Select **OK** when done.

10. Select the **Internet Time** tab and see how your computer's time is currently being synchronized. If you want to change that, select **Change Settings**.

11. Select **Synchronize With An Internet Time Server** if it isn't already selected, open the drop-down list, select a time server, and select **Update Now**. Once turned on, Windows will check the time every seven days. Select **OK** to close the Internet Time Settings dialog box.

12. Select **OK** to close the Date And Time dialog box.

Change Ease-of-Access Settings

Ease-of-access settings provide alternatives to the normal way the mouse and keyboard are used, as well as some settings that make the screen more readable and sounds more understandable.

1. Open the desktop's context menu, select **Personalize**, and select **Ease Of Access Center** in the lower-left area. The Ease Of Access Center window will open, as shown in Figure 2-16.

   –Or–

   Press **WINDOWS+U**.

🔵 **Tip** You can also turn on the most common ease-of-access options from the Windows 8 logon screen by selecting the **Ease Of Access** icon in the lower-left corner of the screen.

2. Select the options you want to use in the common tools area at the top (see Table 2-1 for a description). You can also turn the options on or off using the keyboard shortcuts shown.

3. Select any of the blue text links in the lower part of the window to review, and possibly change, the ease-of-access settings that apply to various areas of the computer. Within links there are a number of assistive tools, shown in Table 2-2, that can be turned on, either in these links or with the keyboard shortcuts shown.

4. When you have set up the accessibility options you want, select **Close**.

Table 2-1: Ease-of-Access Reading Tools

Option	Description	Keyboard Shortcut
Magnifier	Enlarges a part of the screen around the mouse.	
On-Screen Keyboard	Displays an image of a keyboard on the screen, the keys of which can be selected with the mouse.	
Narrator	Reads aloud selected text on the screen.	
High Contrast	Uses high-contrast colors and special fonts to make the screen easy to use.	Press left SHIFT+left ALT+and PRINT SCREEN all together.

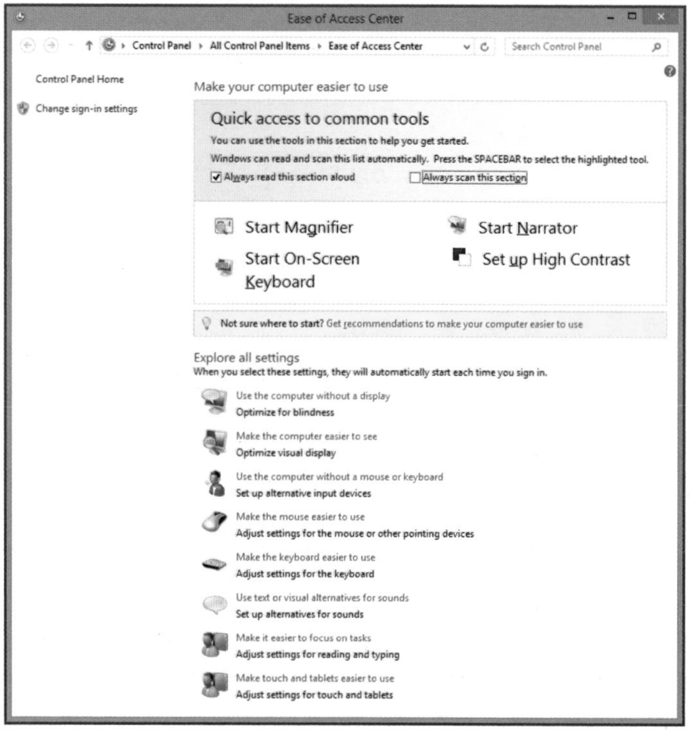

Table 2-2: Ease-of-Access Typing Tools

Option	Description	Keyboard Shortcut
Mouse Keys	Uses the numeric keypad to move the mouse around the screen.	Press left ALT+left SHIFT+NUM LOCK.
Sticky Keys	Simulates pressing a pair of keys, such as CTRL+A, by pressing one key at a time. The keys SHIFT, CTRL, and ALT "stick" down until a second key is pressed. This is interpreted as two keys pressed together.	Press either SHIFT key five times in succession.
Filter Keys	Enables you to press a key twice in rapid succession and have it interpreted as a single keystroke; also slows down the rate at which the key is repeated if it is held down.	Hold down the right SHIFT key for eight seconds.
Toggle Keys	Hear a tone when CAPS LOCK, NUM LOCK, or SCROLL LOCK is turned on.	Hold down the NUM LOCK key for five seconds.

Note If Always Scan This Section is selected and if you have speakers and a sound card, Windows 8 will scan and read aloud the four options in the Quick Access section.

Figure 2-16: Ease-of-access settings let you work with Windows 8 and your apps in ways that facilitate use with various physical limitations.

Customize the Mouse

The mouse lets you interact with the screen and point on, select, and drag objects. You also can start and stop apps and close Windows using the mouse. While you can use Windows without a mouse, many people prefer it, making it important that the mouse operates in the most comfortable way possible.

Switch Buttons and Pointers

Change the way the mouse works through the Control Panel Mouse component.

1. Open the Control Panel as described earlier.

2. In Category view, select **Hardware And Sound**, and under Devices And Printers, select **Mouse**.

   –Or–

   In Large or Small Icons view, select **Mouse**.

   Either way, the Mouse Properties dialog box will appear.

> **Note** Some mice, even some from Microsoft, after installing their unique software, may display their own dialog box with their own settings and tabs when you select **Mouse** in the Control Panel.

3. If you want to use the mouse with your left hand, select **Switch Primary And Secondary Buttons**.

4. Double-click the folder in the middle-right area of the Buttons tab. If the folder opens, your double-click speed is okay. If not, drag the **Speed** slider until the folder opens when you comfortably double-click it.

5. Select the options you want to use on the **Buttons**, **Pointer Options**, **Wheel**, and **Hardware** tabs.

6. Select the **Pointers** tab. If you want to change the way the pointer looks, select a different scheme (see "Use a Different Mouse Pointer," next in this chapter).

7. When you have set up the mouse the way you want, select **OK**.

Use a Different Mouse Pointer

If it is difficult for you to see the mouse pointer, you can change how it looks and behaves in the Mouse Properties dialog box. From the Mouse Properties Pointers tab:

1. Select the **Scheme** down arrow, and choose the scheme you want to use.

2. If you want to customize a particular mouse pointer, select that pointer, select **Browse**, locate/preview and select the pointer you want to use, and select **Open**.

3. Select **OK** to close the Mouse Properties dialog box.

Customize the Keyboard

Depending on your computer and what you do with it, a keyboard may be important. The Keyboard option on the Control Panel allows you to change the length of the delay before a key that is held down is repeated and the rate at which the key is repeated.

1. From the Control Panel in Category view, select **Large** or **Small Icons** view, and then select **Keyboard**. The Keyboard Properties dialog box appears.

![Keyboard Properties dialog box showing Speed tab with Character repeat settings including Repeat delay slider (Long to Short), Repeat rate slider (Slow to Fast), a test text box, and Cursor blink rate slider (None to Fast), with OK, Cancel, and Apply buttons.]

2. Select the text box in the middle of the dialog box, and press a character key to see how long you wait before the key is repeated and how fast the repeated character appears.

3. Move the **Repeat Delay** slider in the direction desired, and then test the repetition again.

4. Move the **Repeat Rate** slider in the direction desired, and then test the repetition again.

5. Move the **Cursor Blink Rate** slider in the direction desired, and observe the blink rate.

6. When you have set up the keyboard the way you want, select **OK**.

Change Sounds

Windows 8 uses sounds to alert and entertain you. Through Control Panel's Sound component, you can select the sound scheme you want.

Configure Your Speakers

1. In the Control Panel's Category view, select **Hardware And Sound**, and then select **Sound**.

   –Or–

   In Large or Small Icons view, select **Sound**.

   In either case, the Sound dialog box appears.

2. Select **Speakers | Configure** in the lower-left corner, select your configuration in the Audio Channels list, and select **Test** to test your setup. When you are ready, select **Next**.

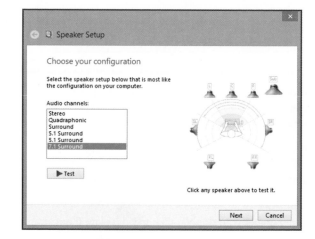

3. If you select a configuration that has more speakers than you actually have—for example, if you have a subwoofer and a pair of speakers—you must select the first 5.1 Surround configuration and select **Next**.

Then select the speakers that aren't present—the Center and Side Pair in this example, and select **Next**. Select the speakers that are full-range speakers, and select **Next**. When you are done, select **Finish**.

4. Open (double-click or double-tap) **Speakers**, select the **Levels** tab, and move the slider(s) in the direction desired to set the volume. Select **OK** to close the Speakers Properties dialog box.

Select the Sounds Windows 8 Plays

You can select the sounds that are played when various events occur, such as a critical stop or Windows shutdown, in the Sound dialog box. From the Personalization window, select Sounds.

1. In the Sounds dialog box, select the **Sounds** tab. Select the **Sound Scheme** down arrow, and select one of the options.

2. Open a **Program Events** option and select **Test** to hear its current sound played.

Region
Formats	Location	Administrative
Format: English (United States)
Match Windows display language (recommended)
Language preferences
Date and time formats
Short date:	M/d/yyyy
Long date:	dddd, MMMM d, yyyy
Short time:	h:mm tt
Long time:	h:mm:ss tt
First day of week:	Sunday
Examples
Short date:	9/4/2012
Long date:	Tuesday, September 4, 2012
Short time:	9:42 PM
Long time:	9:42:29 PM
Additional settings...
OK	Cancel	Apply

3. Select the **Sounds** down arrow to select a different sound for the event. Select **Test** to hear the sound.

4. When you have made all the changes you want to the association of sounds and events, select **Save As** to save your changes as a new scheme. Type a name for the new scheme, and select **OK**.

5. When you are ready, select **OK** to close the Sound dialog box.

▷▷ Change Regional Settings

Windows 8 lets you determine how numbers, dates, currency, and time are displayed and used, as well as the languages that will be used. Choosing a primary language and locale sets all the other settings. You can customize these options through the Regional And Language Options component in the Control Panel.

1. In the Control Panel Category view, select **Clock, Language, And Region**, and then select **Language**.

   –Or–

   In Large or Small Icons view, select **Language**.

   In either case, the Language window will open.

2. Verify that you want to use the language shown. If not, select **Add A Language** | *<the language>* | **Open** | *<the specific country using the language>* | **Add**.

3. Select **Change Date, Time, Or Number Formats** to open the Region dialog box.

Region

Formats | Location | Administrative

Format: English (United States)

Match Windows display language (recommended)

Language preferences

Date and time formats

Short date: M/d/yyyy

Long date: dddd, MMMM d, yyyy

Short time: h:mm tt

Long time: h:mm:ss tt

First day of week: Sunday

Examples

Short date: 9/4/2012

Long date: Tuesday, September 4, 2012

Short time: 9:54 PM

Long time: 9:54:31 PM

Additional settings...

OK   Cancel   Apply

4. Customize the date and time formats by selecting the down arrow associated with each setting and selecting the option that you want.

5. Select **Additional Settings** and then go to the individual tabs for numbers, currency, time, and date; and set how you want these items displayed. Select **OK** when you are done.

6. Review the **Location** and **Administrative** tabs, and make any desired changes.

7. When you have set up the regional settings the way you want, select **OK**. Close the Language window/dialog box.

CAUTION! Changing the format used for dates and times might affect other apps, such as Excel.

⏩ Consider Additional Sets of Controls

As was mentioned earlier in the chapter, while the Control Panel is the primary location to find Windows 8 controls and settings, there are two new facilities that also offer controls: PC Settings, a Windows 8 Style app, and the System menu.

Review PC Settings

PC Settings, shown earlier in Figure 2-4, does not share much with the Control Panel, and even the settings in Ease of Use do not fully duplicate those in the Control Panel. Most of the PC Settings' controls are discussed in later chapters. Here, simply familiarize yourself with the options.

1. Open **Charms** and select **Settings | Change PC Settings**. The PC Settings window will open.

2. Select each of the options in the left column and review the related settings on the right. Many of these will be discussed in later chapters.

Look at the System Menu

The System menu, shown next, is aimed at advanced users, although anybody can use it. The first seven options are contained in the Control Panel, although Disk Management, Event Viewer, and Computer Management are hidden in Administrative Tools, where Disk Management is in Computer Management. The remaining options are all available in Start screen All Apps. Many of the options will be described later in this book.

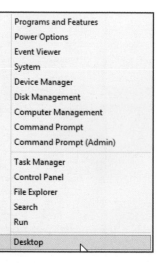

Programs and Features
Power Options
Event Viewer
System
Device Manager
Disk Management
Computer Management
Command Prompt
Command Prompt (Admin)

Task Manager
Control Panel
File Explorer
Search
Run

Desktop

Chapter 3

Storing Information

The information on your computer—documents, email, photographs, music, and programs—is stored in *files.* So that your files are organized and more easily found, they are kept in *folders,* and folders can be placed in other folders for further organization. For example, a folder labeled "Nature," which is contained in the My Pictures folder, contains separate folders for National Parks and Sunsets. The National Parks folder contains folders for the Grand Canyon, Olympic, and Yellowstone National Parks. The Olympic folder contains photos of the park. Such a set of files and folders is shown in Figure 3-1.

In this chapter you'll see how to create, use, and manage files and folders like these. The term "objects" is used to refer to any mix of files, folders, and disk drives.

USE THE WINDOWS FILE SYSTEM

The tool that Windows 8 provides to locate and work with files and folders is *File Explorer* (often called "Explorer," not to be confused with Internet Explorer discussed in Chapter 4). File Explorer has a number of components and features, most of which are shown in Figure 3-2 and described in Table 3-1. Much of this chapter is spent exploring these items and how they are used.

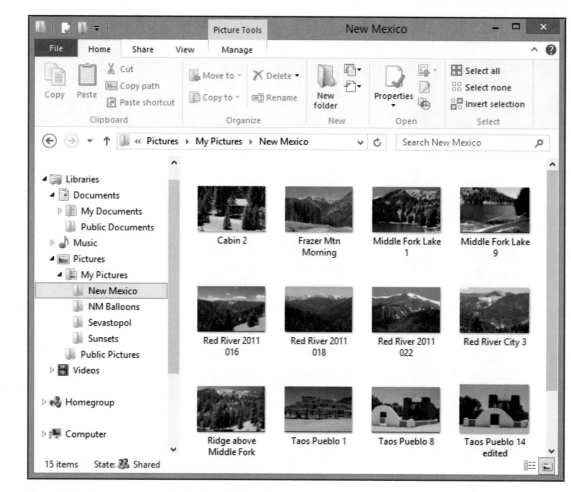

Figure 3-1: *Windows stores files in folders, which can be within other folders. (Courtesy of Tom Beard.)*

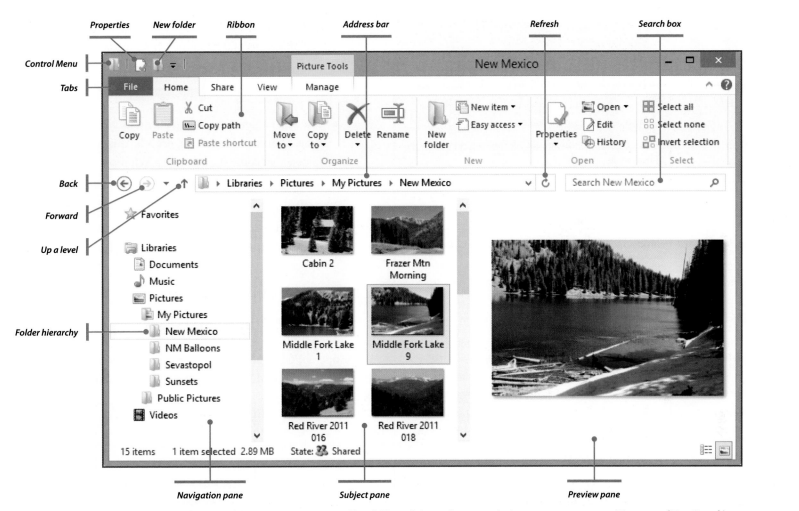

Figure 3-2: *File Explorer provides the means to access files, folders, disks, and memory devices on your computer. (Courtesy of Tom Beard.)*

Table 3-1: File Explorer Components

Component	Function
Properties	Displays the properties of the selected object in the subject pane
New Folder	Creates a new folder in the subject pane
Ribbon	Contains tools to work with the selected object in the subject pane
Address bar	Displays the location of what is being shown in the subject pane
Refresh	Updates what is displayed in the address bar
Search box	Provides for the entry of text you want to search for within the content in the subject pane
Preview pane	Displays the contents of the object selected in the subject pane
Subject pane	Displays the objects stored at the address shown in the address bar
Navigation pane	Facilitates moving around among the objects you have available
Folder hierarchy	Shows the folder within folder within folder hierarchy
Up a level	Moves the view (the contents of the subject pane) up to the containing folder
Back and Forward buttons	Displays an object previously shown
Tabs	Selects from several different groups of ribbon tools
Control menu	Displays control for sizing and moving the window with a keyboard

▷▷ Open File Explorer

The easiest way to open File Explorer is from the desktop.

1. Start your computer, if it's not running, and log on to Windows if necessary.

2. From the Start screen select the desktop, and on the desktop select **File Explorer**, second from the left on the taskbar.

- The File Explorer should open and display your libraries in the subject pane, as shown in Figure 3-3. This gives you access to four folders that come standard with Windows 8. You can
   - **Open** (double-click or double-tap) a folder in the subject pane to display its contents so that you can see and work with them.
   - **Select** (click or tap) an object within the subject pane to get information about it in the details pane, preview it in the preview pane, or use the ribbon tools with that object.

There are three ways of opening File Explorer:

- From the lower-left corner of either the Start screen or the desktop, open (right-click) the System menu and select **File Explorer**. This opens File Explorer and displays its Computer option with its disk drives and shared network devices, as shown in Figure 3-4.

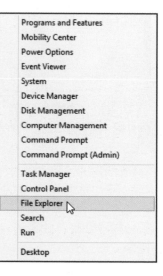

*Figure 3-3: **Windows 8 starts with several standard folders that are a part of the Libraries folder.***

Note As was mentioned in Chapter 2, the System menu can't currently be opened using touch. You could add the Onscreen Keyboard app to the Start screen. Then after opening it, you could press **WINDOWS+X** to open the System menu.

- From the Start screen, open (right-click or swipe up from the bottom of the screen) the App bar and select **All Apps**. From here, under Windows System, you can select

  ■ **Computer** to open File Explorer displaying the Computer option and your disk drives.

■ **File Explorer** to open File Explorer displaying the Libraries option and the four major folders within it.

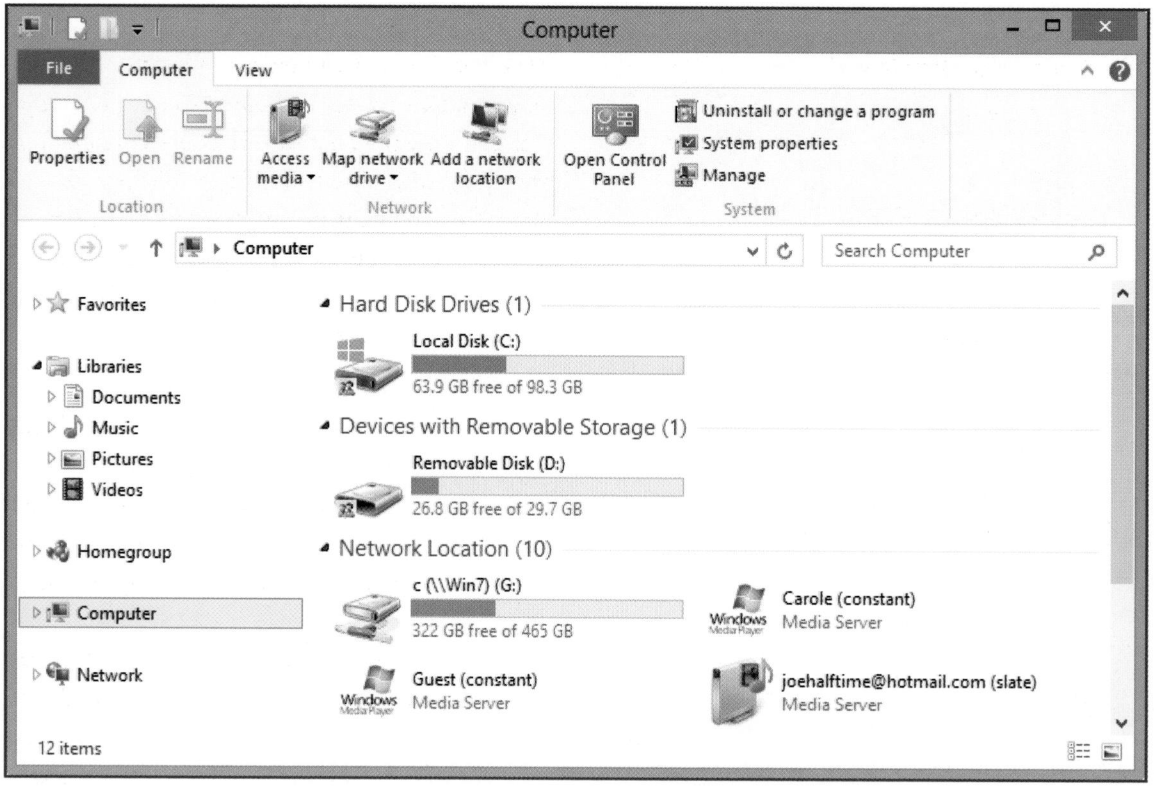

Figure 3-4: Your disk drives, shown in the Computer option, are the primary means of storing information on your computer.

⟫ Change the File Explorer Layout

As you saw in Figure 3-2, the File Explorer window has several different panes that you may want to use. You can turn them on or off through the ribbon's View tab.

Open Layout Options

- In File Explorer, select **View** on the ribbon tabs. The Panes options are displayed for turning on or off the navigation, preview, and details panes. By default, the navigation pane is on and the others are off.

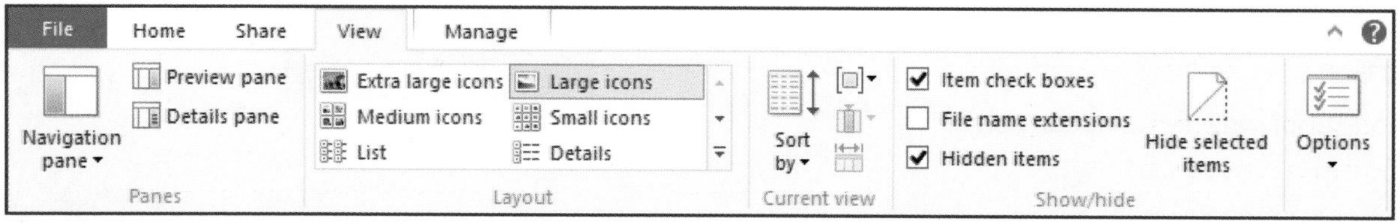

Turn On the Preview Pane

With the View tab displayed, select **Preview Pane**.

Turn On the Details Pane

In the View tab, select **Details Pane**.

Turn Off the Navigation Pane

In the View tab, select **Navigation Pane**, and then select **Navigation Pane** a second time from the menu.

▷▷ Customize File Explorer

You can customize how File Explorer looks and determine which features are available with the ribbon.

1. If File Explorer is not already open, select the desktop and select **File Explorer**.

2. Select **Pictures** in the navigation pane, and then open a folder of photos in the subject pane. That folder should open, as you can see in Figure 3-5.

3. Select one of the pictures. The ribbon changes to something like this:

These ribbon options are specific to the file selected. Selecting other types of files would have generated different options.

Look at the File Explorer Ribbon

The File Explorer ribbon has at least three tabs and can have five or more, as you can see in Figure 3-5. Each tab is opened by selecting the tab above the ribbon. When you open Explorer from the desktop taskbar or by selecting **File Explorer** in All Apps, the Home tab is displayed by default. When you select File Explorer from the System menu or by selecting **Computer** in All Apps, the Computer tab is displayed. The functions that you can perform with each of the tabs and their ribbon include the following:

- **File tab** provides options for the Windows file system. The first option opens a new window to give you two or more copies of File Explorer on the desktop. The second and third options are for accessing and controlling Windows without using the normal Windows interface. The command prompt is touched on in Chapter 5, but generally these options are beyond the scope of this book. Delete History allows you to delete the list of recent places you have visited in the file system (shown when you first open the File tab), and to delete recent entries made in the address bar. Help opens the Windows Help system, and Close closes File Explorer, both of which are also available in the tab and title bars, respectively.

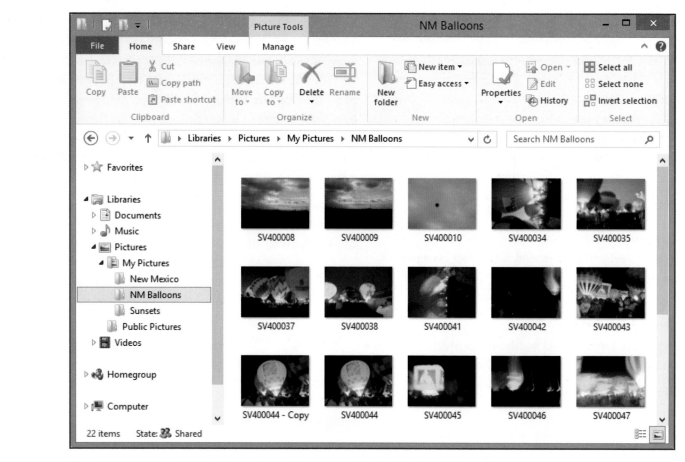

Figure 3-5: *File Explorer's ribbon changes to provide commands for what is selected in the subject pane.*

TIP Selecting the push pin on the list of frequent places will keep the entry on the list until you select the push pin again.

TIP After opening the File tab, you can close it and return to File Explorer by selecting the File tab a second time.

- **Home tab**, which is shown in several earlier figures, allows you to perform operations on the object you have selected, such as Cut, Copy, Paste, Delete, and Rename, as well as Move, Copy, Open, and Edit. You also can perform folder-related operations, such as New Folder, Select All, and Invert Selection. Most of these options are discussed later in this chapter.

- **Share tab** allows you to email, burn to disc, print, and fax an object you have selected. You can also compress one or more objects to make them both easier to store and send over the Internet by selecting them and then selecting **Zip**. You can select who and how you want to share the selected objects, turn off sharing, and set up advanced sharing properties. Controlling sharing is discussed in Chapter 8.

- **View tab**, as you saw earlier, allows you to turn the various panes on and off. It also lets you determine how objects are displayed in File Explorer. Figure 3-5 shows objects displayed as large icons, just one of the eight views. You can also sort and group the items in the subject pane and add and size columns in the Details view. You can add a check box and display file extensions

(like .doc for older Word files), as well as hide objects and display hidden objects. Options, on the right of the ribbon, opens the Folder Options dialog box discussed later in this chapter. Point on each of the other seven view choices, ending with Details to see what they are like. In the Details view, which is shown in Figure 3-6, you can:

1. Select **Name** at the top of the left column in the subject pane. The contents of the subject pane will be sorted alphanumerically by name. Select **Name** again, and the contents will be sorted by name in the opposite direction.

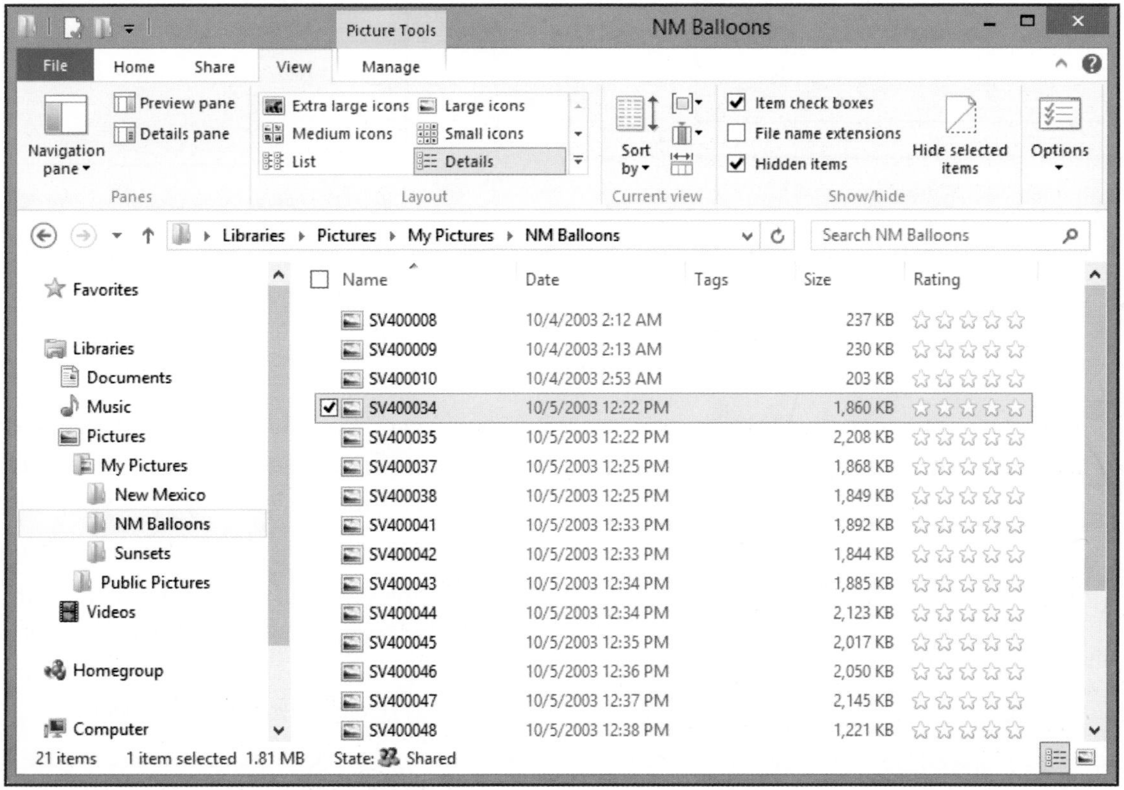

Figure 3-6: Folder Details view gives you further information about the objects in a folder.

2. Select one of the other column headings, and then select the same column heading again to see the contents sorted that way, first in one direction, and then in the other. The Sort By option on the View ribbon tab performs the same purpose.

 TIP Point on a column heading and select the down arrow on its right to see filtering options.

3. Move the mouse pointer until it is between two columns and drag it left or right to dynamically size the column.

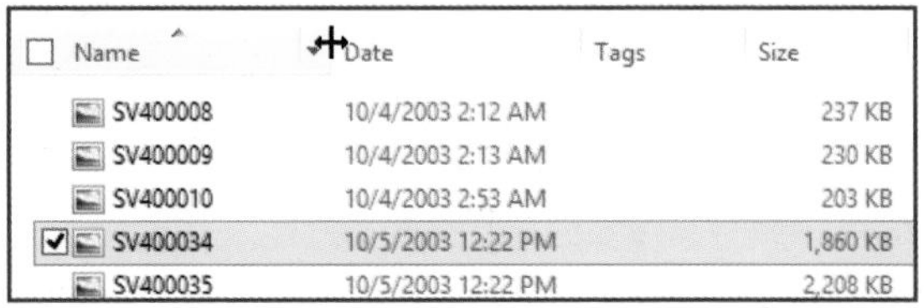

☐ Name	Date	Tags	Size
☐ SV400008	10/4/2003 2:12 AM		237 KB
☐ SV400009	10/4/2003 2:13 AM		230 KB
☐ SV400010	10/4/2003 2:53 AM		203 KB
☑ SV400034	10/5/2003 12:22 PM		1,860 KB
☐ SV400035	10/5/2003 12:22 PM		2,208 KB

 Note The Picture Tools Manage tab in Figures 3-1, 3-2, 3-5, and 3-6 is called a "contextual tab," since it only appears in context with the selected object—in this case, a picture. It provides options for working with the selected object, such as rotating a picture and creating a slide show.

Examine Folder Options

The Folder Options dialog box provides the means to change the way that the Explorer displays and handles files and folders. You open Folder Options from the Explorer's View ribbon.

1. Select the **Options** icon at the top on the right end of the View ribbon. The Folder Options dialog box will appear with the General tab displayed, as shown in Figure 3-7. This allows you to

Note Some options on the ribbon are split in two parts: selecting the icon opens a dialog box; selecting the label and down arrow opens a menu.

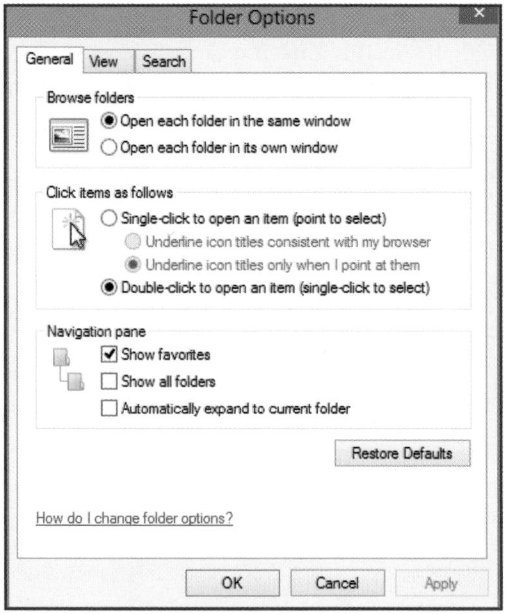

Figure 3-7: Folder Options allows you to determine how folders look and behave.

- Open a new window for each folder you open.
- Use a single click in place of a double click to open a window on the desktop.
- If you choose single click, you can also determine whether to permanently underline an icon title, as in an Internet browser, or underline an icon only when you point on it.
- Display more or fewer folders in the navigation pane.

2. Select the **View** tab, which is shown in Figure 3-8. This gives you a number of options that determine what is displayed for the current folder and allow you to apply these changes to all folders. The default settings generally work for most people.

3. When you are ready, select **OK** to close the Folder Options dialog box. (The Search tab will be discussed under "Search for Apps and Files" later in this chapter.)

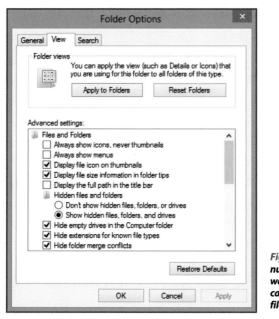

Figure 3-8: There are a number of options in the way that File Explorer can display folder and file information.

LOCATE AND USE FILES AND FOLDERS

The purpose of a file system, of course, is to locate and use the files and folders on your computer, and possibly on other computers connected to yours (accessing other computers is called *networking* and is discussed in Chapters 9 and 10). Within your computer, there is a storage hierarchy that starts with storage devices, such as disk drives, which are divided into areas called folders, each of which may be divided again into subareas called subfolders. Each of these contains files, which can be documents, pictures, music, and other data. Figure 3-1 showed folders containing subfolders and eventually containing files with information in them. Figure 3-9 shows a computer containing disk drives, which in turn contain folders. File Explorer contains a number of tools for locating, opening, and using disk drives, folders, and files.

Identify Storage Devices

Files and folders are stored on various physical storage devices, including hard disk drives, solid-state drives, CD and DVD drives, memory cards and sticks, and Universal Serial Bus (USB) flash memory. You will have some, but not necessarily all, of the following:

- Primary floppy disk, labeled "A:" (most computers no longer have a floppy drive)
- Primary hard disk, labeled "C:"
- CD or DVD drive, labeled "D:"
- Other storage devices, labeled "E:" and then "F:" and so on

Your primary hard disk is always labeled "C:." Other drives have flexible labeling. Often, the

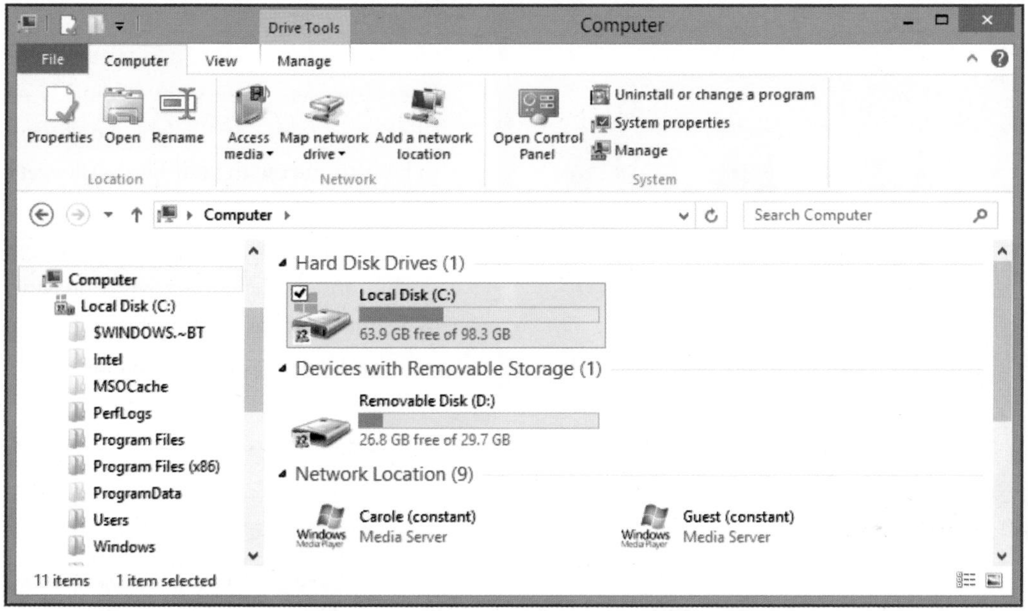

Figure 3-9: Your computer stores information in a hierarchy of disk drives and folders.

CD or DVD drive will be drive "D:," but if you have a second hard disk drive, it may be labeled "D."

Select and Open Drives and Folders

When you open File Explorer and display the items in Computer, you see the disk drives and other storage devices on your computer, as well as several folders, including Program Files, Users, and Windows, as you saw in Figure 3-9. To work with these drives and folders, you must select them; to see and work with their contents, you must open them.

1. In either the Start screen or the desktop, open (right-click) the System menu and select **File Explorer** to open it and display the local disk drives.

2. In the subject pane (right pane), select disk **(C:)**. Disk (C:) will be highlighted.

3. Open (double-click) disk **(C:)** in any pane. Disk (C:) will open and its folders will be displayed in the subject pane.

4. Open **Users** to open that folder and display your folder along with a Public folder.

5. Open your personal folder (the folder with your name on it). The subject pane displays the files and folders in your folder. This will include Contacts, Desktop, My Documents, My Music, and others, as shown in Figure 3-10.

6. Keep opening each folder until you see the contents you are looking for.

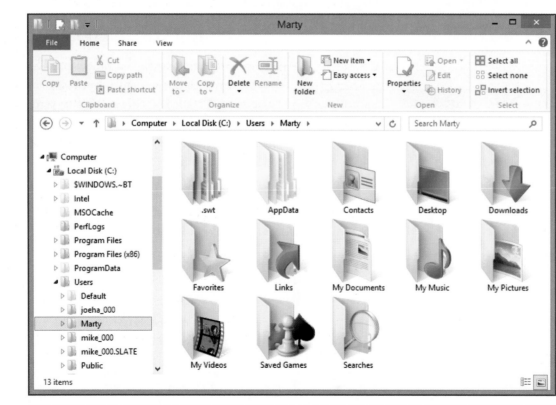

Navigate Folders and Disks

Opening File Explorer and navigating through several folders—beginning with your hard disk—to find a file you want is fine. However, if you want to quickly go to another folder or file, you won't want to have to start with your hard disk every single time. The Windows 8 File Explorer gives you three ways to do this: through the Libraries folder in the navigation pane, by using the folder tree in the navigation pane, or by using the address bar.

Figure 3-10: Opening a drive or folder will open it in the subject pane.

Navigate Using Libraries

The Windows 8 suggested way to navigate is through the Libraries folder, which contains links to the folders within your personal folder (called a "library" in this case, as shown next). By selecting a library in the navigation pane and then opening folders within the subject pane, you can move around the folders and files within your personal folder. For example, given the folder structure shown in Figure 3-1, here are the steps to open the NM Balloon folder.

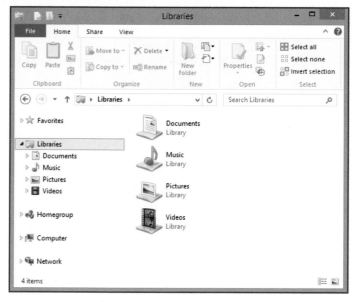

1. From the desktop taskbar, open **File Explorer**, and then open the **Libraries** folder.

2. In the navigation pane, select the right-pointing triangle or arrow opposite the Pictures library to open it.

3. Still in the navigation pane, select the right-pointing arrow opposite **My Pictures** to open it and then select the final folder (NM Balloons here) to open it in the subject pane.

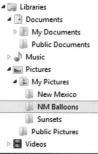

TIP It is easy to become confused by the various folders in the navigation pane. Both Favorites and Libraries are folders with *shortcuts*, or links, to folders and files on your computer. (See "Create Shortcuts" later in this chapter.) The shortcuts in Libraries are links to the actual folders in the C:/Users/*Personal Folder*/My Documents path, as you can see in "Navigate Using Folders."

Navigate Using Folders

The portion of the navigation pane starting with Computer is a folder tree that contains all the disk drives, folders, and files on your computer in a tree, or hierarchical, structure. To open the same folder structure shown in Figure 3-1 through Computer:

1. From the System menu, select **File Explorer**, opening Computer in the navigation pane, as you saw in Figure 3-9.

2. In the navigation pane, select the right-pointing arrow opposite the (C:) disk drive to open it.

3. Still in the navigation pane, select the right-pointing arrow opposite **Users** to open it.

4. Repeat step 3 to open your personal folder and then the My Pictures folder.

5. Finally select the final folder (NM Balloons here) to open it in the subject pane.

You can see that Libraries saves a couple of steps, but at the cost of possible confusion.

TIP The folder tree is also useful for copying and moving files and folders, as you will see in "Copy and Move Files and Folders" later in this chapter.

Navigate Using the Address Bar

Windows 8 gives you another way to quickly navigate through your drives and folders by selecting segments of a folder address in the address bar, as shown here:

> Computer ▸ Local Disk (C:) ▸ Users ▸ Marty ▸ My Pictures ▸ NM Balloons

By selecting the down arrow on the far right of the address bar, you can see how this same address looked in versions of Windows before Windows 7 and use the address bar as it was in the past.

C:\Users\Marty\Pictures\NM Balloons

With Windows 8, if you select any segment of the address, you will open that level in the subject pane. If you select the arrow to the right of the segment, it displays a drop-down list of subfolders that you can jump to. By successively selecting segments and their subordinate folders, you can easily move throughout the storage space on your computer and beyond to any network you are connected to.

My Pictures ▸ NM Balloons
New Mexico
NM Balloons
Sunsets

TIP The small down arrow between the Forward button and the address bar displays a list of disks and folders that you recently displayed. The upward arrow moves the *focus* (what is shown in the subject pane) up one level. For example, if the NW Balloons folder is open in the subject pane and you select the upward arrow, the My Pictures folder will become the focus displayed in the subject pane.

✓ **NM Balloons**
Libraries

⏩ Create New Folders

While you could store all your files within one of the ready-made folders in Windows 8—such as Documents, Music, or Pictures—you will probably want to make your files easier to find by creating several subfolders.

For example, to create a Windows 8 Notes folder:

1. From the desktop taskbar, open **File Explorer**, opening the Libraries folder. Open **Documents**. Make sure nothing is selected.

2. Select **New Folder** on right of the Quick Access toolbar. A new folder will appear with its name ("New Folder") highlighted.

File Home Share View
New folder (Ctrl+Shift+N)
Create a new folder.

3. Type the name of the folder, such as <u>Windows 8 Notes</u>, and press **ENTER**. Open your new folder to open it (you will see it's empty).

Windows 8 Notes

As an alternative to selecting New Folder on the Quick Access toolbar, right-select the open area in the subject pane of File Explorer. Select **New | Folder**. Type a name for the folder, and press **ENTER**.

⏩ Rename and Delete Files and Folders

Sometimes, a file or folder needs to be renamed or deleted (whether it was created by you or by an application) because you may no longer need it or for any number of reasons.

Rename a File or Folder

With the file or folder in view but not selected, to rename it:

- In the subject pane, slowly select the name twice (don't double-select), type the new name, and press **ENTER**.

  –Or–

- In either the navigation or subject pane, open the context menu for the name, select **Rename**, type the new name, and press **ENTER**.

Delete a File or Folder to the Recycle Bin

With the file or folder in view in either the navigation or subject pane, to delete it:

- Select the icon for the file or folder and press **DELETE**.

  –Or–

- Open the context menu for the icon and select **Delete**.

Recover a Deleted File or Folder

To recover a file or folder that has been deleted:

- Open the **Recycle Bin** on the desktop to display it. Select the object to be restored, and select **Restore The Selected Items** in the Recycle Bin Tools tab.

  –Or–

- Open the context menu for the file or folder icon, and select **Restore**.

Permanently Delete a File or Folder

If you're sure you want to permanently delete a file or folder:

- Select the icon, press and hold **SHIFT** while pressing **DELETE**, and select **Yes** to confirm the permanent deletion.

  –Or–

- Open the context menu for the icon, and press and hold **SHIFT** while selecting **DELETE | Yes** to confirm the permanent deletion.

Select Multiple Files and Folders

Often, you will want to do one or more operations—such as copy, move, or delete—on several files and/or folders at the same time. To select several files or folders from the subject pane of an Explorer window:

- Move the mouse pointer or your finger to the upper-left area, just outside of the top and leftmost object. Then drag the mouse or your finger to the lower-right area, just outside of the bottom and rightmost object, creating a shading across the objects.

  –Or–

- Select the first object, and press and hold **CTRL** while selecting the remaining objects, if the objects are noncontiguous (not adjacent to each other). If the objects are contiguous, select the first object, press and hold **SHIFT**, and select the last object.

> **Note** Using the Onscreen Keyboard app (not the default touch keyboard), you can use CTRL and SHIFT to make multiple selections using touch; not so from the default keyboard available on the notification area, though when you press CTRL on it, the "a" character allows you to select all.

> **TIP** To select all objects in the subject pane, select **Select All** on the right of the Home tab; or select any object in the subject pane, and press **CTRL+A**.

Use the Recycle Bin

If you do a normal delete operation in Explorer or the desktop, the deleted item or items will go into the Recycle Bin. Should you change your mind about the deletion, you can reclaim an item from the Recycle Bin, as explained in "Rename and Delete Files and Folders" earlier in this chapter.

The Recycle Bin is a special folder that can contain both files and folders. You can open it and see its contents as you would any other folder by opening its desktop icon. Figure 3-11 shows a Recycle Bin after deleting several files. What makes the Recycle Bin special are the special options in the ribbon:

- **Empty The Recycle Bin**   Permanently removes all of the contents of the Recycle Bin.

- **Restore All Items**   Returns all the contents to their original folders, in effect, "undeleting" all of the contents.

- **Restore The Selected Items**   Returns the selected items to their original folders.

- **Recycle Bin Properties**   Allows you to set the maximum size of the Recycle Bin so it doesn't take up all your disk space.

  1. With the Recycle Bin open in File Explorer, select **Recycle Bin Properties**. The Recycle Bin Properties dialog box will appear, as you can see here.

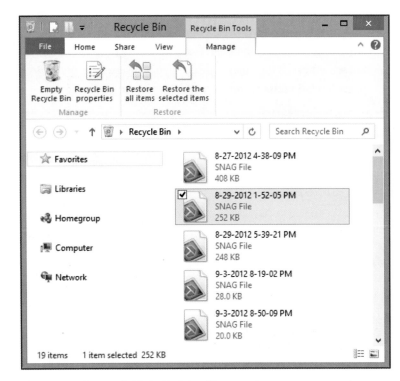

  2. If you have multiple hard disks, select the drive you want to use for the Recycle Bin. With Custom Size selected, select the size, and type the number of megabytes you want to use ("7085" megabytes is 7.085 gigabytes).

  3. If you don't want to use the Recycle Bin, select **Don't Move Files To The Recycle Bin**. This is strongly discouraged since this means that files will be permanently deleted with no hope of recovery.

Figure 3-11: The Recycle Bin holds deleted items so that you can recover them until you empty it.

4. If you want to see a deletion confirmation message, select that check box to check it.

5. When you are ready, select **OK** to close the dialog box.

⏵⏵ Create Shortcuts

A shortcut is a link to a file or folder that allows you to quickly open the file or folder from places other than where it is stored. For example, you can start a program from the desktop even though the actual program file is stored in some other folder. To create a shortcut:

1. In File Explorer, locate the folder or file for which you want to create a shortcut.

2. If it is a program file (one identified as an "application," or with an .exe extension), drag it to a different folder, for example, from a folder to the desktop.

3. If it is any other file or folder:

    With a mouse, hold down the right mouse button while moving the file or folder to a different folder and then release the right mouse button.

    With touch, hold your finger on the object until a rectangle appears, then immediately move the file or folder to a different folder and release your finger.

    In either case, a context menu should appear. Select **Create Shortcuts Here**.

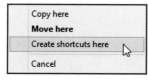

 TIP You may want to have the folders tree visible in the navigation pane and have the destination folder visible so you can drag to it the icon for which you want to create a shortcut.

–Or–

1. In File Explorer, open the folder in which you want to create a shortcut.

2. In a blank area in the subject pane of the folder, open the context menu (right-click or touch and hold the rectangle, then release) and select **New | Shortcut**.

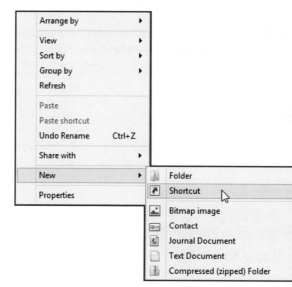

3. In the dialog box that appears, select **Browse** and use the folder tree to locate and select the file or folder for which you want to make a shortcut.

4. Select **OK | Next**. Type a name for the shortcut, and select **Finish**.

 Note You can tell if an object is a shortcut in two ways: "Shortcut" may be in its title (unless you've renamed it), and an upward-pointing arrow is in the lower-left corner of the icon, like this:

Copy and Move Files and Folders

Copying and moving files and folders are similar actions, and can be done with the mouse, with touch, with the mouse or touch and a menu, and with the keyboard.

> **Note** To use touch and the keyboard—for example, holding down **CTRL** or **SHIFT** while moving a file, as in a few places later—you need to use the Onscreen Keyboard app, not the default touch keyboard whose icon is in the notification area of the taskbar. Open the Onscreen Keyboard app from the All Apps, Windows Ease of Access section.

Copy with the Mouse or Touch

- To copy with the mouse or touch, hold down **CTRL** while moving any file or folder from one folder to another on the same disk drive, or simply move without **CTRL** a file or folder from one disk drive to another.

Move Nonprogram Files on the Same Disk with the Mouse or Touch

- Move nonprogram files from one folder to another on the same disk with the mouse or touch by moving the file or folder.

Move Nonprogram Files to Another Disk with the Mouse or Touch

- Move nonprogram files to another disk by holding down **SHIFT** while moving them.

Move Program Files with the Mouse or Touch

- Move program files to another folder or disk by holding down **SHIFT** while dragging them. (Note that program files generally need to be installed and remain in a given location, and moving them may cause them not to run.)

Copy and Move with the Mouse or Touch and a Menu

- To copy and move with a mouse and a menu, hold down the right mouse button while dragging the file or folder. When you release the right mouse button, a context menu opens.

- To copy and move with touch and a menu, touch and hold the object to be moved until you see a rectangle, then quickly move the file or folder. When you release your finger, a context menu opens.

- In the context menu that opens, you can choose whether to copy, move, or create a shortcut (see "Create Shortcuts" in this chapter).

Copy here
Move here
Create shortcuts here
Cancel

Copy and Move with the Keyboard

Copying and moving with the keyboard is done with three sets of keys:

- **CTRL+C** ("Copy") copies the selected item to the Windows Clipboard.

- **CTRL+X** ("Cut") moves the selected item to the Windows Clipboard, deleting it from its original location.

- **CTRL+V** ("Paste") copies the current contents of the Windows Clipboard to the currently open folder. You can repeatedly paste the same Clipboard contents to any additional folders you want to copy to by opening them and pressing **CTRL+V** again.

To copy a file or folder from one folder to another using the keyboard:

- In File Explorer, open the disk and folder containing the file or folder to be copied.

- Select the file or folder, and press **CTRL+C** to copy the file or folder to the Clipboard.

- Open the disk and folder that is to be the destination of the copied item.

- Press **CTRL+V** to paste the file or folder into the destination folder.

TIP You can also use the Cut, Copy, and Paste commands in the object's context menu (by opening the context menu for the object) or from the Home tab in the File Explorer ribbon.

Search for Apps and Files

With large and, possibly several, hard disks, it is often difficult to find apps and files. Windows' Search features address that issue. Windows 8 has two search facilities: on the Start screen and in File Explorer.

Search from the Start Screen

1. From the Start screen (anywhere on it—there is not a specific text box), type all or part of the app or filename. (With touch, you need to open **Charms** and select **Search** to get the touch keyboard, unless you have the Onscreen Keyboard app displayed.) As you type, the Windows 8 Search screen will open and start displaying apps that match some or all of what you typed.

2. If you are looking for files, select **Files** on the right pane, and files will be displayed matching some or all of what you typed, as you can see in Figure 3-12.

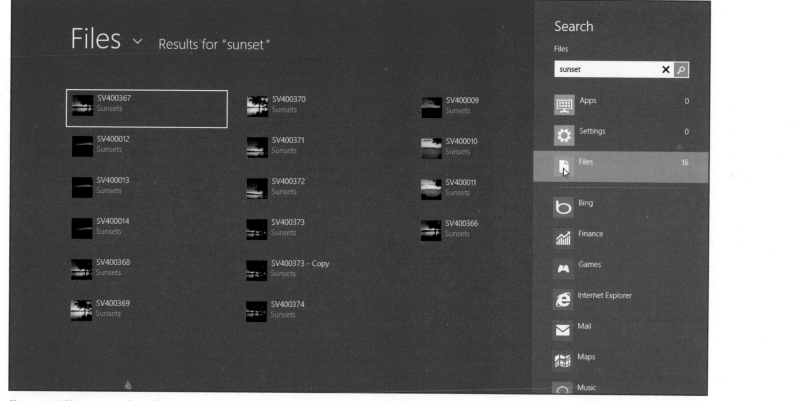

Figure 3-12: You may need to refine your search criteria to get only the files you are looking for.

3. If you see the file or app you are searching for, select it, and if it is a file, it will be displayed in the program that is related to it (Photo for photos, Video for videos, Word for Word documents, and so on). If it is a program, it will start.

4. If you want refine your search, type more information into the Search text box in the upper-right of the Search pane.

Search from File Explorer

1. In the File Explorer Search text box in the upper-right corner (with the magnifying glass), type all or part of the file or folder name, keyword, or phrase you want to find. As you type, File Explorer will start displaying the files and folders that match some or all of what you typed, as you can see in Figure 3-13.

Note The touch keyboard does not appear when you touch the File Explorer Search text box. You have to touch the icon in the notification area to display it.

2. If you see the file or folder you are searching for, double-select it and it will be displayed in File Explorer (if a folder) or in the program that created it or that can display it (if a file).

3. Select **Search Again In** on the left of the Search ribbon, and select one of several specific locations in which to search, or select **Computer** to search your entire computer.

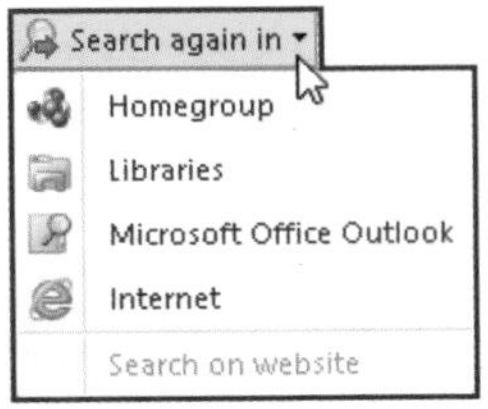

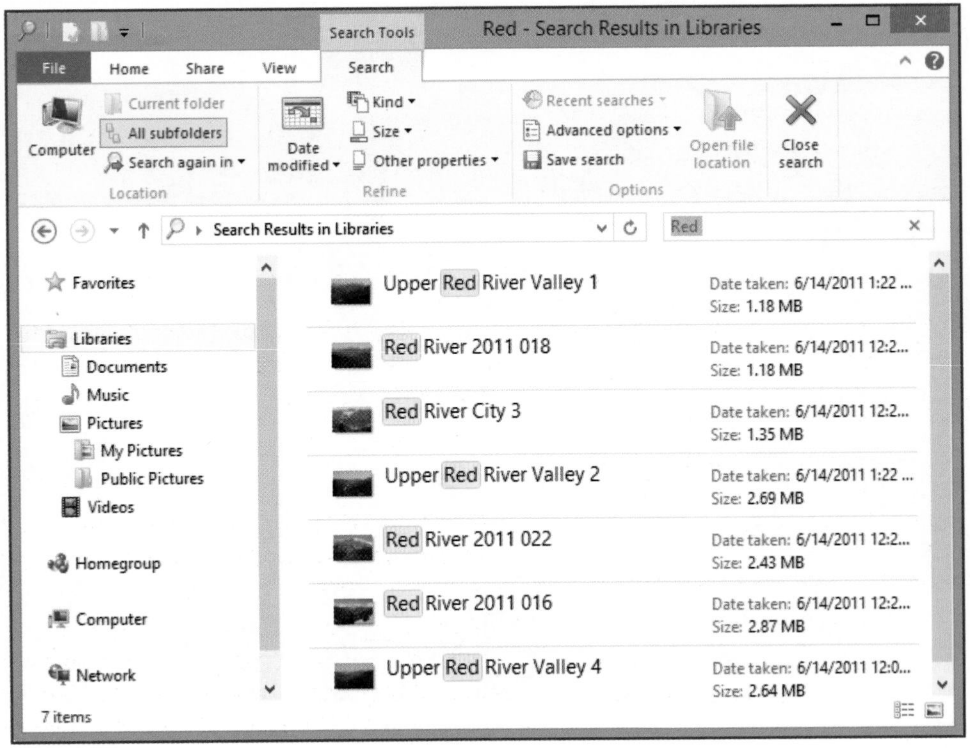

Figure 3-13: *The File Explorer Search ribbon provides a number of options to refine a search.*

4. To filter the search results, select one or more of the options in the Refine area of the Search ribbon. These let you filter the search results by the date it was modified, the kind of file (such as email, Word document, picture, and so on), the size of the file, and other properties (such as type, name, folder path, and tags).

5. You can recall searches you have previously done by selecting **Recent Searches**, and in Advanced Options you can control where and how searches are performed. The Advanced Options are the same as the options available in the Folder Options dialog box Search tab opened from the View ribbon.

6. To change search options, select one of the items in the Options area of the Search ribbon. If you want to save the search, select **Save Search** on the ribbon, select the folder in which you want to store the file, type the filename, and select **Save**. If you don't select another folder, saved searches are available in the Searches folder by default. Saved searches also appear under Favorites in the navigation pane.

7. When you are done, close File Explorer.

▷▷ Create Files

Files are usually created by applications or by copying existing files; however, Windows has an additional file-creation capability that creates an empty file for a particular application.

1. In the desktop select File Explorer in the taskbar, and open the folder in which you want to create the new file.

2. Open the context menu for the subject pane in File Explorer, and select **New**. A menu of all the file types that can be created by the registered applications on your computer will appear.

   –Or–

   Select **New Item** in the New area of the Home ribbon. The same menu of file types will open.

3. Select the file type you want to create. If you want to work on the file, open it in its application.

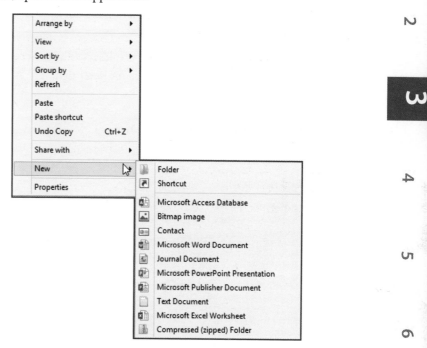

▷▷ Encrypt Files and Folders

Windows 8 Pro and Enterprise editions, but not Windows 8 Core, have the ability to encrypt files and folders so that they cannot be read without a key to decrypt them. The key is attached to the person who performed the encryption. When she or he logs on to the computer, the files can be used as if they were not encrypted. If someone else logs on, the files cannot be accessed. Even if someone takes the disk to another computer, all that will be displayed is gibberish. To encrypt a file or folder:

Note You can let someone else use an encrypted file by giving him or her your logon user name and password. In addition, in many organizations, an administrator will have the ability to decrypt files so that information cannot be lost through encryption.

1. Open the System menu and select **File Explorer** to display the Computer option. In the navigation pane, open the drive and folders necessary to display the files or folders you want to encrypt in the subject pane.

2. Open the context menu for the file or folder, and select **Properties**. In the General tab, select **Advanced** in the lower right. The Advanced Attributes dialog box appears.

3. Select **Encrypt Contents To Secure Data**.

4. Select **OK** twice.

   - If you are encrypting only a file, you will see an Encryption Warning dialog box stating that the file is not in an encrypted folder, which means that when you edit the file, temporary or backup files might be created that are not encrypted. Options include whether to encrypt the file and its parent folder or just the file.

   - If you are encrypting a folder, you will see a Confirm Attribute Changes dialog box that asks if the change applies to this folder only or applies to this folder and its subfolders and files.

5. Choose the option you want, and select **OK**. You may see a message from the Encrypting File System that you should back up your encryption key. Select the icon in the notification area to choose how you want to back up your key. The title under the file or folder icon turns green.

Back Up a File Encryption Key

When you encrypt a file or folder you are reminded to back up your file encryption key. The best way to do this is to use a USB Flash (thumb) drive. You don't need one with very much capacity so it will be very cheap and can be dedicated to this purpose.

> **Back up your file encryption key** ✎ ✕
> This helps you avoid permanently losing access to your encrypted files.

1. Select the reminder message when it pops up to open the Encrypting File System dialog box.

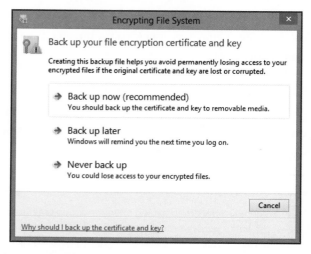

2. Insert a USB Flash drive you want to dedicate to this purpose.

3. In the Encrypting File System dialog box, select **Back Up Now**. The Certificate Export Wizard will open. If you wish, read about certificates (they really don't have much to do with backing up the encryption key) and select **Next**.

4. Accept the default format and select **Next** again. Select Password, enter and confirm a password, and once more select **Next**.

5. Enter a name to the backup file (I use "Enc Key") and select **Next**. Confirm the steps you want to take and select Finish. You are told when the export has completed.

6. In File Explorer, open Computer so you can see your USB Flash drive. Then open Libraries, select Documents, and open **My Documents**, so you can see the encryption key.

Enc Key

7. Drag the encryption key to your USB Flash drive. Open the USB Flash drive to make sure the key is there, and then delete it from My Documents. Remove the USB Flash drive and store it in a safe place.

▷ Change Other File and Folder Attributes

Encryption, described in the previous section, is one of five or six file or folder attributes. The others are shown in Table 3-2.

 Note Using the attribute to compress a file or folder is seldom done since the advent of zipping a file (see "Zip Files and Folders" later in this chapter), which is more efficient (makes smaller files) and can be more easily "unzipped" or decompressed by most people. Also, a file or folder that has been compressed with attributes cannot also be encrypted and vice versa.

Table 3-2: Additional File and Folder Attributes

Attribute	Description
Read-Only	The file or folder cannot be changed.
Hidden	The file or folder cannot be seen unless Show Hidden Files, Folders, And Drives is selected in the Folder Options dialog box View tab.
File Or Folder Is Ready For Archiving	This serves as a flag to backup programs that the file or folder is ready to be backed up.
Allow Files In This Folder Or This File To Have Contents Indexed	This allows the Windows Indexing Service to index the file or folder so that searching for the file can be done quickly. (See Chapter 6 for how to use the Indexing Service.)
Compress Contents To Save Disk Space	The file or folder is rewritten on the disk in compressed format. The file can still be read, but the reading will take a little longer while it is decompressed.

To set the additional attributes:

1. Open the System menu and select **File Explorer** to display the Computer option. In the navigation pane, open the drive and folders necessary to display in the subject pane the files or folders whose attributes you want to set.

2. Open the context menu for the file or folder, and select **Properties**. In the General tab, you can select **Read-Only** and **Hidden**. Do that if you wish, and select **OK**.

3. If you want to set archiving or indexing, select **Advanced**. The Advanced Attributes dialog box appears.

4. Select the attribute you want to set, and select **OK** twice.

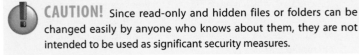 **CAUTION!** Since read-only and hidden files or folders can be changed easily by anyone who knows about them, they are not intended to be used as significant security measures.

Zip Files and Folders

Windows 8 has a way to compress files and folders called "zipping." *Zipped* files have the extension .zip and are compatible with programs like WinZip. Zipped files take up less room on a disk and are transmitted over the Internet faster.

Create a Zipped Folder

You can create a new zipped folder and drag files to it.

1. Open the System menu and select **File Explorer** to display the Computer option.

2. Navigate to the folder that you want to contain the zipped folder.

3. Open the context menu for the subject pane, and select **New | Compressed (Zipped) Folder**. The zipped folder will appear.

New Compressed (zipped) Folder

4. Select the folder name, type a new name, press **ENTER**, and drag files and folders into it to compress them.

Send Files or Folders to a Zipped Folder

1. In File Explorer, select the files and/or folders you want zipped.

2. Open the context menu for the selected objects, select **Send To | Compressed (Zipped) Folder**. A new zipped folder will appear containing the original files and/or folders, now compressed.

 TIP When you zip a group of files, open the context menu for the file whose name you want to give to the zip folder, and then select **Send To**. The file's name will automatically be given to the zip folder.

Extract Zipped Files and Folders

To unzip a file or folder, simply move it out of the zipped folder, or you can extract all of a zipped folder's contents.

1. Open the context menu for a zipped folder, and select **Extract All**. The Extract Compressed (Zipped) Folders dialog box will appear.

2. Enter or browse to the location where you want the extracted files and folders, and select **Extract**.

3. Close File Explorer when you are done.

▷▷ Back Up Files and Folders with File History

Backing up copies important files and folders on your disk and writes them on another device, such as another hard disk, an external hard disk, a recordable CD or DVD, or a USB flash drive, or even to the "cloud" (the term used for offsite, Internet-connected storage). In previous versions of Windows there was an app called Backup and Restore, and there are many third-party apps that fulfill that function. In Windows 8 the Backup and Restore app has been replaced with the new File History app.

File History automatically backs up the files that are in your libraries, contacts, and favorites folders as well as on your desktop. This is done periodically so you can not only restore the most recent copy of a file, but also get a copy of a file as of a particular date. To set up and use File History, you need to

- Set up a drive on which to store your File History
- Determine which files you want to include in File History
- Determine the frequency of saving files and how long to keep them
- Turn on File History
- Restore files from File History

Start and Set Up File History

1. Open the System menu and select **Control Panel** to display it. In Category view, select **System And Security | File History**. The File History window will open, as you see in Figure 3-14.

2. Select **Select Drive**. A list of the drives that you have available on your computer will be displayed, excluding the system drive you are using for Windows 8.

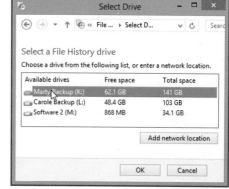

3. Select a local drive on which to store your file history, or select **Add Network Location**.

4. If you chose to save on a network, open the network computer with the drive you want to use to see a list of drives. Open the drive you want to use. Select an existing folder or select **New Folder**, type a name for it, and select **Select Folder**. You are returned to the Select Drive window where the network drive now appears on the list of destination drives. Select it.

5. Select **OK** to return to the File History window. Select **Exclude Folders** to determine what you don't want backed up.

6. Select **Add** to open the Select Folder window. Open the Favorites and Libraries folders to locate and select the folders you don't want backed up. When you have selected a folder you don't want backed up, select **Select Folder**. Repeat this step as necessary. When you are finished, select **Save Changes**. You are returned to the File History window.

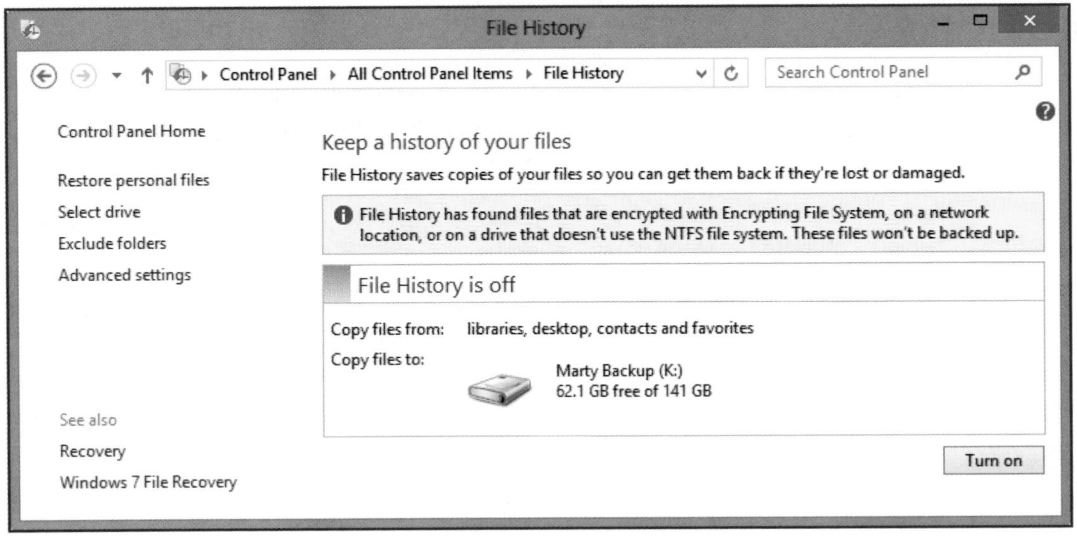

Figure 3-14: *If possible, back up to an external drive.*

7. Select **Advanced Settings** and review the defaults shown next. Select each of the drop-down lists to see the options and select any changes that you wish to make. When you are ready, select **Save Changes**.

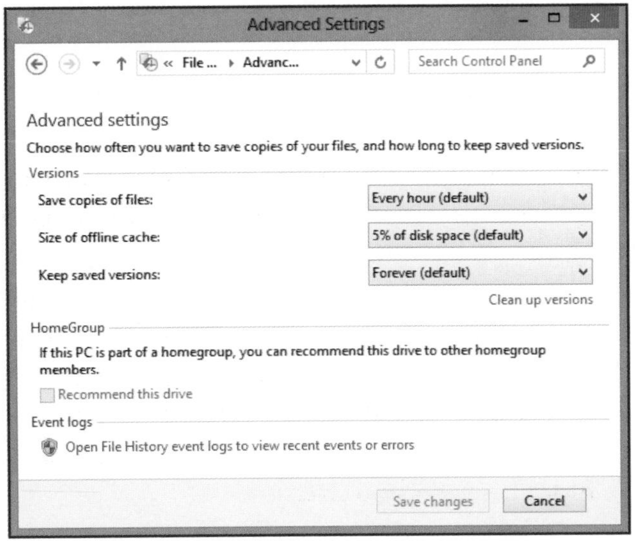

8. Back in the File History window, select **Turn On** to start saving the file history. If you are part of a HomeGroup, you are asked if you want to recommend the drive you selected to your HomeGroup. Select either **Yes** or **No**. You will see a message that the initial file history is being created.

Restore from File History

After you have used File History for a while and you encounter a situation where you need or want to use one or more of the files that have been backed up, you can restore those files with the File History app.

1. Open the System menu and select **Control Panel** to display it. In Category view, select **System And Security | File History**. The File History window will open.

2. Select **Restore Personal Files** to open the Home – File History window shown in Figure 3-15.

3. Open the folders, locate and select the file(s) you want to restore, and select the circular arrow button at the bottom of the window to restore the files to their original location.

Figure 3-15: *File History gives you access to a number of copies of your files over a period of time—a history of your files.*

–Or–

- Open the context menu for the file(s) you want to restore and select either **Restore**, to restore the file to its original location, or **Restore To** to specify the folder in which you want to restore the file.

4. If you select Restore To, the Restore To window will open allowing you to select the folder (or create a new one) in which you want to restore the file. When you have located the folder, select **Select Folder**. The folder will open showing you the file that was restored.

5. Close any or all of the windows that have been opened.

Note System and program files will not be backed up with the automatic File History app.

⏩ Write Files and Folders to a CD or DVD

Windows 8 allows you to copy ("burn" or record) files to a writable or rewritable CD or DVD. You must have a CD or DVD writing drive and blank media.

1. Place a blank recordable disc (a CD in this example) in the drive. A message will appear asking you to "Tap to choose what happens with blank CDs." Tap or click this message to open a dialog box asking if you want to burn files to a disc using File Explorer or burn an audio CD using Windows Media Player, or take no action.

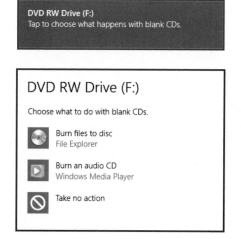

2. Select **Burn Files To Disc**. Type a name for the disc. You will be shown two formatting options based on how you want to use the disc:
   - **Like A USB Flash Drive** This format, called *Live File System,* can only be read on a computer with Windows XP or newer versions of the Windows operating systems. This option allows you to add one file or folder to the CD or DVD at a time, like you would with a hard disk or a USB flash drive. You can leave the disc in the drive and drag data to it whenever you want and delete previously added objects.

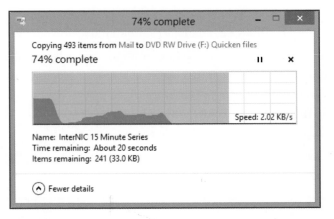

Figure 3-16: *Periodically copying files and folders that are particularly important to a CD or DVD is very easy and can protect you from losing the contents.*

4. Open another File Explorer window, locate in the navigation pane the folders that contain the files you want on the CD or DVD, and then move them to the subject pane in the original Explorer window that opened in step 3, which is the CD/DVD drive, as shown in Figure 3-16.

- If you are using the Live File System format, as you drag the objects to the drive, they will be immediately written on the disc. When you have written all the files you want to the disc, in the navigation pane, open the context menu for the drive and select **Close Session**. After the "Closing Session" message above the notification area disappears and is replaced by "Disc Ready," you can remove the disc from the drive and insert it at a later time to resume adding or removing files and folders.

- **With A CD/DVD Player** This format, called *Mastered,* can be read by most computers, including older Windows and Apple computers and most stand-alone CD and DVD players. To use this format, you must gather all the files in one place and then burn them all at one time. Use this format for music and video files that you want to play on automobile or stand-alone devices, such as MP3 and video players.

TIP The Live File System that lets you use CD-R/DVD-R discs like CD-RW/DVD-RW discs is a capability that you can use like an additional hard disk.

3. Select the option you want and then select **Next**. The disc will be formatted and, depending on the option you chose, either a Media Player will open or a new File Explorer window will appear.

- If you are using the Mastered format, drag all the objects you want written on the disc to the drive. When all files and folders are in the drive's subject pane, in the navigation pane, open the context menu for the drive and select **Burn To Disc**. You are asked to confirm or change the title, select a recording speed, and then click **Next**. When the burn is complete, the disc will be ejected, and you can choose to burn the same files to another disc. In any case, select **Finish**. The temporary files will be erased, which might take a few minutes.

5. When you are done, select **Close** to close File Explorer.

⏩ Manage Disks

Windows 8 provides three tools to help manage the files and folders stored on hard disks: Disk Cleanup, Error Checking, and Optimizing.

Clean Up a Disk

Disk Cleanup helps you get rid of old files on your hard disk. This can speed up your system and make room for other files. Windows looks through your hard disk for types of files that can be deleted and lists them. You can then select the types of files you want to delete.

1. Open the System menu, select **File Explorer**, open the context menu for a disk drive you want to work on, and select **Properties**.

2. Select **Disk Cleanup**. Windows 8 will calculate how much space you could save.

3. Select the types of files to delete and select **OK**. You are asked if you want to permanently delete these files. Select **Delete Files** to permanently delete them.

Check for Errors

Error Checking tries to read and write on your disk, without losing information, to determine if bad areas exist. If it finds a bad area, that area is flagged so that the system will not use it. Error Checking automatically fixes file system errors and attempts to recover bad sectors.

1. In the disk drive's Properties dialog box, select the **Tools** tab and select **Check**. If there is no obvious need to scan the drive, you will be informed of that. You can cancel the scan or go ahead.

2. You will be shown the status of the Error Checking operation and told of any problems that could not be fixed. When Error Checking is complete, your computer may need to restart.

Optimize a Disk

When files are stored on a hard disk, they are broken into pieces (or *fragments*) and individually written to the disk. As the disk fills, the fragments are spread over the disk as space allows. To read a file that has been fragmented requires extra disk activity and can slow down the performance of your computer. To fix this, Windows has an automatic optimizing process that rewrites the contents of a disk, placing all of the fragments of a file in one contiguous area.

Note In the past this optimization process was called defragmentation (or "defrag") and someone, trying to be helpful, might tell you that you might need to "defrag your hard drive." By default, Windows 8 automatically optimizes and thereby defragments your drives on a periodic basis, so under most circumstances, you won't need to do it.

1. In the disk drive's Properties dialog box, select the **Tools** tab and then select **Optimize**. The computer's Optimize Drives window will open and give you the status of each of your drives, as shown in Figure 3-17. Under most circumstances your drives should look like mine with an "OK" status and "0% fragmented."

2. If you wish to go ahead manually, such as with an external drive not otherwise defragmented, select the drive and select **Analyze** to see if the disk needs defragmenting. If you wish to continue, select **Optimize**. The process can take up to a couple of hours. Some fragments may remain, which is fine.

3. Select **Change Settings** to change the frequency of the automatic optimization and/or to select the drives that are optimized.

4. When you are ready, select **Close** to close the Optimize Drives window.

Drive	Media type	Last run	Current status
Windows 8 (C:)	Hard disk drive	9/6/2012 9:55 AM	OK (0% fragmented)
Windows 7 (D:)	Hard disk drive	9/6/2012 9:49 AM	OK (0% fragmented)
Data (E:)	Hard disk drive	9/6/2012 9:49 AM	OK (0% fragmented)
Marty Backup (K:)	Hard disk drive	9/6/2012 10:08 AM	OK (0% fragmented)
Carole Backup (L:)	Hard disk drive	9/6/2012 10:10 AM	OK (0% fragmented)
Software 2 (M:)	Hard disk drive	9/6/2012 10:10 AM	OK (0% fragmented)

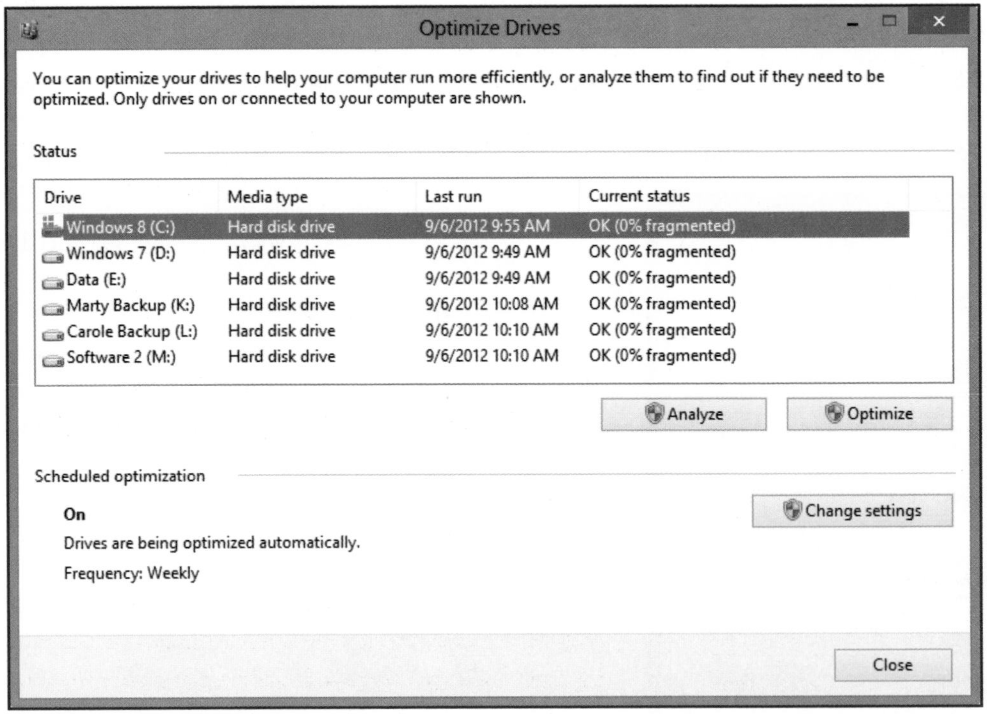

Figure 3-17: Drive optimization is primarily the defragmenting of the drive, which brings pieces of a file together into one contiguous area.

Chapter 4

Using the Internet

The Internet provides a major means for worldwide communication between both individuals and organizations, as well as a major means for locating and sharing information. For many, having access to the Internet is the primary reason for having a computer. To use the Internet, you must have a connection to it using one of the many communications services that are now available, and you need two apps on your computer:

- An **Internet browser** to access the World Wide Web, read the news, look at the weather, use social networking, track your portfolio, watch movies, and shop, among many other things.

- An **Internet mail** app to send and receive email, maintain an address book, and keep track of your appointments.

This chapter will discuss connecting to the Internet, exploring it with both of Windows 8's Internet browsers and sending and receiving email with the new Internet mail apps in Windows 8.

CONNECT TO THE INTERNET

You can connect to the Internet using a telephone line, a cable TV connection, a satellite link, or a wireless link. Across these various types of connections there are a myriad of speeds, degrees of reliability, and costs. The most important factor is what is available to you at the location where you want to use it. In an urban area, you have a number of alternatives from landline phone companies, cell phone companies, and cable TV companies, all with options. As you move away from the urban area, your alternatives will decrease to a telephone dial-up connection and/or a satellite link. With a telephone line, you can connect with a *dial-up* connection, a *DSL* (digital subscriber line) connection, or a high-speed fiber-optic connection. DSL, cable, satellite, and some wireless connections are called *broadband* connections and offer higher speeds and are always on. You must have access to at least one of these forms of communication in order to connect to the Internet. You may need to also set up the Internet connection itself.

In addition to the direct connections that you contract for with a telephone, cable, satellite, or cellular company, you can connect to the Internet through one of two wireless connections:

- **Wi-Fi**, which is just a name and doesn't stand for anything. Wi-Fi *hotspots* are areas where the signals can be received and are set up by organizations such as coffee shops, airports, hotels, or other establishments for their customers, or you can easily have Wi-Fi in your home. You may or may not need a passcode to use a Wi-Fi hotspot (you should have one in your home), and you may or may not have to pay for it.

- **3G/4G data plan** through a cell phone company allows you to connect to the Internet anywhere the company has service. In some cases you can have a choice between Wi-Fi and 3G/4G service. Wi-Fi is generally cheaper, but 3G/4G is often, but not necessarily, faster. To set up and use 3G/4G, you need to seek out the instructions of the cell phone company.

▷▷ Establish an Internet Connection

With most forms of Internet connections, you have a choice of speed and ancillary services, such as the number of free email accounts and possibly a personal website. Also, depending on the type of connection, you may need dedicated equipment, such as a modem, DSL router, or

satellite receiving equipment, which may or may not be included in the price. Ask friends and neighbors about what are the best local Internet connections. Contact your local phone company and cable TV provider.

Review Types of Internet Connections

Table 4-1 provides a summary of Internet connection types to give you a starting place for determining the type you want, if it is available to you. The speeds and costs are representative averages and may not be correct for the Internet service provider (ISP) you are considering or for your location. You must get the correct numbers from your local providers.

 Tip Often, setup, installation, and equipment charges for an Internet connection are waived or reduced if you sign a one- or two-year contract and/or prepay for a year or two of service.

Table 4-1: Comparison of Internet Connection Types

Connection Type	Down/Up Speed	Availability	Reliability	Average Cost/Mo
Telephone dial-up	48 Kbps/34 Kbps	Most places	Fair	$10 to over $20
Telephone DSL	6 Mbps/2 Mbps	Urban/ suburban	Good	$30 to over $60
Telephone fiber	20 Mbps/8 Mbps	Urban	Very good	$50 to over $120
Cable TV	10 Mbps/6 Mbps	Urban/ suburban	Good	$40 to over $100
Cellular Wireless 3G	1 Mbps/750 Kbps	Urban	Good	$40 to over $80
Cellular Wireless 4G	6 Mbps/2 Mbps	Urban	Good	$60 to over $100
Satellite	2 Mbps/250 Kbps	Most places	Fair	$60 to over $300

Set Up Communications

To set up the communications link between your computer and the Internet, you must first choose and contract for a type of connection. The ISP that provides this service normally will help you set it up.

> **Note** To connect to the Internet, you need to have an account with an ISP who will help you establish a user name and password for your account and give you an email address, the type of mail server (POP3, IMAP, or HTTP), and the names of the incoming and outgoing mail servers (such as mail.anisp.net).

A broadband connection—made with a DSL phone line, a TV cable, a satellite connection, or a high-speed wireless connection—if wired, is normally made with a device called a *router* that connects to your computer or to local area network (LAN), which allows several computers on the network to use the connection. (See Chapter 9 to set up a network.) This broadband connection is always on and connected to the Internet. If your computer is turned on and has this connection, there is nothing else you need to do to use it other than start your Internet browser or email app.

Figure 4-1: Many commercial locations have a number of Wi-Fi networks, necessitating knowing which you should use.

Establish a Wi-Fi Connection

When you start a computer in a Wi-Fi (wireless) hotspot, the wireless icon on the right of the taskbar will be dark and have an attention asterisk like this: ▦. This is telling you that you need to set up Wi-Fi. To do that:

1. Select the wireless icon to see a list of Wi-Fi networks that are available at your location, as shown in Figure 4-1.

2. Select the wireless network you want to use. This may open the Security dialog box.

3. If needed, enter the network security key and select **Next**. You will be connected to the network and, in most cases, to the Internet.

Establish a 3G/4G Wireless Connection

Establish a contract with a cellular provider, such as Verizon, T-Mobile, or AT&T, and, in communication with them, make sure your device has the necessary SIM (Subscriber Identity Module) card installed and is set up to use their service. Most cellular providers are very helpful in getting you up and running (you're going to be paying them for at least the next two years).

Once you are connected to the Internet, it doesn't matter the type of connection or whether it is wired or wireless, other than the facts that some connections are faster and more reliable than others.

Explore Windows 8's Internet Browsers

Windows 8 comes with two Internet browsers; both are versions of Microsoft's Internet Explorer (IE), version 10. The first is a Windows 8 style app that is started by selecting the **Internet Explorer** tile on the Start screen. The second is a desktop app that is started by selecting the **Internet Explorer** icon on the desktop taskbar. Both of these browsers allow you to go anywhere on the Internet and use all of its resources, but there are some differences.

Discover Windows 8 IE 10

Windows 8's new Windows 8 style Internet Explorer fills the screen displaying the content of the webpage. When you first open Windows 8 IE there is a command bar with the address box and other controls at the bottom, as you can see on the left in Figure 4-2. Selecting a blank or inactive area on the webpage will close the command bar and its controls, allowing the full screen to be used by the webpage, as shown in the middle of Figure 4-2. The command bar can be returned by right-clicking an inactive area of the screen or swiping down from the top or up from the bottom of the screen. When you do that, if you have viewed other websites, a bar of recent sites will appear at the top of the screen, as you can see on the right in Figure 4-2.

Discover Desktop IE 10

Desktop IE 10 is similar to Internet Explorer in previous versions of Windows. It is inside a window with a set of controls at the top, as you can see in Figure 4-3. You can add toolbars, but the minimum window always has a title bar containing an address box on the left, one or more tabs for different webpages in the center, and a set of controls on the right and far left.

Figure 4-2: Windows 8 style Internet Explorer can give the entire screen to a webpage (center), display a command bar at the bottom (left), or display both the command bar and a tab bar of recent sites (right).

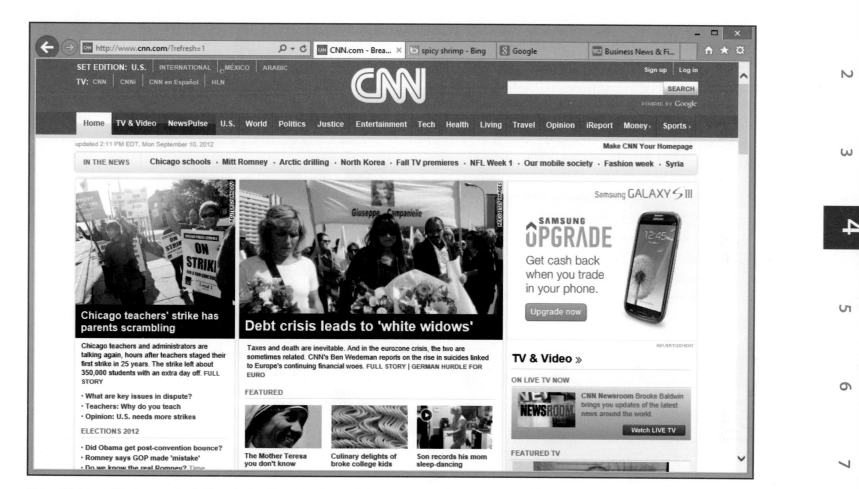

Figure 4-3: Internet Explorer on the desktop always offers a set of controls for you to use on the Internet.

⏩ Reconfigure an Internet Connection

In most circumstances, when you purchase and have installed an Internet connection, it is automatically set up within your computer and you have nothing more to do to use the Internet other than start your browser. The easiest way to check that is to try to connect to the Internet as described in the previous section. If you do that and you do not connect to the

Internet, and you know that your broadband and network connections are all working properly, you need to reconfigure the Internet connection on your computer.

1. If Internet Explorer did not connect to the Internet, open the System menu in the lower-left corner of your screen (right-click or press **WINDOWS+X**), and select **Control Panel**.

2. In Category view, select **Network And Internet**, and then in any view select **Network And Sharing Center**.

3. Select **Set Up A New Connection Or Network**. The Set Up A Connection Or Network dialog box will appear (see Figure 4-4).

4. Select **Connect To The Internet | Next**. Select **Broadband**.

5. If you have a choice between a wireless and a wired connection, choose which you want (if you are using a desktop computer, normally choose wired). If asked, enter your user name, password, a name for the connection, and choose whether to allow others to use it. When you are done, select **Connect**.

6. Once more, select the **Internet Explorer** tile on the Start screen or the desktop's taskbar icon. If you still cannot connect and are using a broadband connection, you may need to go to Chapter 9 and look at potential network problems or contact your ISP, who can probably help you.

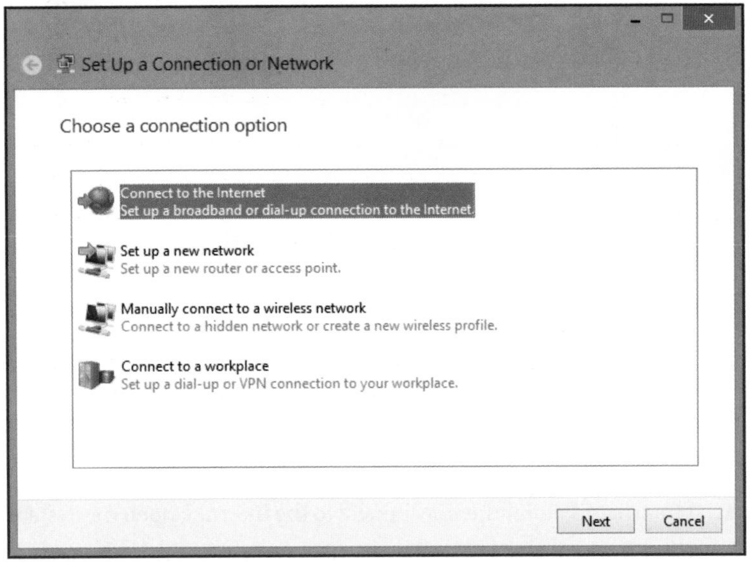

![Set Up a Connection or Network dialog box showing connection options: Connect to the Internet, Set up a new network, Manually connect to a wireless network, Connect to a workplace]

Figure 4-4: Most broadband connections are always on and, after setup, don't require a user name and password.

USE THE WORLD WIDE WEB

The *World Wide Web* (or just the *Web*) is the sum of all the websites in the world—examples of which are CNN (which was shown in Figure 4-2), Google, and Bing. The World Wide Web is what you can access with a *web browser*, such as Internet Explorer.

> **Note** For the sake of writing convenience and because Windows 8 comes with Internet Explorer, this book assumes you are using Internet Explorer to access the Internet. Other browsers, such as Mozilla Firefox (mozilla.com) and Google Chrome (google.com), also work fine.

Browse the Internet

Browsing the Internet refers to using a browser, like Internet Explorer, to go from one website to another. You can browse to a site by directly entering a site address, navigating to a site from another site, or using the browser controls. First, of course, you have to start the browser, as described earlier in this chapter.

Enter a Site Directly

To go directly to a site:

1. Start your browser and select the existing address, or *Uniform Resource Locator (URL)*, in the command bar to select it (at the bottom of the screen in Windows 8 IE or at the top of the window in desktop IE).

2. Type the address of the site you want to open, as shown (Windows 8 IE on the left and desktop on the right), and either select **Go To** (the right-pointing arrow on the right) or press **ENTER** in either version of IE.

> **Tip** The on-screen keyboards that appear when the command bar is tapped change the label of the **ENTER** key to **GO**.

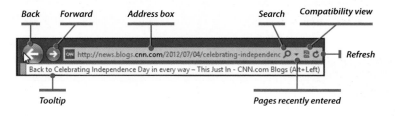

Use Site Navigation

Site navigation uses a combination of links and menus on one webpage to locate and open another webpage, either in the same site or in another site.

- **Links** are words, phrases, sentences, or graphics that always have an open hand displayed when the mouse pointer is moved over them and, when selected, take you to another location. They are often a different color or underlined—if not initially, then when you move the mouse pointer to them.

- **Menus** contain one or a few words in a horizontal list, vertical list, or both that always have an open hand displayed when the mouse pointer is moved over them and, when selected, take you to another location.

Use Browser Navigation

Browser navigation uses the controls within your browser to go to another location. Both versions of Internet Explorer 10 have two controls not discussed elsewhere that are used for navigation:

- **Back** and **Forward** buttons take you to the next or previous page in the stack of pages you have viewed most recently. Moving your mouse over these buttons will display a tooltip showing you the name of the page the button will take you to.

- The **Pages recently entered** button displays a drop-down list of webpages that you have recently entered into the address box, as well as a list of sites you recently visited.

The desktop IE has these controls to the left of and within the command/address bar, as shown here:

Note Older webpages are shown in Compatibility View, as indicated with an additional icon of a broken page at the right end of the desktop address bar.

Tip Open the context menu for a *highlighted* Back or Forward button to open a drop-down menu of recent pages you have visited going in the direction of the button.

Windows 8 IE has these controls split, with Back and Forward on either end of the command bar, as shown next, and the recently entered sites appearing when you start to enter an address, as shown second.

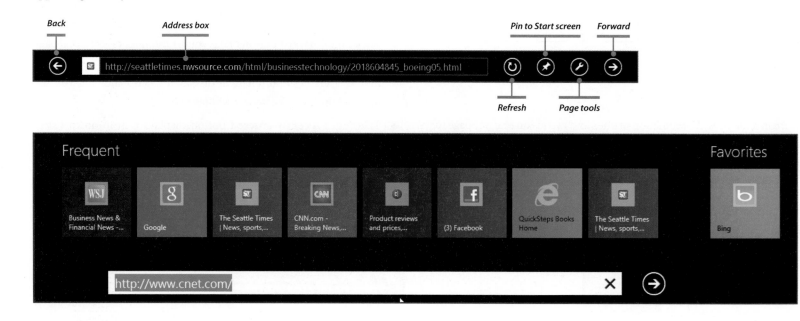

Search the Internet

You can search the Internet in two ways: by using the search facility built into Internet Explorer and by using an independent search facility on the Web.

Search from Internet Explorer

To use Internet Explorer's search facility, in either version, select the contents of the address box and begin typing what you want to search for. What happens next depends on what you typed.

As you are typing, IE looks at sites you have recently visited and, if a possible match is found, a site is suggested, and others are listed. If what you have typed does not look like a site, for example "spicy shrimp," the Bing search site will open with the results of the search, as you can see in Figure 4-5.

When you see a site you want to visit, select the link to go to that site.

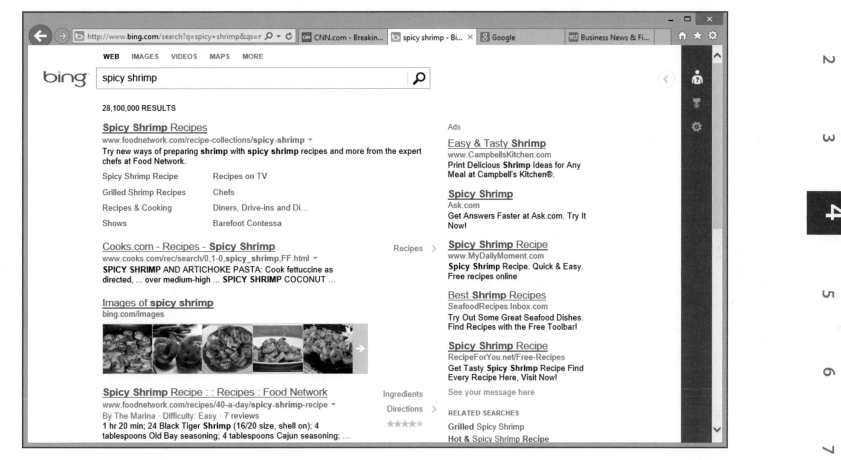

Figure 4-5: The results of a search using Internet Explorer's address box

Search from an Internet Site

There are many independent Internet search sites. The most popular is Google.

1. In either version of Internet Explorer, select the current address in the address box, type google.com, and either select **Go To** (the right-pointing arrow on the right) or press ENTER.

2. In the text box, type what you want to search for, and select **Google Search**. The resulting websites are shown in a full webpage, as illustrated in Figure 4-6.

3. Select the link of your choice to go to that site.

Tip When you enter search criteria, place quotation marks around certain keywords or phrases to get only results that match those words exactly.

+You **Search** Images Maps Play YouTube News Gmail Documents Calendar More ▾

Google

spicy shrimp ✕ 🔍

spicy shrimp
spicy shrimp **recipe**
spicy shrimp **pasta**
spicy shrimp **stir fry**

Search

Web

Images

Maps

Videos

News

Shopping

Recipes

More

Langley, WA
Change location

Ingredients   Yes No
garlic   ☐ ☐
tabasco pepper   ☐ ☐
crushed red pepper   ☐ ☐
steak   ☐ ☐
worcestershire sauce ☐ ☐
lemon   ☐ ☐
paprika   ☐ ☐

Any cook time
Less than 15 min
Less than 30 min
Less than 60 min

Images for **spicy shrimp** - Report images

Spicy Shrimp Recipes
www.foodnetwork.com/recipe-collections/**spicy-shrimp**/index.html
Try new ways of preparing shrimp with **spicy shrimp** recipes and more from the
expert chefs at Food Network.

4 Minute **Spicy** Garlic **Shrimp** Recipe : Rachael Ray : Recipes : Food...
www.foodnetwork.com › Recipes › Seafood
★★★★★ 92 reviews - 17 mins
Get this all-star, easy-to-follow Food Network 4 Minute **Spicy** Garlic
Shrimp recipe from Rachael Ray.

Moroccan **Spicy Shrimp** Recipe - A Recipe for Spicy Sauteed Shrimp
fishcooking.about.com/.../shrimprecipe1/.../maroc_s...
★★★★★ Rating: 5 - 1 review - 20 mins
A recipe for **spicy** sauteed **shrimp** cooked in a Moroccan style, with
cumin, paprika, coriander and a little ginger. This **shrimp** recipe is very
quick, and easy to ...

Spicy Shrimp | The Pioneer Woman Cooks | Ree Drummond
thepioneerwoman.com/cooking/.../spicy_shrimp_yu...
26 mins
Aug 2, 2007 – Its official name is "Barbeque **Shrimp**," but that's actually
a little misleading since this dish doesn't require...

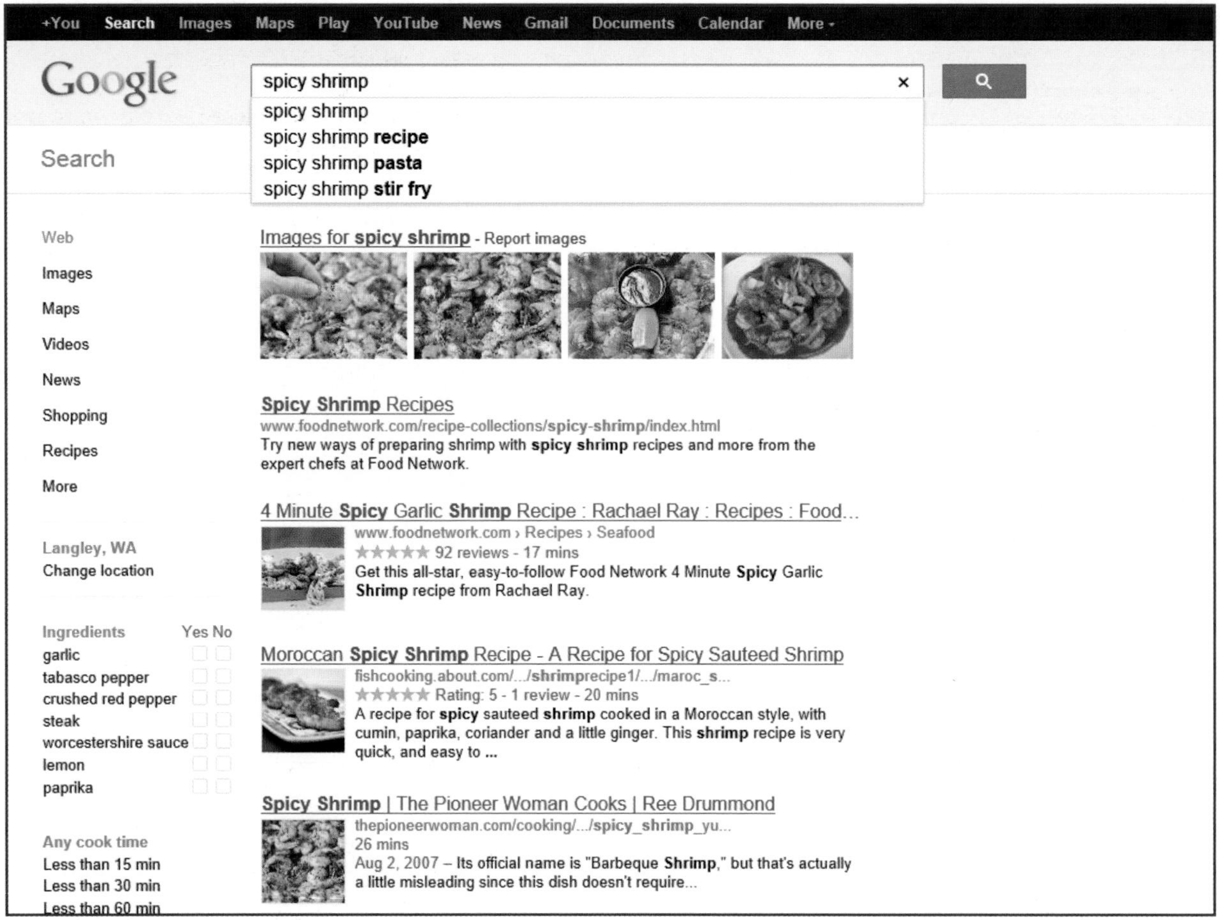

Figure 4-6: The results of a search using Google

▷▷ Save a Favorite Site

Sometimes, you visit a site that you would like to return to quickly or
often. Both versions of Internet Explorer have the ability to save sites
for easy retrieval.

Add a Favorite Site

In desktop IE 10 you save the site to a list called "Favorites."

1. In Internet Explorer, open the webpage you want to add to your
Favorites list, and make sure its correct address (URL) is in the
address box.

2. Select the **Favorites** icon in the middle of the three icons on the right of the tab row.

3. Select **Add To Favorites**. The Add A Favorite dialog box appears. Adjust the name as needed in the text box (you may want to type a name you will readily associate with that site), and select **Add**.

Save to the Start Screen

In Windows 8 IE 10 you save the site to the Start screen.

1. In Internet Explorer, open the webpage you want to add to your Favorites list, and make sure its correct address (URL) is in the address box.

2. Select the **Pin To Start** icon on the command bar.

3. Make any change to the site name that you want, and select **Pin To Start.**

Open a Favorite Site

To open a favorite site you have saved:

In desktop IE, select the **Favorites** icon on the right of the tab row, ensure the **Favorites** tab is selected, and select the site you want to open.

In Windows 8 IE, select the tile on the Start screen.

Tip In desktop IE, if the status bar is turned on (open the context menu for it in the blank area on the right of the tab row and select **Status Bar**), there is a Zoom button and menu in the lower-right corner of the Internet Explorer window. Select the down arrow to open the menu, and select a level of magnification, or select the button to iterate through the levels. On a touch screen, pinch or spread your fingers.

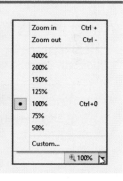

Change Your Home Page

When you open either version of Internet Explorer, a webpage is automatically displayed. This page is called your *home page*. When IE starts, you can have it open several pages in addition to the home page, with the additional pages available through tabs (see "Use Tabs" in this chapter).

> **Note** You can only set the home page or pages in the desktop version of IE, but the home page(s) you set there will normally be reflected in the Windows 8 version.

To change the home page and the other pages initially opened in either version of IE:

Home (Alt+Home)

1. In desktop Internet Explorer, directly enter or browse to the site you want as your home page. If you want additional pages, open them in separate tabs.

2. Open the context menu for the Home Page icon, and select **Add Or Change Home Page**. The Add Or Change Home Page dialog box will appear.

Add or Change Home Page

Would you like to use the following as your home page?

http://www.cnn.com/

○ Use this webpage as your only home page
○ Add this webpage to your home page tabs
○ Use the current tab set as your home page

Yes   No

3. Select:

   - **Use This Webpage As Your Only Home Page** if you wish to have only a single home page.

   - **Add This Webpage To Your Home Page Tabs** if you wish to have several home pages on different tabs.

   - **Use The Current Tab Set As Your Home Page** if you want all the current tabs to appear when you start Internet Explorer or select the Home Page icon (this option is only available if you have two or more tabs open).

4. Select **Yes** to complete your home page selection and close the dialog box.

> **Note** You can also change the home page by selecting the **Tools** icon in desktop IE, selecting **Internet Options** to open the dialog box, and making the desired changes at the top of the General tab.
>
>
> Tools (Alt+X)

> **Tip** You can open the home page in its own tab instead of replacing the current tab by holding down **CTRL** while selecting the **Home Page** icon.

Use Tabs

Both versions of Internet Explorer allow you to have several webpages open at one time and easily switch among them by selecting the tab associated with the page. In desktop IE, the tabs reside on the *tab row*, immediately above the displayed webpage, which also includes the address box, as shown in Figure 4-7.

In Windows 8 IE, the tabs, shown in Figure 4-8, reside in a separate bar that opens above the current webpage when you swipe down from the top of the screen or right-click a blank area of the screen.

Figure 4-7: Tabs allow you to quickly switch among several websites.

Open Pages in a New Tab

To open a page in a new tab instead of opening the page in an existing tab:

1. Open Internet Explorer with at least one webpage displayed.

2. Open the tab bar in Windows 8 IE and then, in either version, select **New Tab** on the right end of the tab row or bar (or press **CTRL+T**) and open a new webpage in any of the ways described earlier in this chapter.

   –Or–

   Type a web address in the address box, and press **ALT+ENTER**. (If you just press **ENTER**, you'll open a page in the same tab.)

–Or–

Hold down **CTRL** while selecting a link in an open page. (If you just select the link, you'll open a page in the same tab.) Then select the new tab to open the page.

3. Repeat any of the alternatives in step 2 as needed to open additional pages.

Switch Among Tabs

To switch among open tabs:

In Windows 8 IE, open the tab bar and in either version, select the tab of the page you want to open.

–Or–

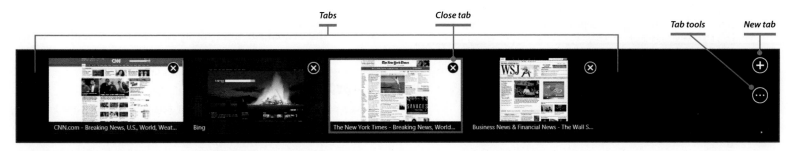

Figure 4-8: Windows 8 style IE tabs must be specifically displayed to use them.

Press **CTRL+TAB** to switch to the next tab to the right, or press **CTRL+ SHIFT+TAB** to switch to the next tab to the left.

–Or–

Press **CTRL+N**, where *n* is a number from one to eight to switch to one of the first eight tabs numbered from the left in the order they were opened. You can also press **CTRL+9** to switch to the last tab that was opened, shown on the right of the tab row.

> **Note** To use **CTRL+N** to switch among Internet Explorer's tabs, you need to use a number key on the top of the main keyboard, *not* on the numeric keypad on the right.

Close Tabs

To close one or more tabs:

In Windows 8 IE, open the tab bar and select the **x** on the right of the tab of the page you want to close. In desktop IE select the tab and then select the **x**.

–Or–

Press **CTRL+W** to close the current page and its tab.

–Or–

Open the context menu for the tab for the page you want to close, and select **Close Tab** on the context menu; or select **Close Other Tabs** to close all of the pages except the one you selected.

> **Tip** In desktop IE, press just the **ALT** key to view Internet Explorer's menus.

▷▷ Organize Favorite Sites

In desktop IE, you will probably find that you have a number of favorite sites and it is becoming hard to find the one you want. Internet Explorer provides two places to store your favorite sites: a Favorites list, which is presented to you in the form of a menu you can open, and a Favorites bar, which is displayed at all times. There are several ways to organize your favorite sites.

> **Tip** The webpages that you have pinned to the Start screen from Windows 8 IE can also be organized in any way you want as described in Chapter 2.

Rearrange the Favorites List

The items on your Favorites list are displayed in the order you added them, unless you move them to a new location.

In desktop IE, select the **Favorites** icon, locate the site you want to reposition, and move it to the location in the list where you want it.

Create New Folders

Desktop Internet Explorer comes with several default folders added by Microsoft or by the computer's manufacturer. You can also add your own folders within the Favorites list.

1. In desktop IE, select the **Favorites** icon, select the **Add To Favorites** down arrow, and select **Organize Favorites** to open the Organize Favorites dialog box, shown in Figure 4-9.

2. Select **New Folder**, type the name for the folder, and press **ENTER**.

3. Move the desired site links to the new folder, move the folder to where you want it on the list, and then select **Close**.

Put Favorites in Folders

You can put a site in either your own folders (see "Create New Folders") or the default ones when you initially add it to your Favorites list.

1. Open the webpage you want in your Favorites list, and make sure its correct address or URL is in the address box.

Figure 4-9: As with files, organizing your favorite websites helps you easily find what you want.

2. Select the **Favorites** icon, select **Add To Favorites**, adjust the name as needed in the text box, select the **Create In** down arrow, select the folder to use, and select **Add**.

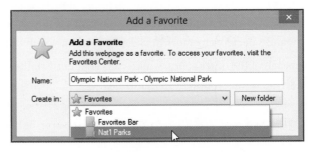

Add a Site to the Favorites Bar

In desktop IE you can turn on the Favorites bar by opening the context menu for any of the three icons (Home, Favorites, and Tools) on the right of the tab row and selecting **Favorites Bar**. By default, the Favorites bar may have several sites on it, but you can delete those and add others.

Open the site you want to add to the Favorites bar. If the Favorites bar is open, select the **Add To Favorites Bar** button on the left of the Favorites bar.

–Or–

Select **Favorites**, select the **Add To Favorites** down arrow, and select **Add To Favorites Bar**.

Tip To delete a favorite site from either the Favorites list or the Favorites bar, right-select it and select **Delete**.

Access Web History

Internet Explorer on the desktop keeps a history of the websites you visit, and you can use that history to return to a site. You can set the length of time to keep sites in that history, and you can clear your history.

Use Web History

To use the Web History feature:

1. In desktop IE, select the **Favorites** icon, and select the **History** tab; or press **CTRL+H** to open the History pane.

2. Select the down arrow on the History tab bar to select how you want the history sorted. Depending on what you select, you will be able to further specify the type of history you want to view. For example, if you select View By Date, you can then select the day and website you want to open, as shown in Figure 4-10.

Delete and Set History

You can set the length of time to keep your Internet history, and you can clear this history.

1. In desktop IE, select the **Tools** icon at the right end of the tab row, and select **Internet Options**.

2. In the General tab, under Browsing History, select **Delete** to open the Delete Browsing History dialog box. If needed, select the **History**

check box to delete your browsing history. Select any other check box to delete that information, although you should keep the Preserve Favorites Website Data check box selected to *keep* that information (it is a confusing dialog box). Select **Delete**.

–Or–

In the General tab of the Internet Options dialog box, under Browsing History, select **Settings | History** and use the **Days** spinner to set the number of days to keep your web history. Select **OK**.

3. Select **OK** again to close the Internet Options dialog box.

Figure 4-10: The Web History feature allows you to find a site that you visited in the recent past.

Control Internet Security

Internet Explorer on the desktop allows you to control three aspects of Internet security. You can categorize sites by the degree to which you trust them, determine how you want to handle *cookies* placed on your computer by websites, and set and use ratings to control the content of websites that can be viewed. These controls are found in the Internet Options dialog box.

In desktop IE, select the **Tools** icon and select **Internet Options**.

Categorize Websites

Desktop IE allows you to categorize websites into zones: Internet (sites that are not classified in one of the other ways), Local Intranet, Trusted Sites, and Restricted Sites (as shown in Figure 4-11).

From the Internet Options dialog box:

1. Select the **Security** tab and select the **Internet** zone. Note its definition.

2. Select **Custom Level**. Select the elements in this zone that you want to disable, enable, or prompt you before using. Alternatively, select a level of security you want for this zone, select **Reset**, and select **Yes** to confirm. Select **OK** when you are finished.

3. Select each of the other zones, where you can identify either groups or individual sites you want in that zone.

> **Note** Protected Mode—which you can turn on or off at the bottom of the Security tab (the notice for which you'll see at the bottom of Internet Explorer)—is what produces the messages that tells you a program is trying to run in Internet Explorer or that software is trying to install itself on your computer. In most cases, you can select a bar at the top of the Internet Explorer window if you want to run the program or install the software. You can also open the notice at the bottom of Internet Explorer to open the Security tab and turn off Protected Mode (clear the **Enable Protected Mode** check box).

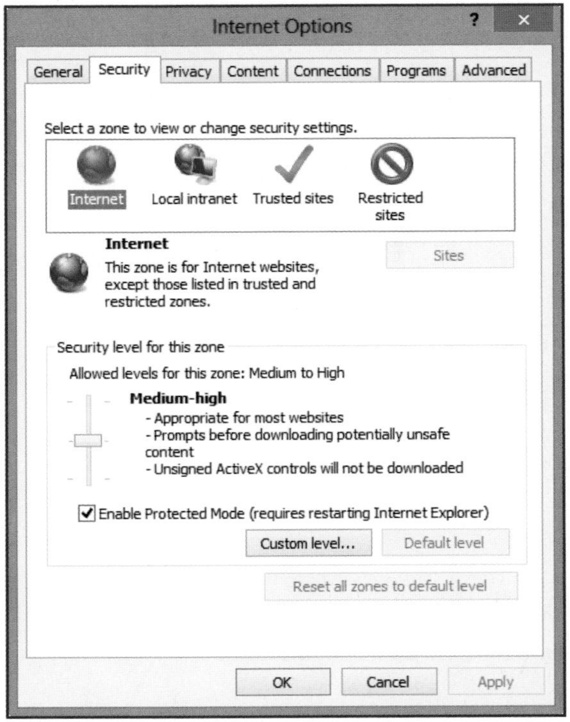

Figure 4-11: Internet Explorer allows you to categorize websites into zones and determine what can be done within those zones.

Handle Cookies

Cookies are small pieces of data that websites store on your computer so that they can remind themselves of who you are. These can save you from having to constantly enter your name and ID. Cookies can also be dangerous, however, letting people into your computer where they can potentially do damage. Internet Explorer on the desktop lets you determine the types and sources of cookies you will allow and what those cookies can do on your computer.

From the Internet Options dialog box:

1. Select the **Privacy** tab and select a privacy setting by moving the slider up or down.

2. Select **Advanced** to open the Advanced Privacy Settings dialog box. If you wish, select **Override Automatic Cookie Handling**, and select the settings you want to use.

3. Select **OK** to return to the Internet Options dialog box.

4. In the middle of the Privacy tab, you can turn off the pop-up blocker, which is on by default (it is recommended that you leave it on). If you have a site that you frequently use that needs pop-ups, select **Settings**, enter the site address (URL), and select **Add | Close**.

5. At the bottom of the Privacy tab, you can determine how to handle InPrivate Filtering and Browsing. See the Note on InPrivate Browsing later in this chapter.

Control Content

You can control the content that desktop IE displays.

From the Internet Options dialog box:

1. Select the **Content** tab and select **Family Safety**. Select the user you want to control to open the User Settings window, shown in Figure 4-12 (there have to be nonadministrative users on the computer in order to set parental controls). Select **On** to turn on Family Safety, and configure any other settings you want to use. Select **Close** to close the User Settings window.

2. Select **Enable** to open the Content Advisor dialog box. Select **Yes** to approve changes to the computer. Individually select each of the categories, and move the slider to the level you want to allow. Detailed descriptions of each area are shown in the lower half of the dialog box.

3. Select **OK** to close the Content Advisor dialog box.

When you are done, select **OK** to close the Internet Options dialog box. (Other parts of this dialog box are discussed elsewhere in this book.)

Figure 4-12: You can place a number of controls on what a particular user can do on a computer using the Family Safety feature.

Note Both versions of Internet Explorer have a way to more safely browse and view websites, called *InPrivate*. Open this in Windows 8 IE by opening the tab bar and selecting **Tab Tools | New InPrivate Tab**. In desktop IE, select the **Tools** icon and then select **Safety | InPrivate Browsing**. This opens a separate browser window with this address box in desktop IE:

or this in Windows 8 IE ![InPrivate address bar]. While you are in this window, your browsing history, temporary Internet files, and cookies are not stored on your computer, preventing anyone looking at your computer from seeing where you have browsed. In addition, with the desktop's ActiveX Filtering, also opened from Safety in Tools, you can control how information about you is passed on to Internet content providers.

▷▷ Copy Internet Information

You may occasionally find something on the Internet that you want to copy—a picture, some text, or a webpage.

CAUTION! Material you copy from the Internet is normally protected by copyright; therefore, what you can do with it is limited. Basically, you can store it on your hard disk and refer to it. You cannot put it on your own website, sell it, copy it for distribution, or use it for a commercial purpose without the permission of the owner.

Copy a Picture from the Internet

To copy a picture from an Internet webpage to a folder on your hard disk:

1. Open either version of Internet Explorer and locate the webpage containing the picture you want.

2. Open the context menu for the picture. In Windows 8 IE, select **Save To Picture Library**. In desktop IE, select **Save Picture As**, locate the folder in which you want to save the picture, enter the filename you want to use and the file type if it is something other than the default .jpg, and select **Save**.

Copy
Copy link
Open link in new tab
Open link
Save to picture library

Copy Text from the Internet to Word or Email

To copy text from a webpage to a Microsoft Word document or email message:

1. Open either version of Internet Explorer and locate the webpage containing the text you want.

2. Move across the text to highlight it, open the context menu for the selection, and select **Copy**.

 Tip To highlight and copy text using touch, slowly double-tap a word in the text to be copied. Two circles will be displayed under the selection. Move each circle in opposite directions to highlight more text. Tap the selection to display the word "Copy." Tap **Copy** to complete the operation.

3. Open a Microsoft Word document or an email message in which you want to paste the text. Open the context menu for where you want the text, and select **Paste**.

4. Save the Word document and close Microsoft Word or your email program if you are done with them.

Copy a Webpage from the Internet

To make a copy of a webpage in desktop IE and store it on your hard disk:

1. Open desktop IE and locate the webpage you want to copy.

2. In desktop IE select the **Tools** icon and then select **File | Save As**.

3. In the Save Webpage dialog box, select the folder in which to save the page, enter the filename you want to use, and select **Save**.

4. Close Internet Explorer if you are done.

▷▷ Play Internet Audio and Video Files

You can play audio and video files on the Internet with Internet Explorer directly from a link on a webpage. Many webpages have links to audio and video files, such as the one shown in Figure 4-13. To play these files, simply select the links. If you have several audio players installed (for example, Windows Media Player and Real Player), you will be asked which one you want to use. Make that choice, and the player will open to play the requested piece.

 Note Chapter 7 discusses working with audio and video files in depth, including how to play these files using Windows Media Player.

 Tip To search for information on an open webpage in desktop IE, press **CTRL+F;** in Windows 8 IE, select **Page Tools | Find On Page**.

Tip To view a page shown on Windows 8 IE in desktop IE, select **Page Tools | View On The Desktop**.

*Figure 4-13: **Play an audio or video file on a webpage by selecting the link.***

USE INTERNET EMAIL

Windows 8 includes a new Windows 8 style mail program, which allows you to send and receive email. You can also send and receive email through a web mail account using Internet Explorer, but this section will primarily describe using Mail. See "Use Web Mail" for a discussion of that subject.

▷▷ Set Up Windows Mail

For email with Windows 8, this book describes the use of the Windows 8 Mail app because it works well, is freely available from Microsoft, and is designed for Windows 8. There are a number of other alternatives that you can buy or get for free, including Outlook from Microsoft, Google, Eudora, Mozilla Thunderbird, and Opera. If you wish to explore the alternatives, do an Internet search on each of these.

To begin the use of Windows Mail you must establish an email account with one of the email providers recognized by Mail and then convey that information to Mail.

Establish an Email Account

To send and receive email with Mail, you must have an Internet connection and an email account established with a recognized email provider.

For an email account, you need:

- Your email address, for example: mike@anisp.com

- The password for your mail account

- You may also need to know the type of mail server you are using, IMAP or POP (probably the majority are POP)

At the time this was written, Mail recognized accounts with Outlook.com (the new Microsoft Internet mail service replacement for Hotmail), Google, and Exchange servers and possibly many others. Since you had to have a Microsoft account to use Windows 8, you can generally use that for your Mail account. You can also open Internet Explorer from either the Start screen or the desktop and go to Outlook.com (not the Office product, but the replacement for Hotmail) and create a new account.

Initiate Windows Mail

With your account information, you can set up an account in Mail.

1. In the Start screen, select the **Mail** tile. Mail will try to set up an account for you based on the email address in your Microsoft account. If your account is not in Hotmail, Outlook.com, or Google, you will be asked what type of account you have: Exchange (generally in larger enterprises), IMAP, or POP (but if you choose POP, you will be told that Mail does not support that). With either of the other choices, select **Connect**.

2. If you have a Hotmail, Google, or Outlook.com account you will automatically be signed in and you can start using Mail, as you can see in Figure 4-14.

3. If you do not have a Hotmail or Outlook.com account, open **Charms** and in **Settings** at the top of the panel, select **Accounts | Add An Account** in the Settings pane.

4. Select the type of email account you have—for example, **Google**— enter your email address, press **TAB**, enter your email password,

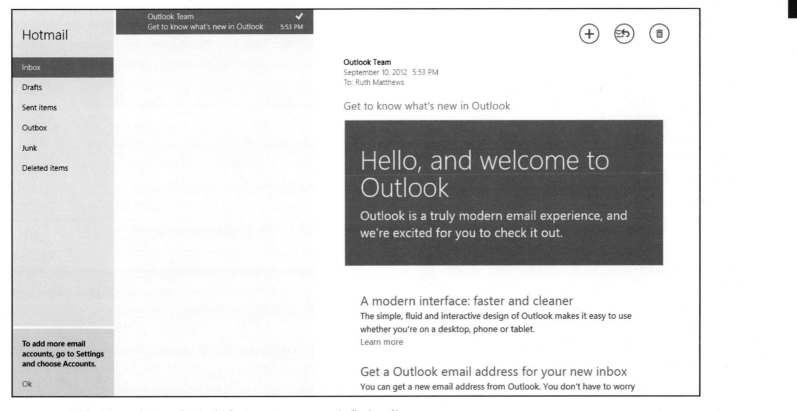

Figure 4-14: With a Microsoft Hotmail or Outlook .com you are automatically signed in.

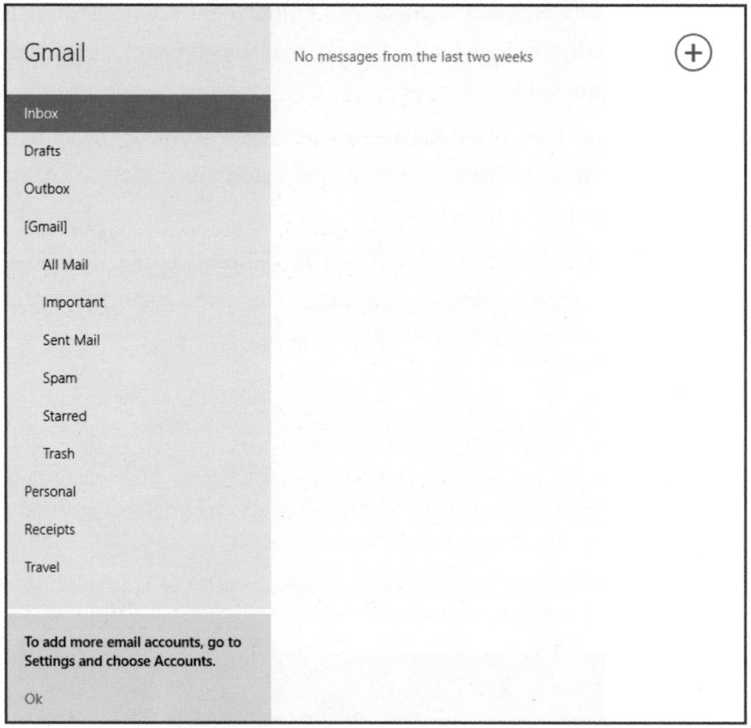

| Gmail | No messages from the last two weeks | ⊕ |

Inbox

Drafts

Outbox

[Gmail]

   All Mail

   Important

   Sent Mail

   Spam

   Starred

   Trash

Personal

Receipts

Travel

To add more email accounts, go to Settings and choose Accounts.

Ok

Figure 4-15: You start in Google with a blank page.

and select **Connect**. Your email account will open as you can see in Figure 4-15.

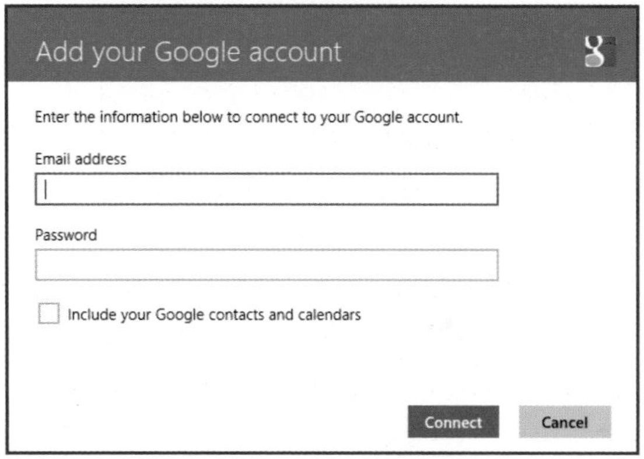

Add your Google account   g

Enter the information below to connect to your Google account.

Email address

| |

Password

| |

☐ Include your Google contacts and calendars

Connect   Cancel

▷▷ Send, Receive, and Respond to Email

The purpose of email, of course, is to send messages to others, receive messages from them, and respond to the messages you receive. Windows 8 Mail does this with a simple elegance.

Create and Send Email

To create and send an email message:

1. Select the **Mail** tile and in the page that opens, select the **New** icon (a plus sign). The New Message window will open, similar to the one in Figure 4-16.

2. Start to enter a name in the To text box. If the name is in your People (see "Use People" in this chapter), it will be completed automatically and you can press ENTER or tap to accept that name. If the name is not automatically completed, finish typing a full email address (such as billg@microsoft.com) and then press ENTER.

3. If you want more than one addressee, after pressing ENTER as directed in step 2 where a space is automatically added (you can also press ; in place of ENTER), simply begin typing a second one as in step 2.

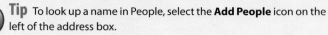

To

help@anisp.com   info@anisp.com   ⊕

Tip To look up a name in People, select the **Add People** icon on the left of the address box.

4. If you want to differentiate the addressees to whom the message is principally being sent from those for whom it is just information, select the **Cc** text box, and enter the desired addressees there as you did in the To text box.

Gmail
marty. | Add a subject   I (≡☑) (✕)

To
[   ] ⊕ | Add a message

Cc   Sent from Windows Mail
[   ] ⊕

Show more

Figure 4-16: Email messages are an easy and fast way to communicate.

5. If you want to send the message to a recipient and not have other recipients see to whom it is sent, select **More Details**, select the **Bcc** text box, and type the address(es) to be hidden. (Bcc stands for "blind carbon copy.")

6. Select **Add A Subject** and type a subject for the message.

7. Select the area beneath the line on the right and type your message.

8. When you have completed your message, select the **Send** icon to the right of the Subject line. For a brief time, you may see a message in your Outbox and then, if you look, you will see the message in your Sent Items folder. If you are done, close Mail.

(≡☑)

Note If you want to copy, edit, or remove an email addressee, open the context menu (right-click or tap and briefly hold) for the addressee and select the option you want.

Receive Email

Mail will automatically receive any messages sent to the accounts you have established in it. To open and read your mail:

1. Open **Mail** and select **Inbox**, which contains all of the messages you have received and haven't deleted. (The number beside the word "Inbox" is the number of unviewed messages.)

Tip Have a friend send you an email message so you know whether you are receiving messages. Then send the friend a message back and ask them to let you know when they get it so you know you are sending messages.

2. Select a message in the inbox Message List to have it displayed and then read it in the reading pane on the right of the Mail window, as shown in Figure 4-17.

3. If you wish, you can delete a message while it is selected by selecting the **Delete** icon (a trashcan) on the far right.

Respond to Email

You can respond to messages you receive.

Select the message in the message list and then select the **Respond** icon on the right of the screen. From the menu that appears, select:

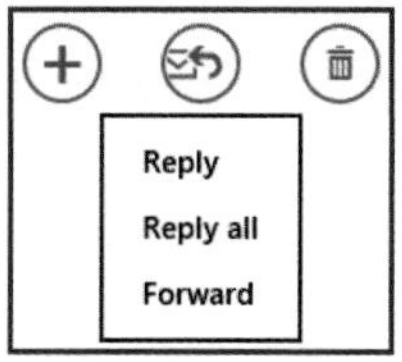

(+) (↩) (🗑)

Reply
Reply all
Forward

- **Reply** to return a message to just the person who sent the original message.

- **Reply All** to return a message to all the people who were addressees (both To and Cc) in the original message.

- **Forward** to relay a message to people not shown as addressees on the original message.

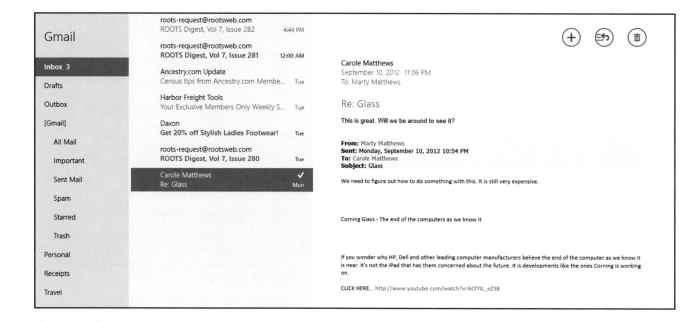

Figure 4-17: The message area in the lower-right corner of the screen shows the chain of emails that lead up to the current one.

In all three cases, a window similar to the New Message window opens and allows you to add or change addressees and the subject and add a new message.

▷▷ Apply Formatting

Windows 8 Mail messages are sent with formatting using Hypertext Markup Language (HTML), the language with which many websites are created. Because of this you can set and change formatting of a message in a number of ways.

To use particular formatting on an email message:

1. Open an email message you want to create or that is in response to a message you received, as described in the previous sections of this chapter.

2. Type the text you want in the message, and then select the text you want specially formatted. When the text is selected, a formatting bar will open as you see in Figure 4-18.

–Or–

You may apply formatting before you enter text by right-selecting the text line where you are about to enter it. The formatting bar will open.

3. Select the font, size, style, effects, color, and other formatting that you want to use, or select **More** to add bulleted or numbered lists, or to undo or redo the formatting you have just applied.

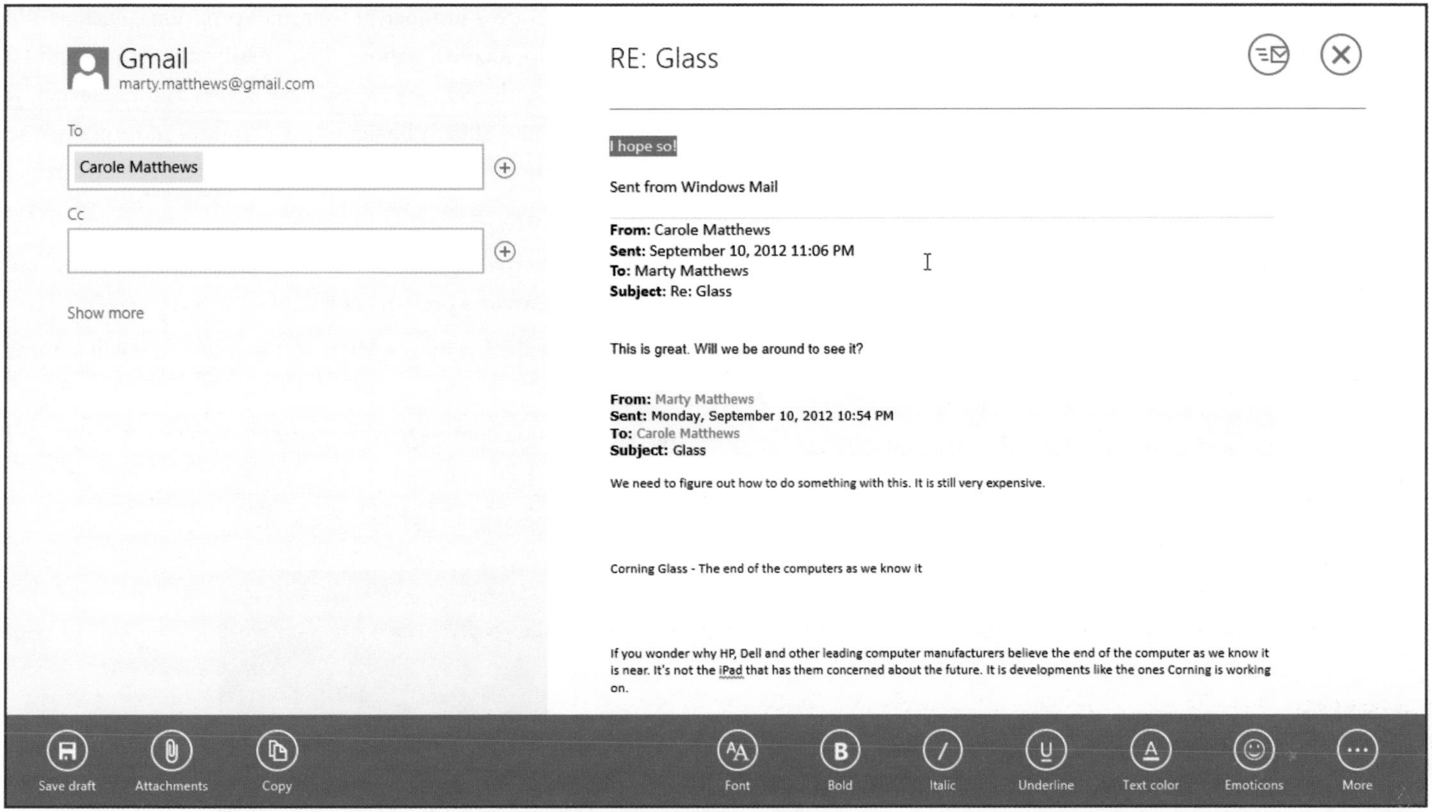

Gmail
marty.matthews@gmail.com

To
Carole Matthews ⊕

Cc
⊕

Show more

RE: Glass ⊟ⓧ

I hope so!

Sent from Windows Mail

From: Carole Matthews
Sent: September 10, 2012 11:06 PM
To: Marty Matthews
Subject: Re: Glass

This is great. Will we be around to see it?

From: Marty Matthews
Sent: Monday, September 10, 2012 10:54 PM
To: Carole Matthews
Subject: Glass

We need to figure out how to do something with this. It is still very expensive.

Corning Glass - The end of the computers as we know it

If you wonder why HP, Dell and other leading computer manufacturers believe the end of the computer as we know it is near. It's not the iPad that has them concerned about the future. It is developments like the ones Corning is working on.

Save draft Attachments Copy   Font Bold Italic Underline Text color Emoticons More

Figure 4-18: Mail allows you to change the fonts, weighting, color, and other formatting.

Tip If you are applying formatting as you type, instead of selecting it after the text is typed, you will probably want to turn off the formatting at some point. Do that by right-selecting where you want it turned off and selecting the formatting attributes that you want to turn off; they should be highlighted.

Attach Files to Email

You can attach and send files, such as documents or images, with email messages.

1. Open an email message you want to create or that is in response to a message you received, as described in the previous sections of this chapter.

2. Select **Attachments** in the left of the command bar at the bottom of the message window. Your most recently opened Library folder will be displayed as shown in Figure 4-19.

3. If what you want is shown in that folder, select as many objects as you want and select **Attach**. The attachment(s) will appear in your email message.

4. If what you want is in another folder, select the down arrow at the top next to **Files**, select the parent and successive folders necessary to display the document you want, and then perform step 3.

–Or–

Repeatedly select **Go Up** until you reach the parent folder you want, and then select successive subordinate folders as needed to reach the document you want and then perform step 3.

5. Repeat steps 3 and 4 as needed. When you are ready, address, enter, and send the message as you would normally.

Use Web Mail

Web mail is the sending and receiving of email over the Internet using a browser, such as Internet Explorer, instead of an email program, such as Mail. There are a number of web mail programs, such as Windows Outlook (outlook.com), Yahoo! Mail (mail.yahoo.com), and Google's Gmail (gmail.com). So long as you have access to the Internet, you can sign up for, or may already be signed up for, one or more of these services. The basic features (simple sending and receiving of email) are generally free. For example, to use Outlook.com:

1. Open either version of Internet Explorer. In the address box, type outlook.com and press **ENTER**.

2. Since you already have a Microsoft account, you will automatically be signed in.

3. The Outlook.com page will open and display your mail, as shown in Figure 4-20.

4. Select a message to open and read it.

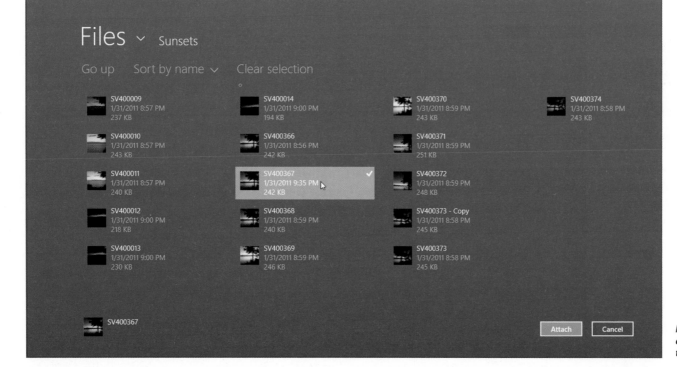

Figure 4-19: You can attach any file on your computer to an email message.

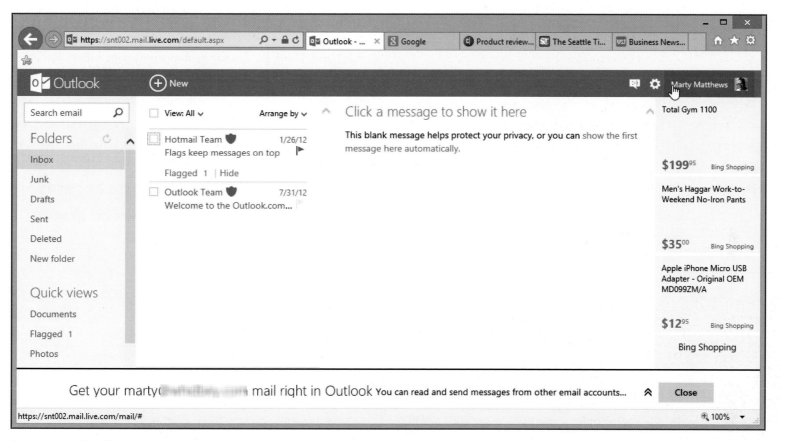

Figure 4-20: Web mail accounts are a quick and free way to get one or more email accounts.

5. Select **New** on the toolbar to write an email message. Enter the address, a subject, and the message. When you are done, select **Send**.

6. When you are finished with Outlook.com, close Internet Explorer.

Tip A way to quickly open Outlook.com is to add it to your Favorites list or Favorites bar. See the earlier discussion to do this.

USE PEOPLE

People, shown in Figure 4-21, allows you to collect email addresses and other information about the people with whom you correspond or otherwise interact. It starts out by looking at the public lists of people you have, such as Facebook and Google, and if you are on an Exchange Server, it will look at that too.

2. If you have existing accounts in the services shown on the left of Figure 4-21, select the service to open its page, where you need to select **Connect** again.

3. When it is done you are returned to People.

4. To add more accounts, select **Connected to** in the top-right corner. The Add An Account list will appear on the right of the screen.

Figure 4-21: People provides a way to collect the people you correspond with across various accounts.

▷▷ Add New People

You can add people by including more accounts to be searched and by adding individuals.

Add People in Accounts

People will connect to and gather people you correspond with from your accounts on Facebook, Hotmail, Twitter, LinkedIn, and Google, and from an Exchange Server if you are connected to one.

1. Select the **People** tile on the Start screen to open the People window. You may or may not have anyone in your People window.

5. Select an account and then select **Manage This Account Online**. A page will open explaining what will transpire between the other account and your Microsoft account. Follow the instructions on the page.

Add People Individually

You can add individuals to People one at a time.

1. Open the command bar at the bottom of the People screen and select **New**. The New Contact window opens as shown in Figure 4-22.

2. Enter as much of the information as you have or want. For email, you need at least an email address, and a name is recommended. If you have additional information, such as a nickname, several email addresses, several phone numbers, or a home address for

the contact, select the plus sign next to those items and fill in the desired information.

3. When you are done, select **Save** to close the New Contact window.

 Tip When you have several email addresses in a single contact's record, they are all displayed when you go to enter the contact in an email message, so you can select the address you want.

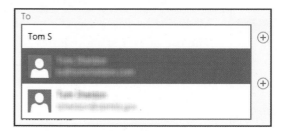

USE CALENDAR

Calendar, which you can use to keep track of scheduled events, is an app on the Start screen. To open and use Calendar:

From the Start screen, select the **Calendar** tile. The Calendar will open as you can see in Figure 4-23.

Add Events to Calendar

To add an event to a calendar date:

1. With the Calendar screen open, select the date on which you want to add the event. If it is in a different month, use the right or left arrows on the edges near the top to select the desired month, and then select the day, or swipe left/right using touch.

   –Or–

   Open the command bar at the bottom of the screen and select **New**.

   In either case, the New Event window will open, as shown in Figure 4-24.

2. Enter the title, when it will start, how long it will run, where it will be held, and what calendar it should be listed on, if you have more than one. You can also enter a message or notes about the event on the right.

3. If the event will happen on a repeated basis, select **Show More | How Often** down arrow and select the period for this event.

4. If you have selected **Show More**, you can select how long before the event you want to be reminded of the event, and you can have the calendar reflect your status during the event.

Figure 4-22: People allows you to store a lot of information about an individual.

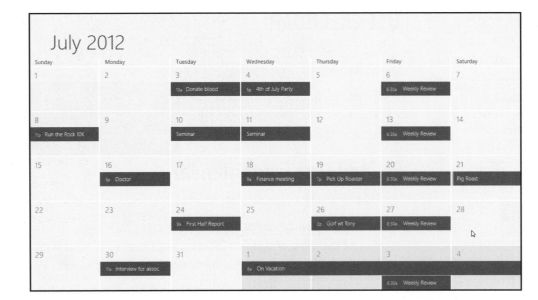

July 2012

Sunday	Monday	Tuesday	Wednesday	Thursday	Friday	Saturday
1	2	3	4	5	6	7
		10a Donate blood	5p 4th of July Party		8:30a Weekly Review	
8	9	10	11	12	13	14
11p Run the Rock 10K		Seminar	Seminar		8:30a Weekly Review	
15	16	17	18	19	20	21
	3p Doctor		9a Finance meeting	1p Pick Up Roaster	8:30a Weekly Review	Pig Roast
22	23	24	25	26	27	28
		9a First Half Report		2p Golf wt Tony	8:30a Weekly Review	
29	30	31	1	2	3	4
	11a Interview for assoc.		9a On Vacation			8:30a Weekly Review

Figure 4-23: The Calendar provides a handy way of keeping track of scheduled events, especially those scheduled through email.

5. When you have completed the event, select **Save This Event**, in the upper-right corner, to store the event on your calendar and store it on your computer.

Tip If you have several calendars, you can control which are shown in Calendar. Open **Charms** and select **Settings | Options** to see a list of your calendars with controls to turn them on or off and select the colors with which they are displayed.

⟵ Options 📅

Whidbey
~~████████~~

My Calendar
Show ████▮

■ Blue ⌄

Birthday calendar
Show ████▮

■ Purple ⌄

USE MESSAGING

Messaging allows you to send and receive instant messages (or *chat*) with others who are online at the same time as you. This is frequently called "instant messaging" or IM.

⟫ Start Messaging

Messaging, by default, has a tile on the Start screen. The use of Messaging requires your Microsoft account, which you have to use Windows 8. As a result of that, you will automatically be signed in when you open Messaging.

1. On the Start screen, select the **Messaging** tile. Messaging will open as you see in Figure 4-25.

2. Select **New Message** in the upper-left of the screen. The People app will open. Select **Online Only** to see the people in the app who are online at that moment.

People ⌄

All   Online only
C
   CB Matthews ✓

J
   john cronan

Connected to ▣ ▣ ▣ ⤤

Select   Cancel

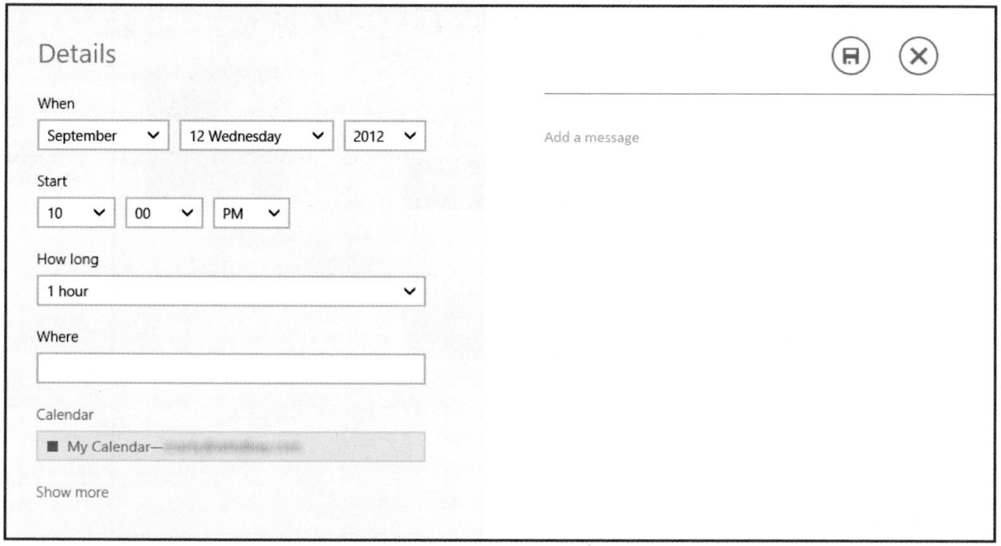

Details

When

| September ⌄ | 12 Wednesday ⌄ | 2012 ⌄ |

Start

| 10 ⌄ | 00 ⌄ | PM ⌄ |

How long

| 1 hour ⌄ |

Where

| |

Calendar

■ My Calendar—

Show more

Add a message

Figure 4-24: Calendar allows you to send scheduled events to others to put on their calendars.

3. Select one of the people and select **Select**. The new message screen will open. Type your message in the text box at the bottom of the screen and press **ENTER**.

4. Continue the conversation as your correspondent replies, as shown in Figure 4-26.

5. If you have text in another location that you want in the message, you can copy it in its original location and then open the message text box's context menu and select **Paste**.

Connected to 👥 f

Messaging

⊕ New message

Windows team
When you sign in to you...   10:04 PM

To add or manage an account, go to
Settings and choose Accounts.

Ok

Windows
team

Today, on Messenger

Hi! 😊
                                    10:04 PM

When you sign in to your PC, you'll be signed in to
your messaging services so you can chat with all your
friends.
                                    10:04 PM

Marty
Matthews

Available

You can't reply to this message.

Figure 4-25: With Messaging, you can chat in real time with friends and associates over the Internet.

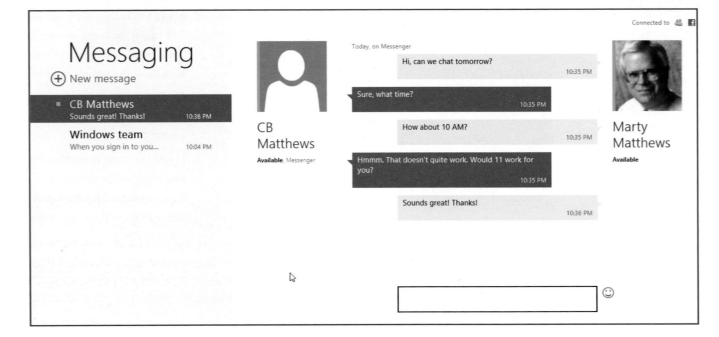

Figure 4-26: Messaging provides a trail of a conversation that can be useful.

▷ Set Messaging Options

Messaging allows you to set your status that others will see, to invite people to sign up for Messaging, to delete message threads, and to turn Messaging on or off.

1. If Messaging is not already open, select its tile in the Start screen.

2. Open the command bar at the bottom of the screen, select **Status**, and choose between Available and Invisible.

3. Delete a message thread by selecting it in the left column, opening the command bar, and selecting **Delete | Delete**.

4. When you are done with Messaging, close the app.

Chapter 5

Managing Windows 8

Windows 8, as you can imagine, is a very complex and sophisticated program that Microsoft has put a great deal of effort into making easy to use. Behind that ease-of-use façade there are several levels of increasingly detailed controls that determine how Windows operates. Previous chapters, especially Chapter 2, have briefly touched on a few of the controls in PC Settings and the Control Panel. In this chapter we'll expand on that, looking in particular at how to maintain and enhance Windows. The chapter will also cover how to set up Remote Assistance so that you can have someone help you without that person actually being in front of your computer, and several different ways to start and stop apps.

MAINTAIN WINDOWS 8

Windows 8 maintenance consists of periodically updating fixes and new features, restoring Windows 8 when hardware or other software damages it, getting information about it, and installing new hardware and software.

▶▶ Update Windows 8

Microsoft tries hard to encourage you to allow Windows 8 to update itself, from the point of installation, where you are asked to establish Automatic Updates, to periodically reminding you to do that. If you turn on Automatic Updates, on a regular basis, Windows will automatically determine if any updates are available, download the updates (which come from Microsoft) over the Internet, and install them. If Automatic Updates was not turned on during installation, you can do that at any time and control the updating process once it is turned on.

Turn On Automatic Updates

To turn on, off, and control Windows Update:

1. From the Start screen open the command bar and select **All Apps | Control Panel** (under Windows System on the right). In Category view, select **System And Security**, and in any view, select **Windows Update**.

> **Note** Periodically throughout this chapter you will be asked to open the Control Panel. You can do this from the Start screen by opening the command bar and selecting **All Apps | Control Panel**, or from either the Start screen or the desktop, by opening the System menu (right-clicking the lower-left corner of the screen or pressing **WINDOWS+X**) and selecting **Control Panel**. In future instances in this chapter, I'll simply say "open **Control Panel**." Also, I'll always start from Category view and not repeat that.

2. Select **Change Settings**, determine the amount of automation you want, and select one of the following four choices after selecting the **Important Updates** down arrow (see Figure 5-1):

   - The first and recommended choice, which is the default, automatically determines if updates are available, downloads them, and then installs them in the background when your computer is not on a metered Internet connection (for example, over a 3G or 4G cellular link where you are charged by the second or MB).

   - The second choice automatically determines if updates are available and downloads them; it then asks you whether you want to install them.

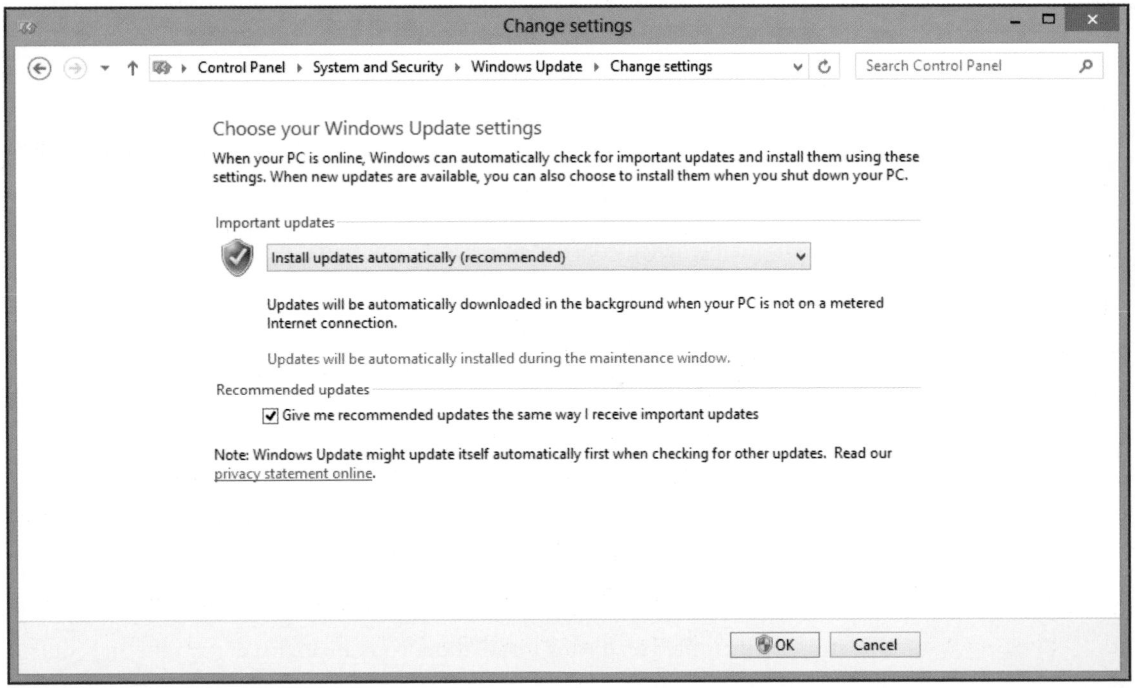

*Figure 5-1: **Automatic Updates determines which updates you need and can automatically download and install them.***

- The third choice automatically determines if updates are available, but asks you before downloading them, and asks you again before installing them.

- The fourth choice, which is not recommended, never checks for updates.

3. Choose whether to include recommended updates when you receive important updates.

4. Select **OK** when you are finished, and close Windows Update.

Apply Updates

If you choose either the second or third option for handling updates, you may periodically see on the desktop a notice that updates are ready to download and/or install.

When you see the notice:

1. Select the notice. The Windows Updates dialog box will appear and show you the updates that are available.

2. Select the individual updates to see detailed information for the updates being proposed.

3. Select the check boxes for the updates you want to download and/or install, and then select **OK**.

4. After you have selected all the updates you want, select **Install Updates**. You will see a notice that the updates are being installed.

5. When the updates have been downloaded and installed, Windows Update will reopen, tell you of this fact, and often ask to restart your computer.

6. Close any open apps, and select **Restart Now**.

▷▷ Use the Action Center

The Windows Action Center in the desktop's notification area contains messages that have been sent to you from Windows and other apps

that, at least from the viewpoint of the app, you need to respond to. When a message is sent to you by an app, a flag with a red X appears in the notification area.

Open the Action Center

Select the notification area Action Center flag to open the Action Center jump list. Select any option on the jump list to go directly to the window or dialog box, where you can view the message and possibly take corrective actions.

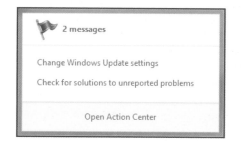

–Or–

1. Select **Open Action Center** to review recent messages and resolve problems, as you can see in Figure 5-2.

2. Select the relevant item to address the issue, and when you are ready, close the Action Center.

Change Action Center Settings

You can change how the Action Center informs you of an alert message.

1. From the Action Center, select **Change Action Center Settings**.

2. Select the security and maintenance messages you want to see. Open any of the related settings that seem pertinent, returning to the Action Center when you are ready.

3. When your Action Center settings are the way you want them, select **OK** and close the Action Center.

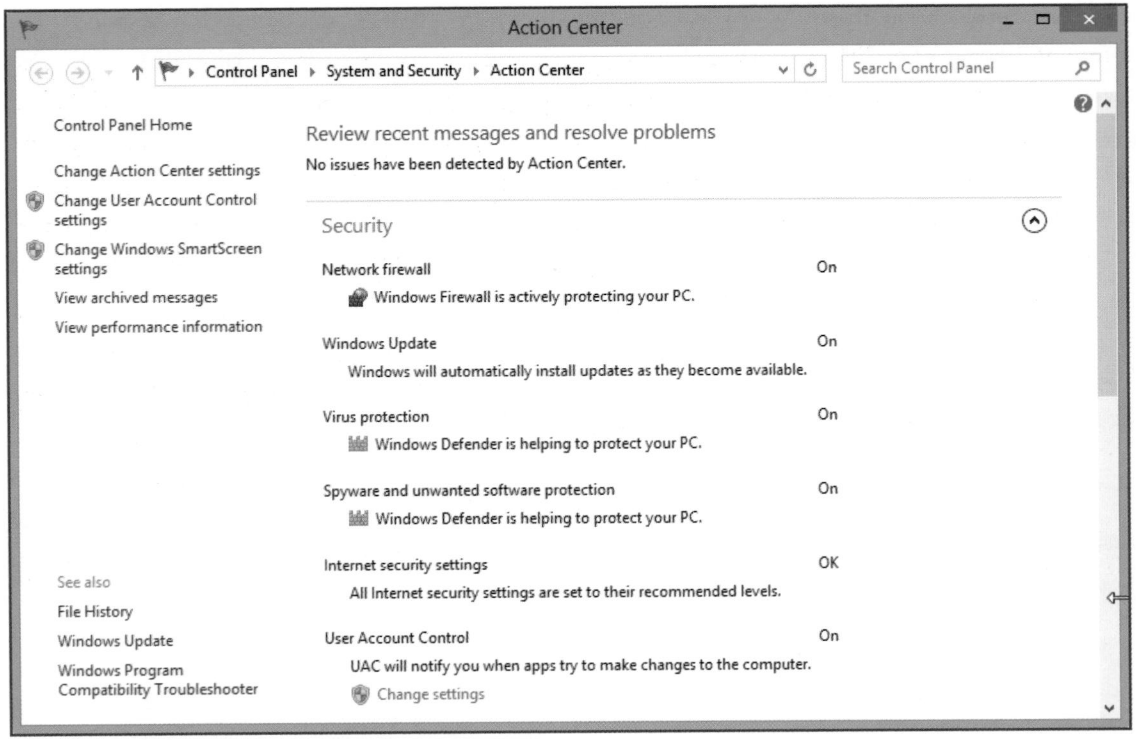

Action Center

Control Panel ▸ System and Security ▸ Action Center

Search Control Panel

Control Panel Home

Change Action Center settings

Change User Account Control settings

Change Windows SmartScreen settings

View archived messages

View performance information

Review recent messages and resolve problems

No issues have been detected by Action Center.

Security

Network firewall	On
Windows Firewall is actively protecting your PC.	
Windows Update	On
Windows will automatically install updates as they become available.	
Virus protection	On
Windows Defender is helping to protect your PC.	
Spyware and unwanted software protection	On
Windows Defender is helping to protect your PC.	
Internet security settings	OK
All Internet security settings are set to their recommended levels.	
User Account Control	On
UAC will notify you when apps try to make changes to the computer.	

See also

File History

Windows Update

Windows Program Compatibility Troubleshooter

Change settings

*Figure 5-2: **The Action Center consolidates and maintains alert messages that are sent to you by the apps you run.***

▶▶ Restore Windows 8

System Restore keeps track of the changes you make to your system, including the software you install and the settings you make. If a hardware change, a software installation, or something else causes the system not to load or not to run properly, you can use System Restore to return the system to the way it was at the last restore point.

Note System Restore does not restore or make any changes to data files, only to system and app files. Data files must be backed up, using either the Windows 8 File History app or a third-party backup program, and then restored from a backup (see Chapter 3).

Set Up System Restore

In a default installation of Windows 8, System Restore is automatically installed. If you have at least 300MB of free disk space after installing Windows 8, System Restore will be turned on and the first restore point will be set. If System Restore is not enabled, you can turn it on and set a restore point.

Note System Restore actually needs at least 300MB on each hard drive that has the feature turned on, and may use up to 15 percent of each drive. If a drive is smaller than 1GB, System Restore cannot be used.

1. Open Control Panel and select **System And Security | System | System Protection** in the left pane. The System Properties dialog box will appear with the System Protection tab displayed, as you can see in Figure 5-3.

   By default, the disk on which Windows 8 is installed should have System Protection turned on, indicating that System Restore is automatically operating for that disk. Again by default, your other hard drives are not selected.

2. If any drive does not have protection on and you want it on, select the disk, select **Configure | Turn On System Protection**, adjust the disk space usage as desired, and select **OK**.

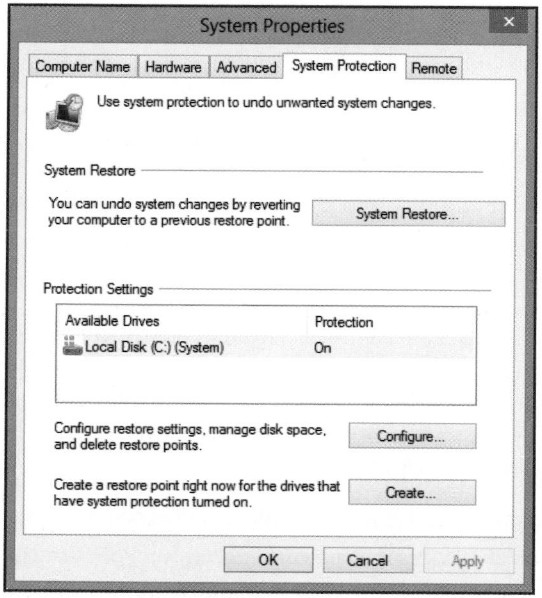

Figure 5-3: *System Restore returns the system to a previous time when it was functioning normally.*

Create Restore Points

A *restore point* is an identifiable point in time when you know your system was working correctly. If your computer's settings are saved at that point, you can use those settings to restore your computer to that time. Normally, Windows 8 automatically creates restore points for the system drive on a periodic basis. But if you know at a given point in time that your computer is operating exactly the way you want it to, you can create a restore point.

1. In the System Properties dialog box with the System Protection tab displayed, which was opened in the previous section, select **Create** and type a name for the restore point. The date and time are automatically added, and you cannot change the name once you create it.

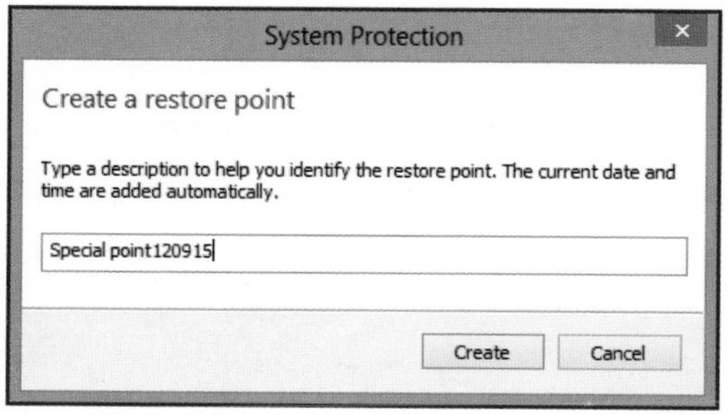

2. Select **Create** again. You will be told when the restore point is created. Select **Close** to close the System Protection message box.

Run System Restore

1. In the System Properties dialog box with the System Protection tab displayed, which was opened in a previous section, select **System Restore**; a message explains the restore.

2. Select **Next** to open the System Restore dialog box shown in Figure 5-4. Select the restore point you want to use and then select **Scan For Affected Programs**. This will tell you if any apps have been updated or had a driver installed after the restore point. If you go ahead with the restore, these apps will be restored to their state before the update.

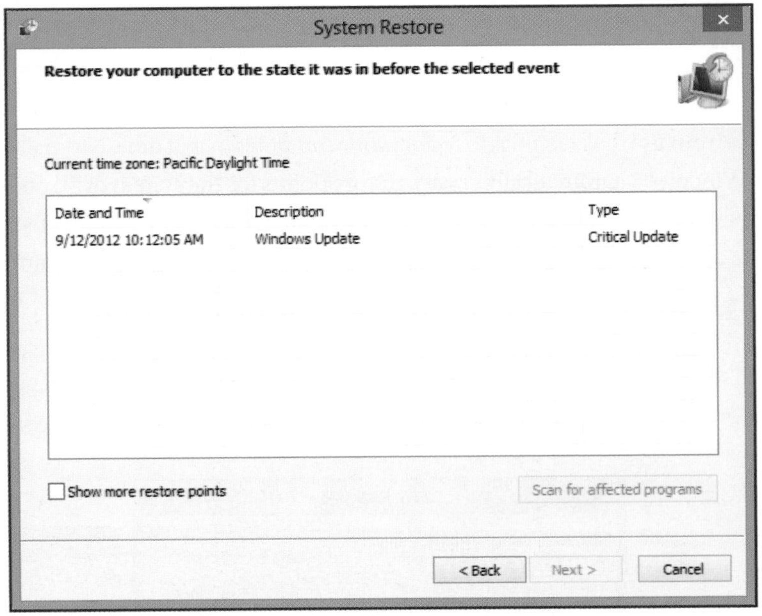

Figure 5-4: You can do a system restore at any of the restore points on the computer and return all of the Windows 8 settings and registry to that point in time.

3. Select **Close | Next**. You are asked to confirm the restore point the system will be returned to and given information about that point. If you do not want to restore to that point, select **Back** and return to step 2.

4. System Restore will need to restart your computer, so make sure all other apps are closed. When you are ready to restore to the described point, select **Finish**.

5. A confirmation dialog box appears, telling you that the restore process cannot be interrupted or undone until it has completed. Select **Yes** to continue. Some time will be spent saving files and settings for a new restore point, and then the computer will be restarted.

6. When the restore is completed, you will be told on the desktop that it was successful. Select **Close**.

Tip You can restore the system after doing a system restore. Immediately before doing a system restore, a restore point is created and can be used to return to the point the system was at prior to performing this action. Simply re-run System Restore as described in the "Run System Restore" section in this chapter, select **Undo System Restore**, and follow the remaining instructions.

Tip You can also run System Restore by opening **Charms | Settings** and selecting **Change PC Settings | General | Advanced Startup – Restart Now | Troubleshoot | Advanced Options | System Restore**.

Get System Information

When you are working on a computer problem, you, or possibly a technical support person working with you, may want some information about your computer. The two primary sources are basic computer information and advanced system information.

Basic Computer Information

Basic computer information provides general system information, such as the Windows edition, the processor and memory, and the computer name and workgroup (see Figure 5-5). To see the basic computer information:

Open Control Panel and select **System And Security | System**. The System window will open. After you have reviewed the information, select **Close**.

Advanced System Information

Advanced system information provides detailed system information and lets you look at services that are running, Group Policy settings, and the error log. To see the advanced system information:

Open Control Panel and select **System And Security | Administrative Tools | System Information**. The System Information window

Figure 5-5: Basic computer information provides an overview of the computer and its operating system.

will open. Select any of the topics in the left pane to display that information in the right pane. Figure 5-6 shows the summary-level information that is available. Select **Close** when you are done.

▷▷ Set Power Options

Setting power options is important on laptop and tablet computers that run at least some of the time on batteries. It can also be useful on desktop computers to conserve power. The Windows 8 Power Options feature provides a number of settings that allow you to manage your computer's use of power.

1. Open Control Panel and select **System And Security | Power Options**.

2. Choose one of the power plans, depending on whether you want to emphasize battery life (energy savings on desktops) or performance (see Figure 5-7). You can also reduce the screen brightness on a laptop or notebook computer to reduce the power drain.

	System Information	_ □ ✕

File   Edit   View   Help

Item	Value
System Summary	
⊟ Hardware Resources	OS Name	Microsoft Windows 8 Pro
Conflicts/Sharing	Version	6.2.9200 Build 9200
DMA	Other OS Description	Not Available
Forced Hardware	OS Manufacturer	Microsoft Corporation
I/O	System Name	SLATE
IRQs	System Manufacturer	SAMSUNG ELECTRONICS CO., LTD.
Memory	System Model	700T
⊟ Components	System Type	x64-based PC
⊞ Multimedia	System SKU	SAMSUNG-PC
CD-ROM	Processor	Intel(R) Core(TM) i5-2467M CPU @ 1.60GHz, 1601 Mhz, 2 Core(s), 4 Logical Pr...
Sound Device	BIOS Version/Date	American Megatrends Inc. 08FW.M084.20120202.SSH, 2/2/2012
Display	SMBIOS Version	2.7
Infrared	Embedded Controller Version	255.255
⊞ Input	BIOS Mode	Legacy
Modem	BaseBoard Manufacturer	SAMSUNG ELECTRONICS CO., LTD.
⊞ Network	BaseBoard Model	Not Available
⊞ Ports	BaseBoard Name	Base Board
⊞ Storage	Platform Role	Mobile
Printing	Secure Boot State	Unsupported
Problem Devices	PCR7 Configuration	Binding Not Possible
USB	Windows Directory	C:\WINDOWS
⊟ Software Environment	System Directory	C:\WINDOWS\system32
System Drivers	Boot Device	\Device\HarddiskVolume1
Environment Variables	Locale	United States
Print Jobs	

Find what: _____   [Find]   [Close Find]

☐ Search selected category only   ☐ Search category names only

*Figure 5-6: **Advanced system information provides a great deal of information useful in troubleshooting.***

3. To see a more detailed setting, select **Choose When To Turn Off The Display**. If you are using a laptop or notebook computer, your power options will look like those in Figure 5-8. (A desktop computer won't have the battery, display dimming, or brightness settings.)

4. Select each of the drop-down lists, select the setting that is correct for you, and adjust the screen brightness. If you would like to control individual pieces of hardware (disk drives, USB ports, and so on), select **Change Advanced Power Settings** and then the plus signs to open the lists; then select the action you want to change and then select the spinners to adjust the values. Select **OK** when you are finished.

5. When you are ready, select **Save Changes** to accept the changes you have made to your power options settings.

 Note   See Chapter 1 for a discussion of the differences between shutting down a computer and putting it to sleep.

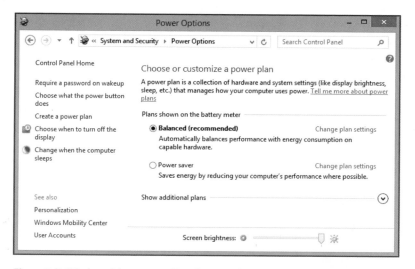

Figure 5-7: *Windows 8 has two preferred power plans that let you emphasize either performance or energy consumption.*

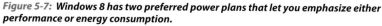

Figure 5-8: *You can set the amount of idle time before the display and/or the computer are turned off or put to sleep, respectively.*

Add and Remove Software

Today, almost all app and utility software comes in one of two ways: on a CD or DVD, or downloaded over the Internet, with downloading being the predominant method.

> **Note** In medium to larger organizations, app software might be available over the local area network (LAN) from a server. Generally, it is better to download the software and then do the installation from your computer than to do the installation over the network in case the network connection is lost during installation (the same can be said for online software; better to download and then install rather than installing directly through an Internet connection).

Install Software from a CD/DVD

If you get software on a CD/DVD and your computer is less than ten years old, all you need to do is put the CD/DVD in the drive, wait for the install app to automatically load, and follow the displayed instructions, of which there are usually only a few and often begin with something like "Run Setup" or "Run Start." When the installation is complete, you may need to acknowledge that by selecting **OK** or **Finish**. Then remove the CD/DVD from its drive. That is all there is to it.

> **Tip** If you are having trouble installing an app for no discernable reason, make sure you are logged on with administrative permissions. Some apps or installation situations require these permissions; without them, the app refuses to install. See Chapter 8 to learn how to establish and work with administrative permissions.

Install Software from the Internet

To download and install an app from the Internet:

1. From the desktop, select the **Internet Explorer** icon on the taskbar. In the address bar, type the URL (Uniform Resource Locator, also

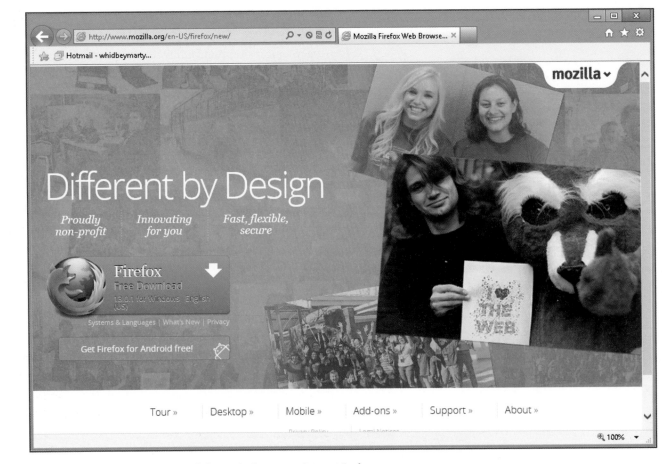

Figure 5-9: Mozilla's Firefox is a good alternative browser to Internet Explorer.

called the address) for the source of the download, and press **ENTER**. (For this example, I'm downloading the Firefox web browser whose URL is mozilla.com.)

2. Locate the link for the download, and select it, as shown in Figure 5-9.

3. A dialog box will appear, asking if you want to run or save the app. Select **Run** (an exception to the previous Note because every time you install Firefox, you want to get the latest app). Select **Yes** in the User Account Control dialog box to continue to install the app.

Do you want to run or save **Firefox Setup 15.0.1.exe** (16.9 MB) from **download.cdn.mozilla.net**?   ×

Run   Save ▼   Cancel

4. In the Welcome dialog box, select **Next** and follow the app's installation instructions, making the choices that are correct for you.

5. When the installation is complete, you will be asked if you want to launch (start) the app. Select **Finish** and you will see Firefox open on your screen and a shortcut to the app.

Remove Software

There are at least two ways to get rid of an app you have installed and one way not to do it. You do not want to just delete the app files in File Explorer. That leaves files in other locations and all the settings in the registry (where Windows stores all the settings that tell it how to run).

To correctly remove an app, you need to use Windows 8's Uninstall Or Change A Program feature. To do the latter:

1. Open Control Panel and select **Programs** | **Programs And Features**. The Uninstall Or Change A Program window will open.

2. Open the context menu for the app you want to uninstall, and select **Uninstall**, as you can see in Figure 5-10. Follow the instructions as they are presented, which vary from app to app.

3. When the uninstall has successfully completed, close the Uninstall Or Change A Program window.

> **Note** The "change" part of the Uninstall Or Change A Program window is used to install updates and patches to apps. It requires that you have either a CD with the changes or have downloaded them. With some apps, you will get a third option: Repair.

Programs and Features

Control Panel ▸ Programs ▸ Programs and Features

Search Programs and F...

Control Panel Home

View installed updates

Turn Windows features on or off

Uninstall or change a program

To uninstall a program, select it from the list and then click Uninstall, Change, or Repair.

Organize ▾   Uninstall

Name	Publisher	Installed On	Size
🗄 Intel® HD Graphics Driver	Intel Corporation	9/8/2012	74.2 MB
🖊 Microsoft IntelliPoint 8.2	Microsoft Corporation	9/15/2012	
▢ Microsoft Office Professional Plus 201...	Microsoft Corporation	8/18/2012	
◉ Mozilla Firefox 15.0.1 (x86 en-US)	Mozilla	9/15/2012	39.0 MB
☑ 🗄 Mozilla Maintenance Service	Mozilla	9/15/2012	215 KB
▨	TechSmith Corporation	8/18/2012	113 MB
▨ thinkorswim from TD AMERITRADE	TD AMERITRADE, Inc.	8/18/2012	

Uninstall

Mozilla Product version: 15.0.1   Comments: Mozilla Maintenance Service 1...
Size: 215 KB

Figure 5-10: **It is important to remove software that you are not using as a form of housecleaning.**

▷▷ Add Hardware

Most hardware today is *Plug and Play*. That means that when you plug in a device, Windows recognizes it and installs the necessary driver software automatically and you can immediately begin using it. Often, when you first plug in the device or turn on the computer after installing the hardware, on the desktop taskbar you may see an icon with possibly a Device Setup message indicating that Windows is installing the device. Frequently, you need do nothing more; the installation will complete by itself. With other equipment, you may need to select a message for the installation to proceed. You may or may not be told when it has successfully completed. The best test is to try and use the hardware.

Device Setup

Installing Logitech® Unifying Receiver

Please wait while Setup installs necessary files on your system. This may take several minutes.

Close

FantomHD (E:)
Tap to choose what happens with removable drives.

Problems may occur when you have older hardware and the apps that run it, called *drivers,* are not available with Windows 8. In that case, you will see a dialog box saying you must locate the drivers. Here are some options for locating drivers:

- Let Windows see what it can do by itself by selecting the appropriate option to do that. Windows will scan your computer and see what it can find. The original dialog box appears only because a driver wasn't in the standard Windows 8 driver folder. It may well be in other locations or available online.

Microsoft has drivers for the most popular and recent devices and, as a part of Windows Update (discussed earlier in this chapter), has the ability to scan your system and see if it has any drivers to help

you. The first step is to look at Windows Update by opening Control Panel and selecting **System And Security** | **Windows Update**. Select **Check For Updates** in the upper-left area, and see if a driver for your device is found.

- The manufacturer of the device is generally a good source, but as hardware gets older, manufacturers stop writing new drivers for more recent operating systems. The easiest way to look for manufacturer support is on the Internet. If you know the manufacturer's website, you can enter it; or you may have to search for it. If you must search, start out by typing the manufacturer's name in the Internet Explorer address bar. This uses Bing and gives you a list of sites.

- Third-party sources can be found using search engines like Google (google.com) and searching for "device drivers." You should find a number of sources, as you can see in Figure 5-11. Some of these sources charge you for the driver; others are free. Make sure the driver will work with Windows 8.

USE REMOTE ASSISTANCE

Remote Assistance allows you to invite someone to remotely look at your computer and control it for the purposes of assisting you. The other person must be using Windows 8, Windows 7, Windows Vista, Windows XP, or Windows Server 2012, 2008, or 2003, and it will be helpful if both of you have an email account. To use Remote Assistance, you must set it up, and then you can be either the requester or the helper.

Note If you are using Windows 8 and want to use Remote Assistance with someone using Windows XP or Windows Server 2003, you must be on the receiving end of the assistance and you cannot use Windows 8's Pause feature. Also, the person using Windows XP/Server 2003 cannot use Start Talk for voice capability.

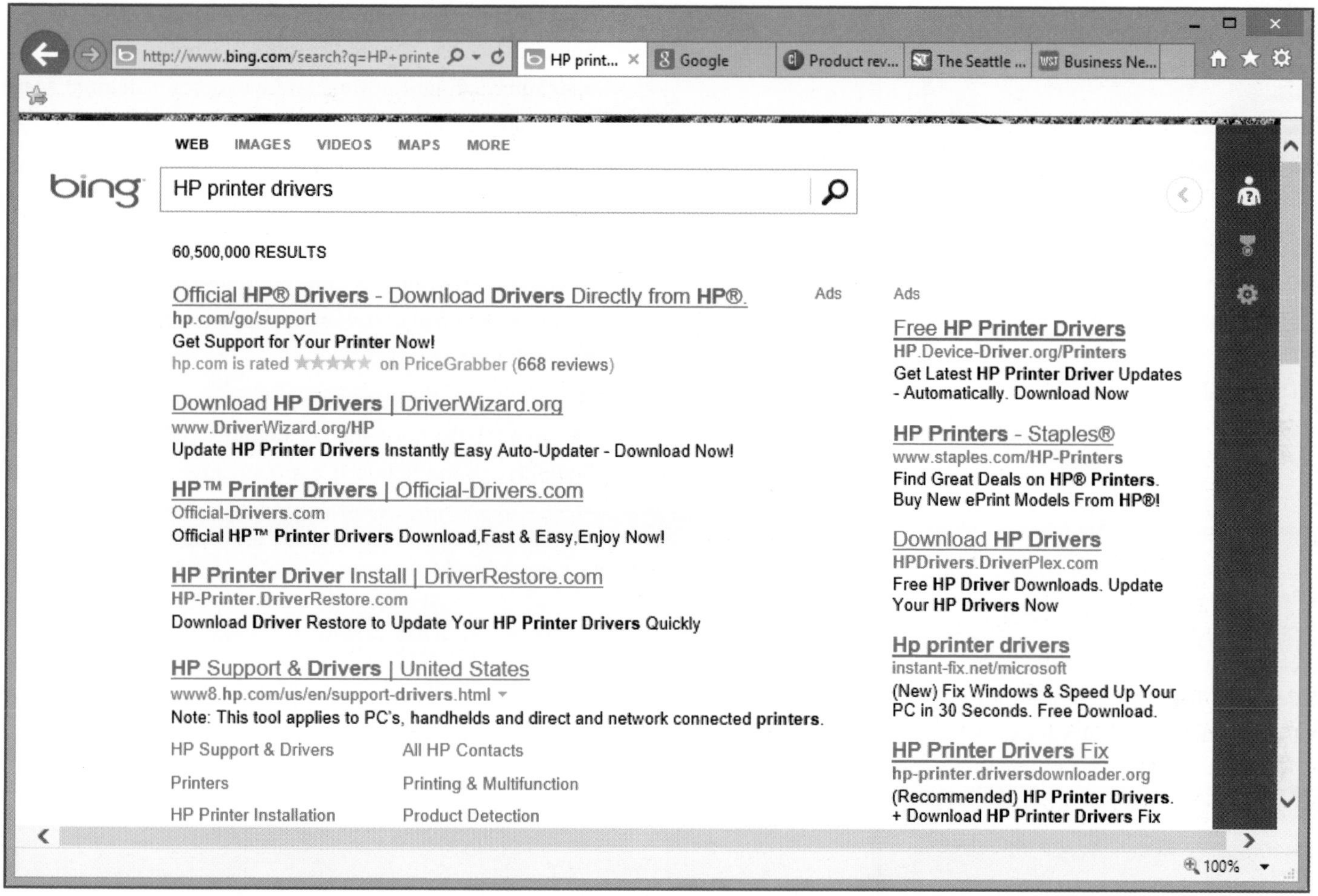

*Figure 5-11: **Many device drivers can be found by searching the Internet, although you may have to pay for them.***

Set Up Remote Assistance

Although Remote Assistance is installed with Windows 8, you must turn it on and set your firewall so that Windows 8 will allow it through. Both of these tasks are done in Control Panel.

1. Open Control Panel and select **System And Security | System | Remote Settings** in the left pane. The System Properties dialog box will appear with the Remote tab displayed (see Figure 5-12).

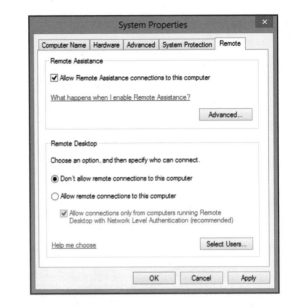

Figure 5-12: *Before using Remote Assistance, it must be turned on.*

2. Select **Allow Remote Assistance Connections To This Computer**, if it isn't already, and then select **Advanced**.

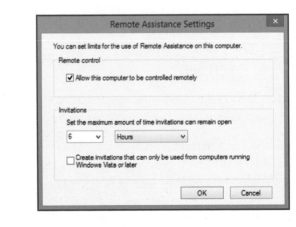

3. Determine if you want a person to control your computer, and select the check box under Remote Control accordingly. Set the maximum amount of time an invitation for Remote Assistance is to remain open.

4. Select **OK** twice to close the two open dialog boxes. In Control Panel's address bar select **System And Security | Windows Firewall**.

5. Select **Allow An App Or Feature Through Windows Firewall**. The Allow Programs To Communicate Through Windows Firewall window will open and show the apps and features that are allowed through the firewall.

6. Select **Change Settings** toward the top of the window, then scroll through the list until you see **Remote Assistance**, and select it for both Private and Public, if it isn't already selected (see Figure 5-13).

Figure 5-13: *Before you can use Remote Assistance, you must make sure that your firewall will let it through.*

7. Select **OK** to close the dialog box, close the Windows Firewall window, and then close Control Panel.

> **Note** Remote Desktop, which is discussed in Chapter 10, is different from Remote Assistance, even though, when enabled, it is on the same Remote tab of the System Properties dialog box. Remote Desktop lets you sit at home, log on, and use your computer at work as though you were sitting in front of it.

Request Remote Assistance

To use Remote Assistance, first find someone willing to provide it and request the assistance. Besides the obvious invitation text, the request-for-assistance message will include a password to access your computer and the code to allow the encryption of information to be sent back and forth. All this is provided for you with Windows Remote Assistance. To begin a Remote Assistance session:

1. Open the **System** menu and select **Control Panel | System And Security**. Under System, select **Launch Remote Assistance** to open the Windows Remote Assistance dialog box.

2. Select **Invite Someone You Trust To Help You**, and then select one of the following methods:

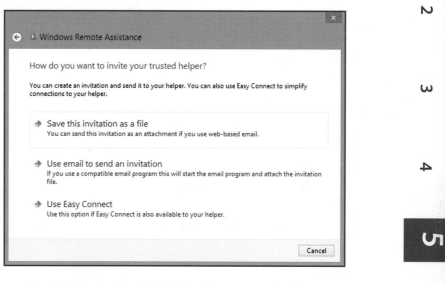

- **Save This Invitation As A File**   You can transfer the invitation as an attachment to an email message using any email app or web-based email such as Google's Gmail, or via a CD or USB flash drive.

- **Use Email To Send An Invitation**   Select this if you are using Windows Mail, Microsoft Office Outlook, or another compatible email package.

- **Use Easy Connect**   Select this if the other computer is using Windows 8.

3. If you select **Use Email To Send An Invitation**, your email app will open and display a message to your helper and contain the invitation as an attachment, as shown in Figure 5-14. Address the email and select **Send**. Skip to step 6.

4. If you select **Save This Invitation As A File**, select the drive and folder where you want to store the invitation—it may be across a network on your helper's computer. Select **Save**.

FILE **MESSAGE** INSERT OPTIONS FORMAT TEXT REVIEW

Paste | B I U | Address Check Book Names | Attach File, Attach Item, Signature | Follow Up, High Importance, Low Importance | Zoom

Clipboard | Basic Text | Names | Include | Tags | Zoom

To...

Cc...

Send

Subject: You have received a Remote Assistance invitation

Attached: Invitation.msrcincident (5 KB)

Hi,

I need help with my computer. Would you please use Windows Remote Assistance to connect to my computer so you can help me? After you connect, you can view my screen and we can chat online.

To accept this invitation, double-click the file attached to this message.

Thanks.

Note: Do not accept this invitation unless you know and trust the person who sent it.

*Figure 5-14: **You need to send an invitation that asks a person for assistance and gives him or her the means to communicate in an encrypted manner.***

5. Attach the saved file to an email message or store it on a CD or flash drive, and send or deliver it to your helper.

6. If you select **Easy Connect**, or in either of the other two cases, a Windows Remote Assistance window will open, providing you with the password you must also communicate to your helper, say, via phone. This window will wait for your helper to answer.

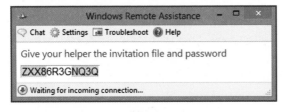

7. When your helper answers, you will be asked if you want to allow the person to see your computer. Select **Yes** if you do. Your computer screen will appear on your helper's computer.

Windows Remote Assistance

Would you like to allow Marty Matthews to connect to your computer?

After connecting, Marty Matthews will be able to see whatever is on your desktop.

Yes | No

What are the privacy and security concerns?

8. Select **Chat** and then select the text box at the bottom, and type a message to the other person, who can see everything on your computer (see "Provide Remote Assistance," next). Select **Send**.

9. If the other person requests control of your computer, you'll see a message asking if that is what you want to do. If you do, select the check box, and then select **Yes**. If you become uncomfortable, you can select **Stop Sharing** or press **ALT+T** at any time.

10. To end the session, send a message to that effect, and close the Remote Assistance window.

⯈⯈ Provide Remote Assistance

If you want to provide Remote Assistance:

1. Upon receiving an invitation as a file, drag it to the desktop, and open it.

2. If you are using Easy Connect, open the **System** menu and select **Control Panel | System And Security**. Under System, select **Launch Remote Assistance** to open the Windows Remote Assistance dialog box. Select **Help Someone Who Has Invited You**. It may take a couple of minutes to connect.

3. Enter the password you have been given, select **OK**, and, if the other person approves, you are shown his or her screen and can request control of the other person's computer. You can view the screen in its actual size or scale it to fit your screen, as shown in Figure 5-15.

Figure 5-15: *The remote screen is shown on the assistance provider's screen.*

4. To request control of the other computer, select **Request Control**. Select **Stop Sharing** to give up control.

5. Select **Close** to end the session and close the Remote Assistance window.

 Note You are protected from misuse of Remote Assistance in five ways: Without an invitation, the person giving assistance cannot access your computer; you can limit both the time the invitation remains open and the time the person can be on your computer; you can determine whether the person can control your computer or just look at it; you can select **Stop Sharing** or press **ALT+T** at any time to immediately terminate the other person's control; and you can select **Close** to instantly disconnect the other person.

 Note Many apps, such as backup and antivirus apps, use their own scheduler to run automatically on a scheduled basis.

1. Open Control Panel and select **System And Security | Administrative Tools** and open **Task Scheduler**. The Task Scheduler window will open, as you can see in Figure 5-16.

2. Select **Create Basic Task** in the Actions pane or in the Action menu. The Create Basic Task Wizard opens. Type a name and description, and select **Next**. Select what you want the frequency of the task to be and therefore its trigger, and again select **Next**.

START AND STOP APPS

Previous chapters discussed starting apps from the Start screen, through a shortcut on the desktop, and by locating the app with File Explorer. All of these methods require a direct action by you. Windows also provides several other ways to start apps and to monitor and manage them while they are running.

▷▷ Schedule Apps

You can schedule an app to run automatically using Windows 8's Task Scheduler, although you may need to specify how the app is to run using command-line parameters or arguments. See how to use Help in step 2 of "Start Older Apps" later in this chapter to learn what parameters are available for the app you want to run.

Figure 5-16: The Task Scheduler is used by Windows 8 for many of its tasks, but you can also use it to repeatedly perform a task you want.

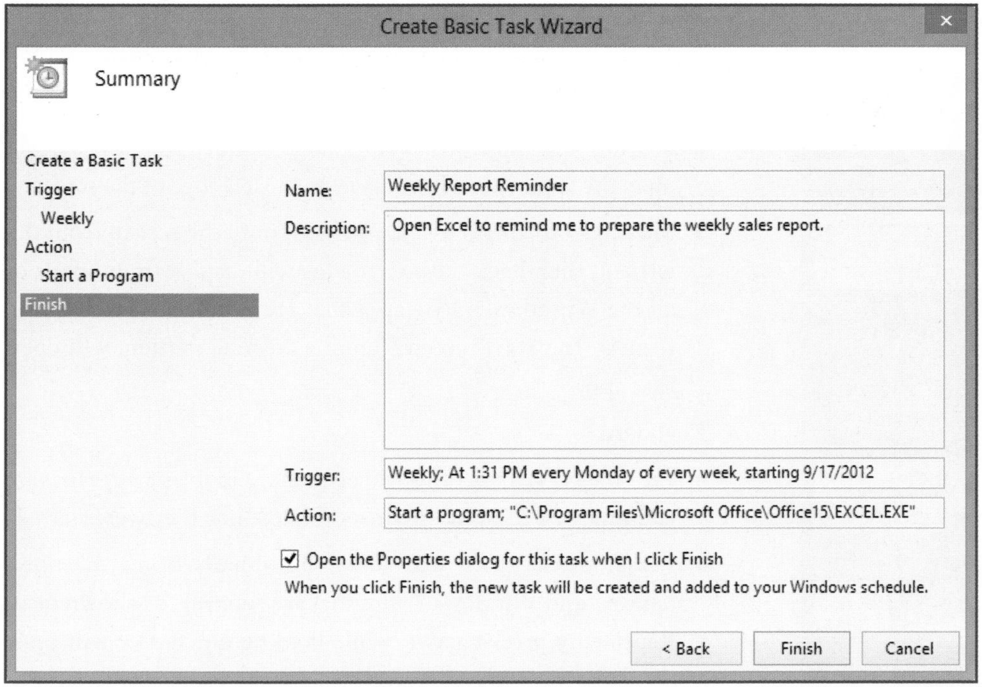

Create Basic Task Wizard ⊠

Summary

Create a Basic Task
Trigger
  Weekly
Action
  Start a Program
Finish

Name: | Weekly Report Reminder

Description: | Open Excel to remind me to prepare the weekly sales report.

Trigger: | Weekly; At 1:31 PM every Monday of every week, starting 9/17/2012

Action: | Start a program; "C:\Program Files\Microsoft Office\Office15\EXCEL.EXE"

☑ Open the Properties dialog for this task when I click Finish

When you click Finish, the new task will be created and added to your Windows schedule.

< Back | Finish | Cancel

*Figure 5-17: **The Task Scheduler should only be used to start an app.***

3. Depending on what you choose for the trigger, you may have to select the start date and time and enter additional information, such as the day of the week for a weekly trigger. Select **Next**.

4. Choose whether you want to start an app, send an email, or display a message (at the time of this writing, Microsoft has marked the Send An Email and Display A Message options as "deprecated," meaning they are obsolete and may be removed; therefore, only Start A Program should be used), and select **Next**.

5. If you want to start an app, select **Browse**, navigate to it and select it, then select **Open**, add any arguments that are to be passed to the app when it starts, and indicate if you would like the app to be looking at a particular folder when it starts (Start In).

6. Select **Next**. The Summary dialog box will appear, as shown in Figure 5-17. Select **Open The Properties Dialog For This Task When I Select Finish** and then select **Finish**. The Task Properties dialog box will appear.

7. Look at each of the tabs, review the information you have entered, and determine if you need to change anything.

8. When you are done reviewing the scheduled task, select **OK**. Select **Task Scheduler Library** in the left pane (called the console tree). You should see your scheduled task in the middle pane. Close the Task Scheduler window.

Tip Select a task in the center pane of the Task Scheduler to work with it. Select **Properties** in the right pane to edit the task's settings.

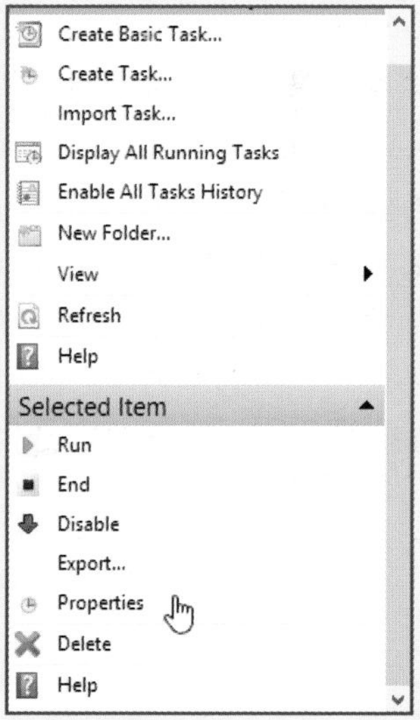

Create Basic Task...
Create Task...
Import Task...
Display All Running Tasks
Enable All Tasks History
New Folder...
View ▶
Refresh
Help

Selected Item ▲
▷ Run
■ End
⬇ Disable
Export...
Properties
✕ Delete
Help

⏩ Switch Apps

You can switch apps that are running in Windows 8 Style, on the desktop, on the taskbar, and on the task list. You can also switch them using the Task Manager (see "Control Apps with the Task Manager" later in this chapter). There are some significant differences between Windows 8 Style apps and desktop apps, but also some similarities.

Switch Windows 8 Style Apps

If you have several Windows 8 Style apps running, you can switch among them in several ways with the mouse, touch, and the keyboard:

- **Mouse**
  - Pointing at the top-left corner of the screen will display a thumbnail of the previous app that was displayed. Clicking that image will open the app. Continuing to click the top-left corner will open the other applications that are running, one at a time, in the order they were started.
  - Pointing at the top-left corner of the screen and then moving the mouse down the left edge will display thumbnails of all the Windows 8 Style apps that are running, as well as the icon for the Start screen. Clicking any one of the thumbnails will open that app. Right-clicking an app opens a context menu allowing you to close the app or to snap a narrow image of the app on the left or right edges of the screen.

- **Touch**
  - Swiping from the left edge of the screen opens one app at a time in the order they were originally opened.
  - Moving your finger just barely onto the screen from the left will open the app in a narrow image on the left edge of the screen.
  - Moving your finger a small amount onto the screen from the left and then back to the left edge will display thumbnails of all the Windows 8 Style apps that are running, as well as the icon for the Start screen. Tapping any one of them will open that app.

- **Keyboard**
  - Pressing **WINDOWS+TAB** will open the Windows 8 apps that are running, one at a time, in the order in which they were started.
  - Pressing **ALT+TAB** will show thumbnails of all the open desktop and Windows 8 apps that are running, as shown next. Repeatedly pressing **TAB** while holding down **ALT** will cycle through the apps. Wherever you are when **ALT** is released will open that app.

Tip Snapping the desktop app to the edge of the screen will display thumbnails of the *desktop* apps that are running.

Switch Apps on the Desktop

If you have several apps running on the desktop, arrange them so that you can see all of them.

Switch from one to another by selecting the app you want to be active.

However, if you have more than two or three apps running, it may be hard to see them on the desktop and, therefore, to select the one you want.

Switch Apps on the Taskbar

If you have up to five or six apps running on the desktop, you should be able to see their tasks on the taskbar.

Select the task to switch to that app.

If you have multiple instances of a single app open, they will, by default, be grouped in a single icon. For example, a taskbar icon for an app can show that there are multiple instances open, like this:

To select a particular instance of an app when there are multiple instances running, mouse over the icon on the taskbar to open thumbnails of the several instances, and then mouse over the one you want to see enlarged. Finally, when you are ready to fully open one particular instance, select the thumbnail for that instance, as you can see in Figure 5-18.

Switch Apps on the Task List

The oldest method of switching apps, which predates Windows 95 and the taskbar, is using the task list, which will include both Windows 8 and desktop apps, as mentioned earlier.

1. Press **ALT+TAB** and hold down **ALT**. The task list will appear.

2. While continuing to hold down **ALT**, press **TAB** repeatedly until the highlight moves to the app and instance you want or the desktop on the right. Then release **ALT** or select an icon to select the app you want.

 Tip If you don't want tasks grouped on the taskbar, open the context menu for an empty area of the taskbar, select **Properties** and then select the **Taskbar Buttons** down arrow, and select **Never Combine**. Select **OK** to close the Properties dialog box. This not only doesn't combine tasks, it also adds a title to each task or icon—taking up a lot of room. This method is not recommended.

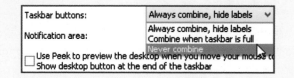

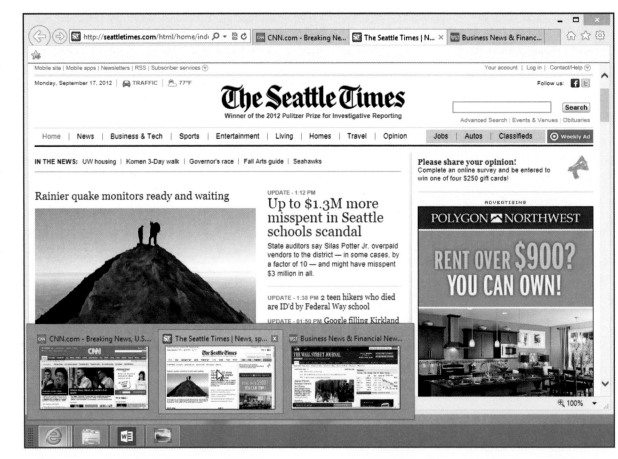

Figure 5-18: **You can select one of several instances of a running app by mousing over the taskbar icon and the thumbnails and then selecting the thumbnail you want.**

▷▷ Stop Apps

You may choose to stop an app simply because you are done using it or in an attempt to keep an app from harming your data or other apps.

Close Windows 8 Apps

Windows 8 Style apps do not have the obvious ways to close that are explained in the next several sections and can actually be left in the background while you are working on other apps without taking up very many, if any, computer resources. If you wish, though, there are several ways to close a Windows 8 app:

- With either a finger or the mouse, drag the top of the screen to the bottom of the screen.

- With the mouse, right-click a thumbnail on the left and click **Close**.

Use the Close Button with Desktop Apps

One of the most common ways to close an app is to select the **Close** button on the upper-right corner of all desktop windows.

Use the Exit or Close Command with Desktop Apps

Many desktop apps have an Exit command in a menu on the left of the menu bar; often, this is the File menu (in Microsoft Office 2010 or 2013, the File tab is the "menu" and the exit [or Close in 2013] command is located in the lower-right corner). Open this menu and select **Exit** or **Close**.

Close Desktop Apps from the Taskbar

There are two ways to close a desktop app from the taskbar.

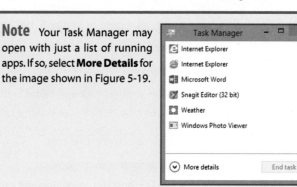

Mouse over the icon, move the mouse to the upper-right corner of the thumbnail, and select the red **X** that will appear.

–Or–

Open the context menu for a task on the taskbar, and select **Close Window** or **Close All Windows** if multiple windows are open.

Close Windows 8 and Desktop Apps from the Keyboard

With any app you want to close open and selected, press **ALT+F4**.

If none of these options work, see "Control Apps with the Task Manager."

Note It could be that none of the stop options mentioned previously will work if the app is performing a task or has some fault. In that case, if you want to force the app to stop, shut down Windows itself, and when told that there are apps running, select **Shut Down Anyway**.

▷▷ Control Apps with the Task Manager

The Windows Task Manager, shown in Figure 5-19, performs a number of functions, but most importantly, it allows you to see what apps and processes (individual threads of an app) are running and to unequivocally stop both. A display of real-time graphs and tables also shows you what is happening at any second on your computer, as you can see in Figure 5-20. To work with the Task Manager:

1. Open the Task Manager in one of these ways:

   ■ From the Start screen, open the command bar and select **All Apps | Task Manager** in the Windows System group on the far right.

   ■ Press **CTRL+ALT+DELETE** and select **Task Manager**.

   ■ Open the context menu for a blank area of the taskbar, and select **Task Manager**.

   ■ Open the **System** menu and select Task Manager.

Note Your Task Manager may open with just a list of running apps. If so, select **More Details** for the image shown in Figure 5-19.

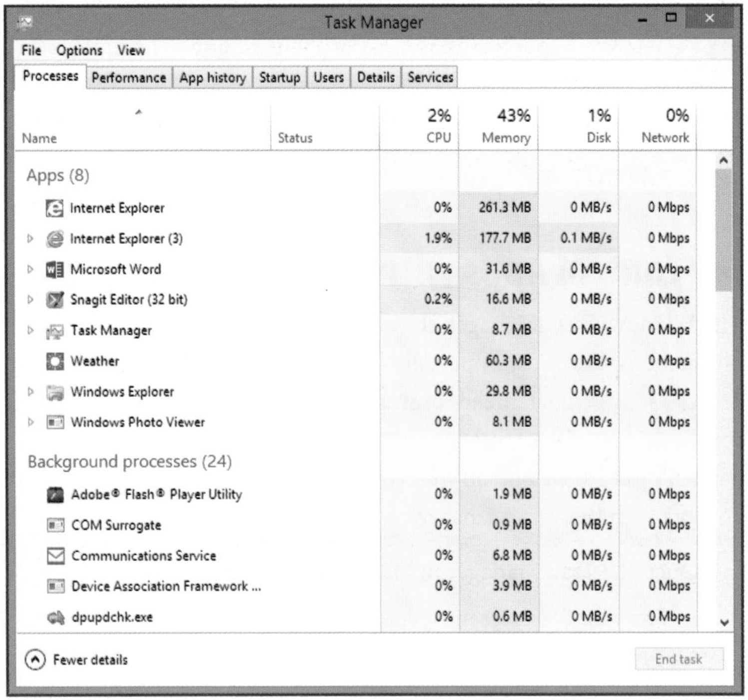

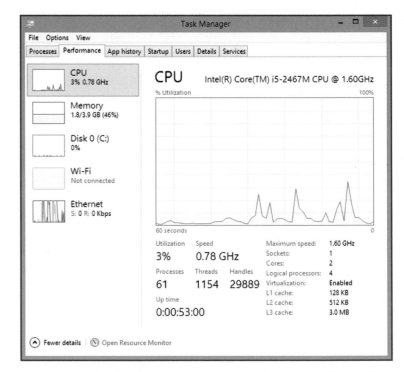

Figure 5-19: *The Task Manager shows you what apps are running and allows you to stop them.*

Figure 5-20: *Under most circumstances, on a personal computer, only a small fraction of the computer's resources are being used.*

2. Select the **Processes** tab if it isn't already displayed. You'll see a list of the apps as well as all the processes (mainly elements of Windows 8) that are running, as shown in Figure 5-19.

3. Select an app in the list, then:

   ■ Select **End Task** to stop the app.

   ■ Open the context menu for another task and select **Switch To**.

   –Or–

   Double-select another task to activate that app.

4. Select each of the other tabs to review their contents:

   ■ The **Performance** tab graphically shows the central processing unit (CPU), memory, disk, and network usage (see Figure 5-20).

   ■ The **App History** tab shows each app's resource consumption since a given date.

   ■ The **Startup** tab shows the apps that are being automatically started. To stop an app from automatically starting, select it and then select **Disable**.

   ■ The **Users** tab shows the users that are logged on to the computer. You can disconnect them by selecting them and then selecting **Disconnect**.

   ■ The **Details** tab lists all of the detail apps that are available and their status. Several of these may join to perform a process. You can end a running task by selecting the app and then selecting **End Task**.

- The **Services** tab is a list of the Windows 8 and other app services that are active and their status. There is nothing that you can do here except observe.

5. When you are done, close the Windows Task Manager.

 CAUTION! It is generally not a good idea to end a detail app or a background process. Instead, stop the app that is using the process (that is, those apps in the Processes tab that show their unique icon next to their executable filename).

Start an App in Run

Run is a dialog box from which you can start most apps if you know the path to the app and its name and don't mind typing all that information. Its primary purpose is to start certain diagnostic tools that don't require a path, like Msconfig, which opens the System Configuration dialog box to change Windows start-up parameters. To open and use Run:

![Run dialog box showing "Type the name of a program, folder, document, or Internet resource, and Windows will open it for you." with msconfig typed in the Open field, and OK, Cancel, Browse buttons]

1. Open the **System** menu and select **Run**.

   –Or–

   From the Start screen, type <u>run</u> and press **ENTER**.

   –Or–

   From the Start screen, open the command bar and select **All Apps |
   Run** in the Windows System group on the far right.

2. In the Run dialog box that appears, type the path (if needed) and filename of the app you want to run, and press **ENTER**.

Tip In many instances, the Run dialog box is no longer necessary. Simply type the app's name on the Start screen, such as Msconfig that was mentioned earlier.

CAUTION! Unless you are trying to diagnose a problem and have some experience doing this, you normally do not want to change the settings in the System Configuration dialog box. However, you can safely stop obvious known Windows-related apps without harm.

Start Older Apps

While you can start most apps from the desktop or Start menu, older, less sophisticated apps require that they be run in their own isolated window named Command Prompt (also called a DOS, or Disk Operating System, window). Here, you can type DOS commands at the flashing underscore, which is called the *command prompt.* To open and use the command prompt:

1. Open the **System** menu and select **Command Prompt**.

   –Or–

   From the Start screen, type <u>command prompt</u> and press **ENTER**.

   –Or–

   From the Start screen, open the command bar and select **All Apps |
   Command Prompt** in the Windows System group on the far right.

   The Command Prompt window will open.

2. Type <u>help</u> and press **ENTER**. A list of commands that can be used at the command prompt will be displayed, as shown in Figure 5-21 (the colors of the background and text have been switched for printing purposes; see the accompanying Note).

```
CMD                    Command Prompt                    - □ ×

Microsoft Windows [Version 6.2.9200]
(c) 2012 Microsoft Corporation. All rights reserved.

C:\Users\Marty>help
For more information on a specific command, type HELP command-name
ASSOC          Displays or modifies file extension associations.
ATTRIB         Displays or changes file attributes.
BREAK          Sets or clears extended CTRL+C checking.
BCDEDIT        Sets properties in boot database to control boot loading.
CACLS          Displays or modifies access control lists (ACLs) of files.
CALL           Calls one batch program from another.
CD             Displays the name of or changes the current directory.
CHCP           Displays or sets the active code page number.
CHDIR          Displays the name of or changes the current directory.
CHKDSK         Checks a disk and displays a status report.
CHKNTFS        Displays or modifies the checking of disk at boot time.
CLS            Clears the screen.
CMD            Starts a new instance of the Windows command interpreter.
COLOR          Sets the default console foreground and background colors.
COMP           Compares the contents of two files or sets of files.
COMPACT        Displays or alters the compression of files on NTFS partitions.
CONVERT        Converts FAT volumes to NTFS. You cannot convert the
               current drive.
COPY           Copies one or more files to another location.
DATE           Displays or sets the date.
DEL            Deletes one or more files.
DIR            Displays a list of files and subdirectories in a directory.
DISKCOMP       Compares the contents of two floppy disks.
DISKCOPY       Copies the contents of one floppy disk to another.
DISKPART       Displays or configures Disk Partition properties.
DOSKEY         Edits command lines, recalls Windows commands, and
               creates macros.
DRIVERQUERY    Displays current device driver status and properties.
ECHO           Displays messages, or turns command echoing on or off.
ENDLOCAL       Ends localization of environment changes in a batch file.
ERASE          Deletes one or more files.
EXIT           Quits the CMD.EXE program (command interpreter).
FC             Compares two files or sets of files, and displays the
               differences between them.
FIND           Searches for a text string in a file or files.
FINDSTR        Searches for strings in files.
FOR            Runs a specified command for each file in a set of files.
FORMAT         Formats a disk for use with Windows.
FSUTIL         Displays or configures the file system properties.
FTYPE          Displays or modifies file types used in file extension
               associations.
GOTO           Directs the Windows command interpreter to a labeled line in
               a batch program.
GPRESULT       Displays Group Policy information for machine or user.
GRAFTABL       Enables Windows to display an extended character set in
               graphics mode.
```

Figure 5-21: **At the command prompt, you can type DOS commands, which Windows 8 will carry out.**

3. To run an app in the Games folder on the C: drive (if you have one—it is not there by default), type <u>cd c:\games</u> (change directory to c:\games), press **ENTER**, type <u>dir /p</u> (display the contents of the directory), press **ENTER** to see the name of the app, type the name of the app executable, and press **ENTER**. The app should run, although not all apps will run in Windows 8.

4. When you are done with the Command Prompt window, type <u>exit</u> and press **ENTER**.

Run Accessory Apps

Windows 8 comes with a number of accessory apps. You can open these from the Start screen by opening the command bar and selecting **All Apps** or simply by typing their name from the Start screen and pressing **ENTER**. Under Windows Accessories you'll see the list of accessory apps, shown in Figure 5-22, each of which can be selected. Many of these

Figure 5-22: **The accessory apps provide a number of useful tools.**

apps are discussed elsewhere in this book, but Calculator, Character Map, Notepad, and Paint will be briefly looked at here. You should also explore these on your own.

 Tip If you use any of the accessory apps a lot, you can put them on the Start screen by opening the command bar for the app and selecting **Pin To Start**.

Calculator

The Calculator has four alternative calculators, each with its own view:

- Standard desktop calculator
- Scientific calculator, shown in Figure 5-23
- Programmer calculator
- Statistics calculator

A unit converter; a date calculator; and four worksheets for calculating a mortgage, a vehicle lease, and fuel economy in both mpg and L/100 km

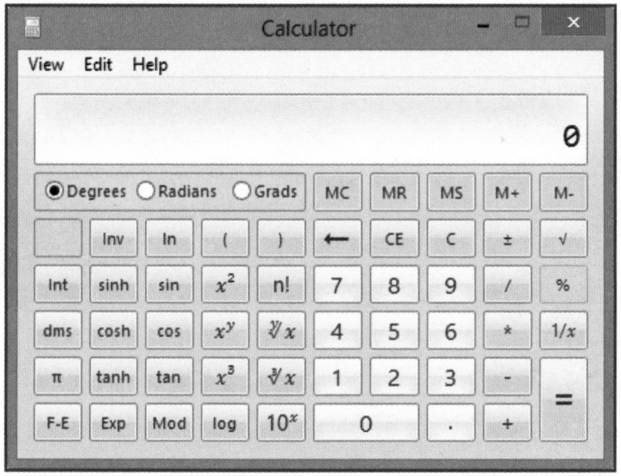

![Scientific view of the Calculator window]

Figure 5-23: The Scientific view of the Calculator provides a number of advanced functions, including several extensions such as the unit converter.

are included that are extensions to the current view. To switch from one view to the other, select **View** and then the other view. To use a calculator, select the numbers on the screen or type them on the keyboard.

Character Map

The Character Map allows you to select special characters that are not available on a standard keyboard.

1. Select the **Font** down arrow and then select the font you want for the special character.

2. Scroll until you find it, and then open the character; or select the character and select **Select** to copy it to the Clipboard.

3. In the app where you want the character, open the context menu for an open area (for example, in Notepad, discussed next), and select **Paste** or press CTRL+V.

Notepad

Notepad is a simple text editor you can use to view and create unformatted text (.txt) files. If you open a text file from File Explorer, Notepad will likely open and display the file. If a line of text is too long to display without scrolling, select **Format | Word Wrap**. To create a file, simply start typing in the Notepad window. When you are done, select **File | Save**. Before printing a file, select **File | Page Setup**; and select the paper orientation, margins, header, and footer (the default header is the filename and the default footer is the page number). When you are ready, select **File | Print**, select the printer to use and other settings, and select **Print**.

Paint

Paint lets you view, create, and edit bitmap image files in .bmp, .dib, .gif, ico, .jpg, .png, and .tif formats. Several drawing tools and many colors are available to create simple drawings and illustrations (see Figure 5-24).

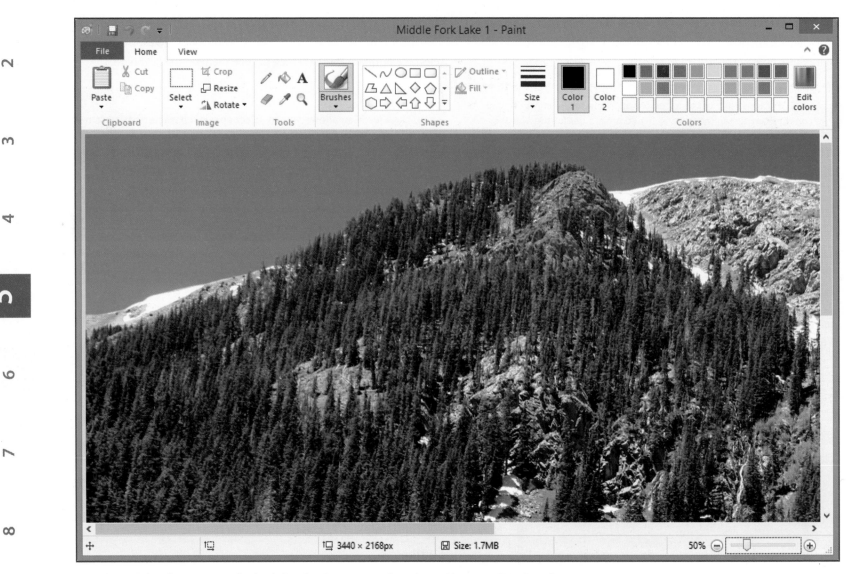

Figure 5-24: *Paint allows you to make simple line drawings or to touch up photos. (Courtesy of Tom Beard)*

Chapter 6

Working with Documents and Pictures

In this chapter you will discover many aspects of creating documents and pictures, installing and using digital cameras and scanners, and installing and using printers and their fonts with documents and pictures.

CREATE DOCUMENTS AND PICTURES

Creating documents and pictures is primarily done with apps outside of Windows 8, although Windows also has simple apps to do this. Windows 8 also has facilities to bring documents and pictures in from other computers, from the Internet, and from scanners and cameras.

▶▶ Acquire a Document

The documents in your computer got there because they were created with an app on your computer, or they were brought to the computer on a disk, transferred over a local area network (LAN), or downloaded from the Internet.

Create a Document with an App

To create a document with an app:

1. Start the app. For example, start Microsoft Word from the Start screen by selecting the **Word** tile if it is there or by opening the command bar and selecting **All Apps | Word 2013** (or **Microsoft Word 2010**).

Start screen tile    **All Apps listing**

2. Create the document using the facilities in the app. In Word, for example, type the document and format it using Word's formatting tools.

3. In Word, save the document by selecting the **File** tab. Then select **Save As | Computer**, if needed; select **Browse**; and select the disk drive and folder in which to store the document. Enter a filename and select **Save**, as shown in Figure 6-1.

4. Close the app used to create the file.

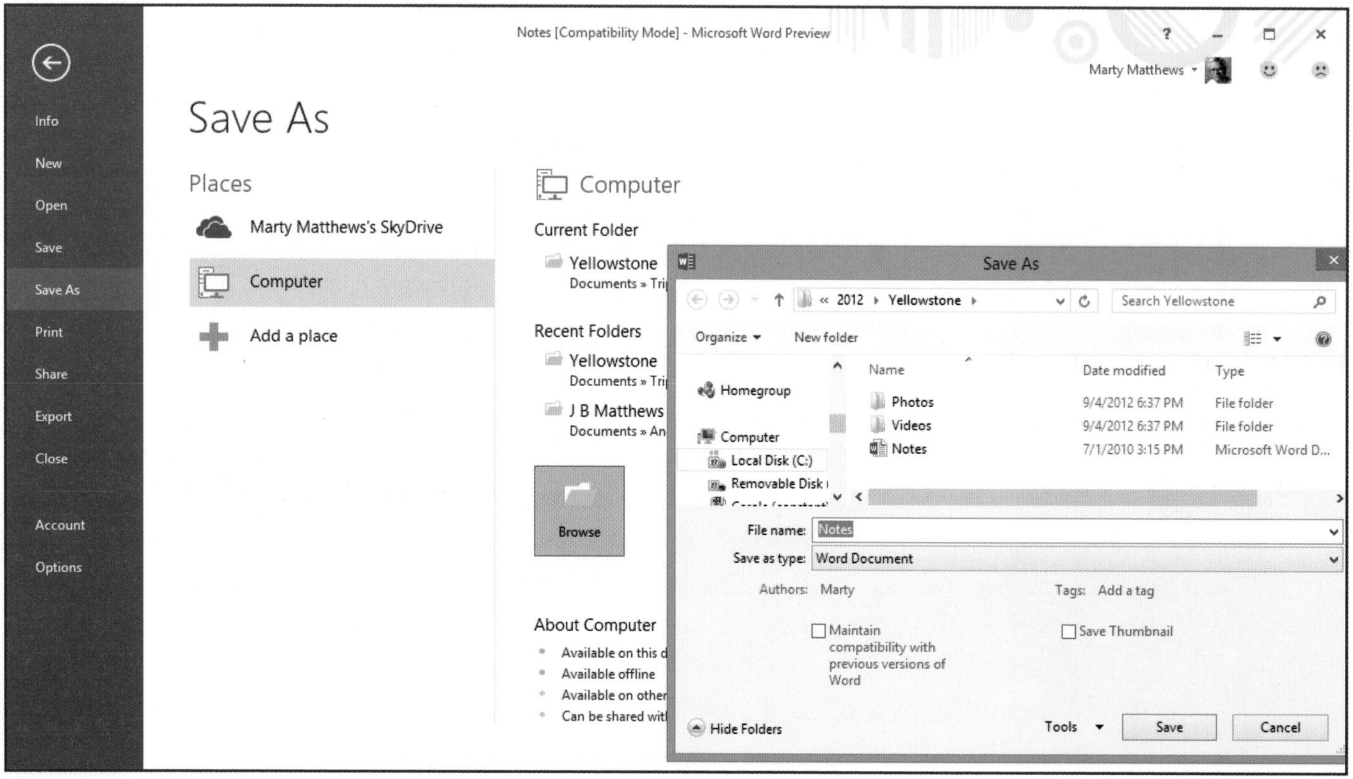

Figure 6-1: **Most document-creation apps let you choose where you want to save the files you create.**

Bring in a Document from a Disk

Use File Explorer to bring in a document from a disk or other removable storage device.

1. Open the **System** menu and select **File Explorer** to open it displaying the Computer window.

2. Open the folder or drive from which you want to retrieve a document (this could be a hard drive, floppy disk, CD, DVD, flash drive, or other device), and open any necessary folders to locate the document

file and display it in the subject (middle) pane (assuming your File Explorer window displays a three-pane view: navigation, subject, and preview).

3. In the navigation pane, display (but do not select or open) the drive and folder(s) in which you want to store the file by selecting their respective triangles on the left.

4. Drag the document file to the displayed folder, as illustrated in Figure 6-2. When you are done, close File Explorer.

*Figure 6-2: **You can drag a document file from either a disk on your computer or from another computer on your network.***

Download a Document Across a Network

Use File Explorer to bring in a document from another computer on your network (the folder on the other computer will need to be shared; see Chapter 8 for more information on sharing files and folders).

1. Open the **System** menu and select **File Explorer | Network** in the left column.

2. Open the other computer from which you want the document, and open any necessary drives, folders, and subfolders to locate the document file.

3. In the navigation pane, display (but do not select or open) the drive and folder(s) in which you want to store the file by selecting their respective triangles on the left.

4. Drag the document file to the displayed folder. When you are done, close File Explorer.

Download a Document from the Internet

Use Internet Explorer to bring in a document from a site on the Internet.

1. Select the **Internet Explorer** icon on the desktop's taskbar.

2. Type an address, search, or browse to a site and page from which you can download the document file.

3. Use the links and tools on the website to select and begin the file download. For example, open the context menu for a picture and select **Save Picture As**. Some sites have download links for transferring the image or document to your computer.

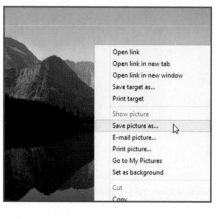

4. In the Save Picture dialog box, select the disk and open the folder(s) in which you want to store the file on your computer.

5. Type or edit the filename, and press **ENTER** to complete the download. When you are done, close your browser.

Create a Picture

Pictures are really just documents that contain an image. They can be created or brought into your computer in the same way as any other document (see "Acquire a Document" earlier in this chapter). For example, to create and save a picture in Windows Paint:

1. From the Start screen, open the command bar and select **All Apps | Paint** under Windows Accessories.

2. Create a picture using the tools in Paint. For example, select the **Pencil** tool, choose a color, and create the drawing.

3. Save the document by selecting **File | Save As** and then select the disk drive and folder in which to store the document, enter a filename, select a Save As type, and select **Save**. Close Paint.

Install Cameras and Scanners

Installing cameras and scanners depends a lot on the device—whether it is Plug and Play (you plug it in and it starts to function), what type of connection it has, and so on. Most recent cameras and scanners are Plug and Play devices. To use them:

1. Plug the device into the computer, and turn it on. If it is Plug and Play, the first time you plug it in, you will see an icon [icon] indicating that that a device driver is being installed and then a message asking if you want to choose what happens with the device.

> **Canon PowerShot SD1300 IS**
> Tap to choose what happens with this device.

2. Select the message to choose what happens. This opens a device-specific dialog box and allows you to choose what you want to do. If you plugged in a scanner, skip to the next section, "Scan Documents." If you plugged in a camera, skip to "Import Camera Images" later in this chapter. Otherwise, continue to step 3.

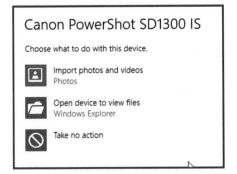

3. Open the **System** menu and select **Control Panel | Hardware And Sound | Devices And Printers**. If you see your device, installation is complete, and you can skip the remainder of these steps.

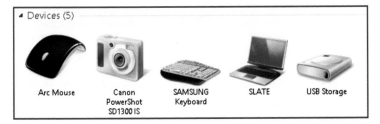

4. Select **Add A Device**. The Add A Device Wizard starts. Select the device you want to install and then select **Next**. Scroll through the manufacturer and model lists, and see if your device is there. If so, select it and select **Next**. Confirm the name you want to use, select **Next**, and then select **Finish** to complete the installation.

5. If you don't see your device on the lists and you have a disk that came with it, select **Cancel** and close the Devices And Printers window, place the disk in the drive, and use the manufacturer's installation app on the disk.

Scan Documents

Scanners allow you to take printed images and convert them to digital images on your computer. The scanner must first be installed, as described in "Install Cameras and Scanners" in the previous section. If you ended up using the manufacturer's software to install the scanner, you might need to use it to scan images, too. If you used Windows to install the scanner, use the following steps to scan an image.

Tip The scanning software in Windows may or may not be superior to the software that comes with your scanner.

1. Turn on your scanner, and place what you want to scan onto the scanning surface.

2. From the Start screen, open the command bar and select **All Apps | Windows Fax And Scan** under Windows Accessories. The Windows Fax And Scan window opens.

3. Select **New Scan** on the toolbar. The New Scan dialog box appears. The scanner you installed should be displayed in the upper-left area. Change the scanner if you wish.

4. Choose the color, file type, and resolution you want to use; and select **Preview**. The image in the scanner will appear in the dialog box.

5. Adjust the margins around the page by dragging the dashed lines on the four sides, as shown in Figure 6-3. When you are ready, select **Scan**.

6. The scanned image will appear in the Windows Fax And Scan window (see Figure 6-4). Select the image in the list at the top of the window, and, using the toolbar, choose to:

- **Forward As Fax** using the Windows fax capability described later in this chapter

- **Forward As E-mail** using your default email app

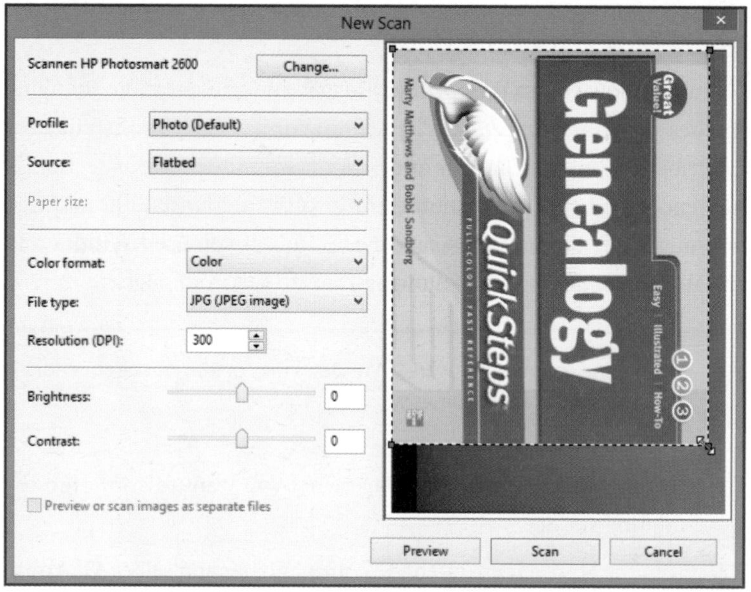

Figure 6-3: *In the Windows 8 scanning software, you can change several of the parameters, including the margins of what to include, and see the results in the preview pane.*

- **Save As** using File Explorer to save the image as a file on one of the storage devices available to you
- **Print** using a printer available to you
- **Delete** the image

7. Work through the related dialog box(es) that appear to complete the scanning process. When you are ready, close the Windows Fax And Scan window.

Tip Documents that you scan into your computer are automatically saved in Libraries\My Documents\Scanned Documents.

Import Camera Images

When most digital cameras or their memory cards are plugged into the computer (see "Install Cameras and Scanners" earlier in this chapter), the device-specific dialog box (shown earlier) appears and asks if you want to:

- **Import Photos And Videos**, in essence, copying them to your hard disk
- **Open Device To View Files** in your camera using File Explorer
- **Take No Action** to ignore the camera or memory card that was plugged in

Note If the Devices dialog box didn't appear, open the **System** menu and select **File Explorer** to display the Computer window. In the navigation column on the left look for the device or an extra removable disk (if you have more than one of them, it would be the most recently accessed one), and open the necessary folders to see images of the pictures in your camera.

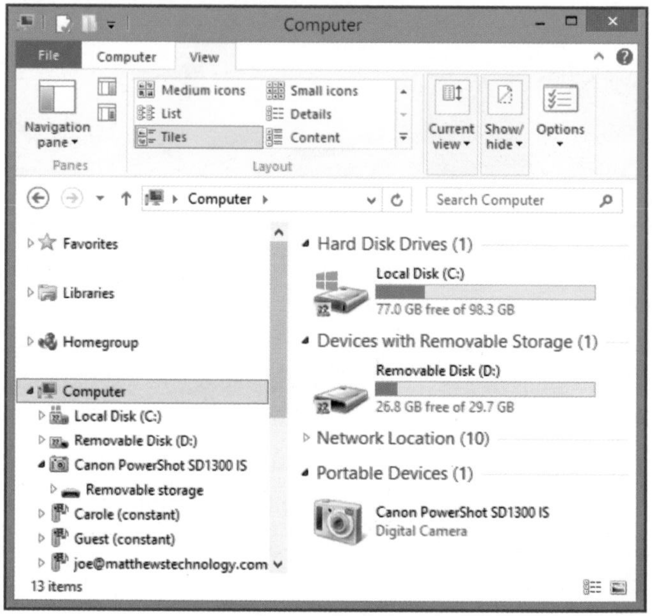

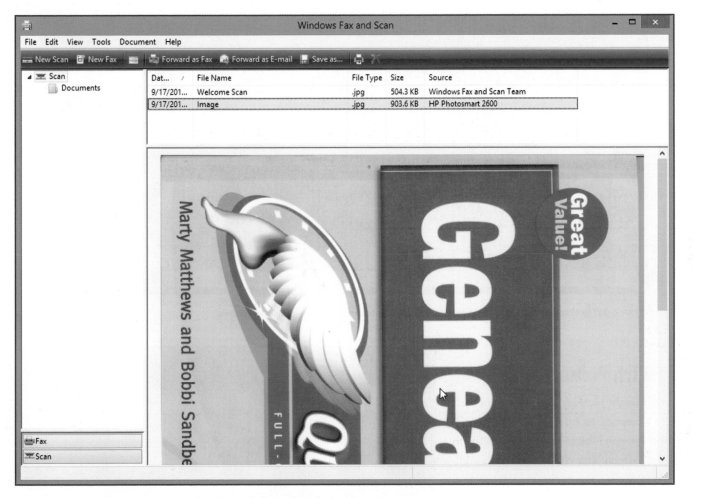

Figure 6-4: *Images that you scan can be faxed, emailed, saved, and printed.*

1. Select **Import Photos And Videos**. The Photos screen should appear displaying the pictures on the camera. By default, all are checked to be imported, as you can see in Figure 6-5.

2. Select to uncheck any pictures you do *not* want to import, make any desired changes to the folder name in the text box at the bottom of the screen, and then select **Import**.

3. You will see a thermometer bar showing you the progress of the importing. You will be told when the process is completed. Select **Open Album**; the Photos app will open and display the pictures that were imported.

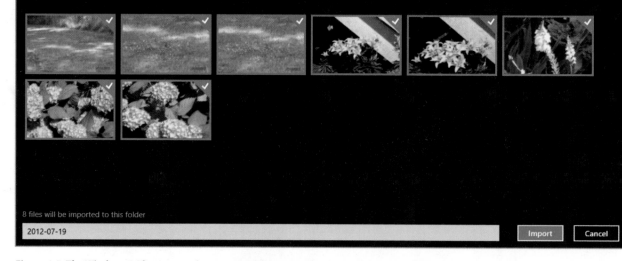

Figure 6-5: *The Windows 8 Photos app gives you a quick way to organize and view your pictures.*

▷▷ Work with Pictures

Once you have brought pictures into your computer
from a camera, a scanner, an Internet download, or a
removable disk, you can look at and work with them
on your computer screen. The Windows 8 Photos app,
as discussed in "Import Camera Images," provides a
quick way to view your pictures.

1. From the Start screen, select **Photos**. The Photos
app will open.

2. Open one or more folders until you are displaying
the pictures you want to view.

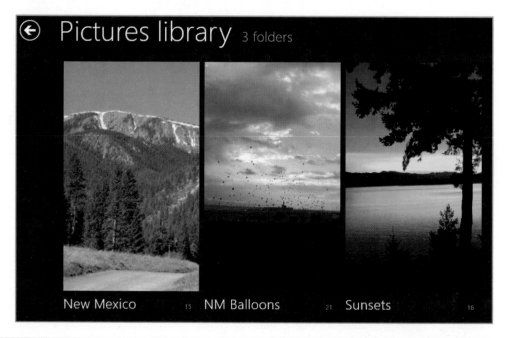

3. To see a larger image, select the picture, then, with touch, repeatedly spread two fingers; or with the mouse, repeatedly click the plus sign in the bottom-right corner of the screen.

4. If you have several pictures you want to view, select the right and left arrows in the middle of the left and right edges of the screen to go through them sequentially.

⏩ View Other Pictures

The Photos app will display photos that are in your Pictures library, your SkyDrive Photos folder, possibly in your Facebook page, and in devices (such as a camera) attached to your computer. If your pictures are not in Photos, you can locate and view them.

1. From the desktop, select **File Explorer**, and open the drive and folders necessary to locate your pictures.

2. Select the **View** tab and select **Extra Large Icons** so that you can adequately see the thumbnail images, as shown in Figure 6-6.

Tip If the preview pane is open, close it to see more extra-large icons, as shown in Figure 6-6.

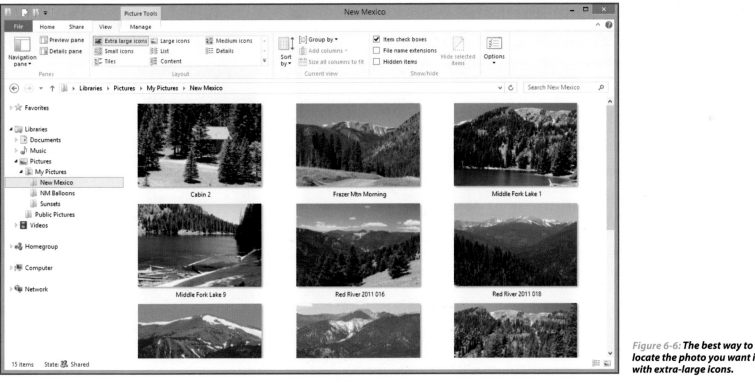

Figure 6-6: **The best way to locate the photo you want is with extra-large icons.**

3. Open the picture you want to view in a larger size. The Windows Photo Viewer will open and display the picture. Select **File**, **Print**, **E-mail**, or **Burn** to perform any of those functions. You can also select **Open** to open the picture in Photos or another program you may have on your computer.

▷▷ Capture Snips

Windows 8 includes the Snipping Tool to capture images of the screen, called "screen shots" or "snips." This can capture four areas of the screen:

- **Full screen** captures the entire screen.
- **Window** captures a complete window.
- **Rectangular area** captures a rectangle you draw around objects.
- **Free-form area** captures any area you draw around objects.

Once you have captured an area, it is temporarily stored on the Clipboard and displayed in the mark-up window where you can write and draw on the snip to annotate it and, when you are ready, save the snip where you want it. To do all of that:

1. Display the windows or other objects on the screen whose images you want to capture (see the Note on capturing a menu).

2. From the Start screen, open the command bar and select **All Apps | Snipping Tool** under Windows Accessories. The Snipping Tool dialog box will appear.

3. If you want to capture a rectangular area, select **New** and drag the cross-hair from one corner of the rectangle to the opposite corner, as shown in Figure 6-7.

4. To capture a different type of area, select the **New** down arrow and select one of the other three types of areas. Then, with:

- **Free-Form Snip**, drag the cross-hair around the area to be captured
- **Window Snip**, select the window to be captured
- **Full-Screen Snip**, the screen is automatically captured

5. In all cases, the mark-up window opens, showing you the area that was captured and allowing you to use the pen, highlighter, and eraser to annotate the snip.

6. From the mark-up window, you can also directly email the snip to someone by selecting **Send Snip**, which opens an email message with the snip in it (to send the snip as an email attachment, open the **Send Snip** down arrow); save the snip by selecting **Save Snip**, select a folder, enter a name, select a file type, and select **Save**.

Tip To capture a snip of a menu, open the Snipping Tool, press **ESC**, display the menu to be captured, press **CTRL+PRINT SCREEN**, select the **New** down arrow, select the type of area to be captured (Free-Form, Rectangle, and so forth), and delineate that area as you would otherwise.

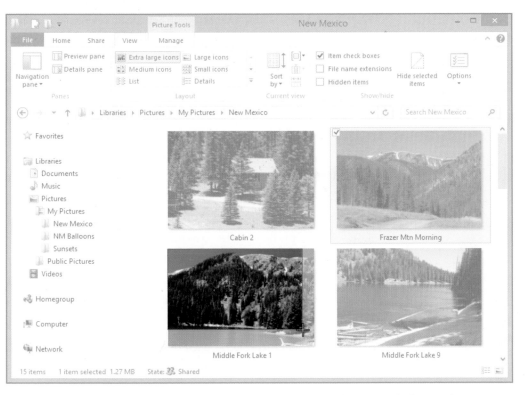

2. If you already have one or more notes on the desktop, the most recent one will be selected. If you want a new note, select **New Note** (the plus sign in the upper-left corner).

3. On the new note, type the message you want it to contain; or, having copied some text from another source, open the context menu for the note and select **Paste**. (You can resize a Note like a window.)

4. Open the context menu for the note (right-select in the note outside the title bar), select the color you want it to be, and then drag the note to where you want it.

5. When you no longer want the note on the desktop, select **Delete Note** (the X in the upper-right corner) and select **Yes**.

*Figure 6-7: **The Snipping Tool allows you to capture an image of an area of the screen for future reference or use.***

Use Sticky Notes

Sticky Notes are exactly what the name implies: little notes to yourself that you can place anywhere on your screen. You can type messages on these notes; change their color; cut, copy, and paste the text on them with the Clipboard to and from other apps; create additional notes; and delete the note.

1. From the Start screen, open the command bar and select **All Apps** | **Sticky Notes** under Windows Accessories. If you don't already have a note on your desktop, one will appear.

PRINT DOCUMENTS AND PICTURES

It is important to be able to install and fully use printers so that you can transfer your digital documents to paper.

Install a Printer

All printers are either automatically installed or done so using the Devices And Printers window. Because there are differences in how the installation is done, look at the sections in this chapter on installing local Plug and Play printers, installing other local printers, installing network printers, and selecting a default printer. Also, if you are installing a local printer, first consider the following checklist.

Printer Installation Checklist

A local printer is one that is attached to your computer with a cable or wireless connection. Make sure that your printer meets the following conditions *before* you begin the installation:

- It is plugged into the correct port on your computer (see manufacturer's instructions).
- It is plugged into an electrical outlet.
- It has fresh ink, toner, or ribbon, which, along with the print heads, is properly installed.
- It has adequate paper.
- It is turned on.

Note Some laptop computer-and-printer combinations are connected through an infrared beam or other wireless connection. In this case, "plugging the printer into the computer" means to establish that wireless connection.

Install a Local Plug and Play Printer

Installing Plug and Play printers is supposed to be fairly automatic, and, for the most part, it is.

1. With your computer and printer turned off, connect the devices to each other. Then make sure the other points in the previous checklist are satisfied.

2. Turn on your computer, let it fully boot, and then turn on your printer. Your computer should find and automatically install the new printer and briefly give you messages to that effect, as discussed earlier in this chapter.

3. Open the **System** menu and select **Control Panel | Hardware And Sound | Devices And Printers**. The Devices And Printers window will open, and you should see your new printer. Hover the mouse pointer over that printer, and you should see something like "Status: Letter, Portrait," as shown in Figure 6-8. (If you don't see your printer or the status says "Offline," it was not fully installed. Go to the next section.)

4. Open the context menu for the new printer, select **Printer Properties** (not "Properties"), and select **Print Test Page**. If the test page prints satisfactorily, select **Close**. Otherwise, select **Get Help With Printing**, follow the suggestions, and close the Help and printer windows when you are done. When you are ready, select **OK** to close the printer Properties dialog box.

5. If you want the new printer to be the default printer used by all apps on the computer, open the context menu for the printer and select **Set As Default Printer**.

6. Close the Devices And Printers window.

Install a Local Printer Manually

If a printer isn't automatically installed and verified in the process of using steps 1 through 3 in the previous section, you must install and verify it manually.

1. If a CD came with your printer, place that CD in the drive, and follow the on-screen instructions to install the printer. When this is complete, go to step 3 in "Install a Local Plug and Play Printer," and determine if the printer will print a test page. If so, skip to step 7.

2. If you don't have a manufacturer's CD or the CD didn't work with Windows 8, open the Devices And Printers window, as described in the previous section.

3. In the Devices And Printers window select **Add A Printer** on the toolbar. If the printer you want to install is listed, select it and select **Next**.

4. If the printer wasn't listed, select **The Printer That I Want Isn't Listed | Add A Local Printer Or Network Printer With Manual Settings | Next**.

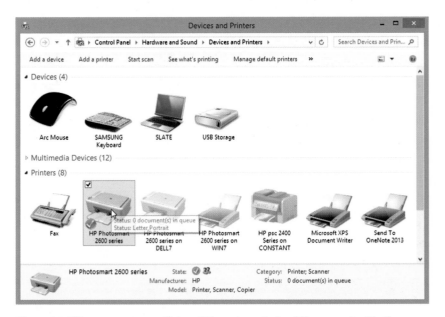

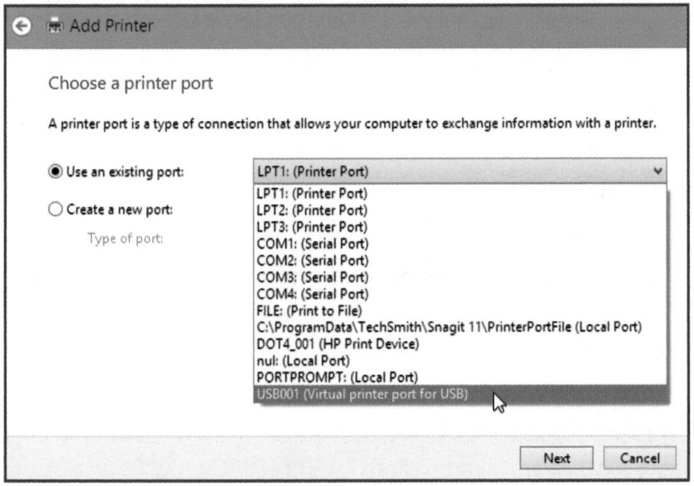

6. Select the manufacturer and model of the printer you want to install (see Figure 6-9). If you can't find your printer, select **Windows Update** to download the latest printer drivers. Then, once more, search for the manufacturer and model. When you find the correct printer, select **Next**.

7. Confirm or change the printer name, and select **Next**. Determine if you want to share this printer; if so, enter its share name, location, and comments. Select **Next**.

8. Choose whether you want this printer to be your default printer. Select **Print A Test Page**. If the test page prints satisfactorily, select **Close**. Otherwise, select **Get Help With Printing**, follow the suggestions, and close the Help and Printer windows when you are done. When you are ready, select **Finish** to close the Add Printer dialog box, and close the Devices And Printers window.

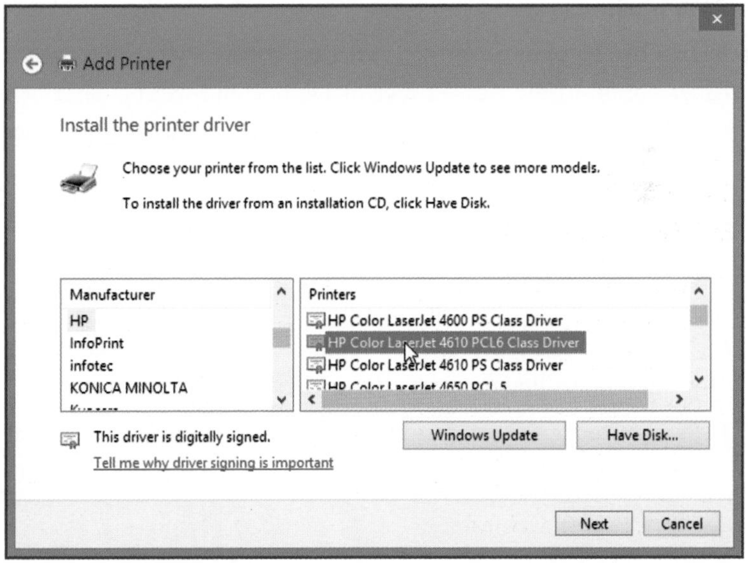

Figure 6-8 **When you connect a Plug and Play printer, it should be recognized by the computer and automatically installed.**

5. Select **Use An Existing Port**, open the drop-down list, and select the correct port (on newer printers, it is probably USB001; on the majority of older printers, it is LPT1), and select **Next**.

Figure 6-9: **Manually installing a printer requires that you know some facts about the printer.**

Tip If your printer was automatically installed but a CD came with your printer and you wonder if you should install using the CD, the general answer is no. Most printer drivers in Windows 8 originally came from the manufacturers and have been tested by Microsoft, so they should work well. Unless the printer came out after the release of Windows 8 (October 2012), the driver in Windows 8 should be newer, and in the installation dialog boxes, you can choose to update the drivers.

Install a Network Printer

Network printers are not directly connected to your computer, but are available to you as a result of your computer's connection to a network and that the printers have been shared. There are three types of network printers:

- Printers connected to someone else's computer, which are shared

- Printers connected to a dedicated printer server, which are shared

- Printers directly connected to a network (which, in effect, have a built-in computer)

The first two types of network printers are installed with the Network Printer option in the Add Printer dialog box and will be described here. The third option is installed with the Local Printer option, often automatically.

1. Open the **System** menu and select **Control Panel | Hardware And Sound | Devices And Printers**. The Devices And Printers window will open.

2. Select **Add A Printer** on the toolbar. Windows will search for printers, including network printers, as shown in Figure 6-10.

3. Scroll through the printers to locate the one you want. Select that printer and select **Next**. If you have found the printer you want, skip to step 5.

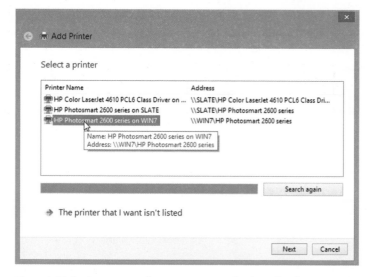

Figure 6-10: *A printer on another computer must be shared by that computer before you can use it.*

Note The search for network printers will find those printers that: (1) have been published to Active Directory—normally in larger organizations; (2) are attached to computers on your network; (3) use a Bluetooth wireless system, and a Bluetooth transceiver is connected to the computer doing the search; and (4) are directly connected to the network (not through another computer) and have their own IP address (probably automatically assigned).

4. If the search did not find the network printer you were looking for, select **The Printer That I Want Isn't Listed**. Select **Select A Shared Printer By Name | Browse**, open the necessary computer to locate and select the printer you want, and select **Next**.

5. Adjust the name of the printer if you want, and select **Next**. Select **Set As The Default Printer**, if you want to do that. Select **Print A Test Page**. If the test page prints satisfactorily, select **Close**. Otherwise, select **Get Help With Printing**, follow the suggestions, and close the Help window when you are done. When you are ready, select **Finish** to close the Add Printer dialog box and close the Devices And Printers window.

Identify a Default Printer

If you have several printers available to you, one must be identified as your default printer—the one that will be used for printing whenever you don't select another one. To change your default printer:

1. Open the **System** menu and select **Control Panel | Hardware And Sound | Devices And Printers**. The Devices And Printers window will open.

2. Open the context menu for the printer you want to be the default, and select **Set As Default Printer**.

3. Close the Devices And Printers window when finished.

Share a Printer

If you have a printer attached to your computer and you want to let others use it, you can share the printer.

1. In the Devices And Printers window, open the context menu for the printer you want to share, and select **Printer Properties**. The printer's Properties dialog box will appear.

2. Select the **Sharing** tab, select| **Share This Printer**, enter a share name, and click **OK.**

3. Close the printer Properties dialog box.

Print

Most printing is done from an app. This section uses Microsoft Office Word 2013, whose Print window is shown in Figure 6-11, as an example.

Print Documents

To print the document currently open in Word:

Select **Quick Print** on Word's Quick Access toolbar to immediately print using the default settings.

> **Tip** If Quick Print isn't on your Quick Access toolbar, select the **Customize** down arrow to the right of the Quick Access toolbar and select **Quick Print**.

Choose a Printer

To choose which printer you want to use:

Select the **File** tab and select **Print** to open Word's Print window shown in Figure 6-11. Select the **Printer** drop-down list, and choose the printer you want.

Figure 6-11: **The Microsoft Office Word 2013 Print window has options similar to many other apps.**

Determine Specific Pages to Print

In the first section of the Print window under Settings, by selecting the down arrow on the right, you can select:

- **Print All Pages** to print the entire document
- **Print Selection** to print the text that has been selected

- **Print Current Page** to print only the currently viewed page
- **Custom Print** to print a series of individual pages and/or a range of pages by specifying the individual pages separated by commas and specifying the range with a hyphen. For example, typing 4,6,8-10,12 will cause pages 4, 6, 8, 9, 10, and 12 to be printed.

Note You can print just the even or odd pages in a document by opening the print range drop-down list immediately under Settings in the Print window and making the relevant selection at the bottom of the list.

Print Pictures

Printing pictures from an app is exactly the same as described in "Print" in the preceding section. In addition, Windows has a Print Pictures dialog box used to print pictures from File Explorer.

1. From the desktop, open **File Explorer**.

2. Open the drives and folders needed to locate and select the picture(s) you want to print. You can select only one picture if you want.

However, to select a contiguous set of pictures, select the first one, hold down **SHIFT**, and select the last picture. To select noncontiguous pictures, hold down **CTRL** while selecting the pictures you want. (Both **SHIFT** and **CTRL** work with the mouse and with touch.)

3. Select the **Share** tab and select **Print** in the Send group to open the Print Pictures dialog box, as shown in Figure 6-12.

4. Select the printer, paper size, quality, paper type, number of photos on a page, number of copies, and whether to fit the picture to a frame. You can also select **Options** above the Cancel button to look at, and possibly change, several print settings. Select **OK** after looking at (and possibly selecting) the options.

5. When you are ready, select **Print**. The pictures will be printed. When you are done, close File Explorer.

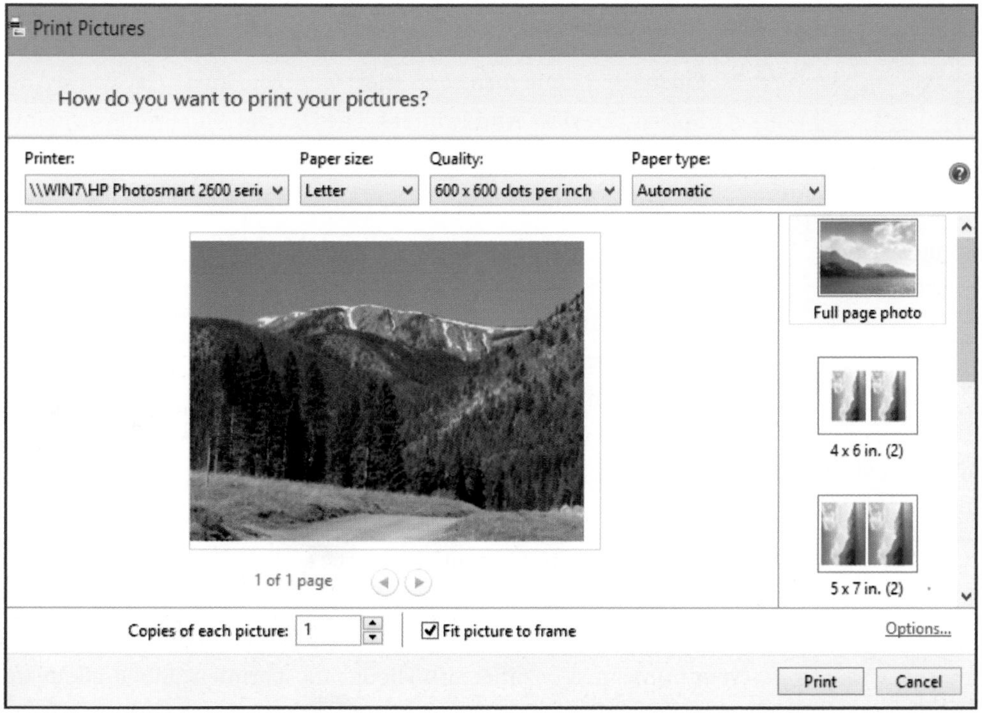

Print to a File

There are two primary reasons to print to a file: to have a file you can take to a remote printer or another computer, and to get information out of one app and into another. The first requires formatting the information for a printer and then sending it to a file. The actual printer must be installed on your computer even though it is not physically connected to your computer. In the second case, you must create a "printer" to produce unformatted generic text. The following sections explain first how to create a text file printer and then how to print to a file.

Print Pictures

How do you want to print your pictures?

Printer:	Paper size:	Quality:	Paper type:
\\WIN7\HP Photosmart 2600 serie ∨	Letter ∨	600 x 600 dots per inch ∨	Automatic ∨

Full page photo

4 x 6 in. (2)

5 x 7 in. (2)

1 of 1 page ◄ ►

Copies of each picture: 1 ☑ Fit picture to frame

Options...

Print Cancel

Figure 6-12: **If you use high-quality photo paper and a newer color printer, you can get almost professional-grade pictures. (Courtesy of Tom Beard.)**

Create a Text File Printer

1. Open the **System** menu and select **Control Panel | Hardware And Sound | Devices And Printers**. The Devices And Printers window will open.

2. Select **Add A Printer** on the toolbar. Then select **The Printer That I Want Isn't Listed | Add A Local Printer Or Network Printer With Manual Settings | Next**. Select **Use An Existing Port**, click the down arrow, select **| File (Print To File)**, and select **Next**.

3. In the Install The Printer Driver dialog box, scroll down and select **Generic** as the manufacturer and **Generic/Text Only** as the printer. Select **Next**.

4. Enter a name for the printer, and select **Next**. Determine if you want to share this printer and, if so, enter a share name. Select **Next**.

5. Select **Set As The Default Printer** (if you want to do that), skip printing a test page, and select **Finish**. A new icon will appear in your Devices And Printers window. Close the Devices And Printers window when you are done.

Generic / Text Only

Select Print To File

Whether you want to print to a file so that you can print on a remote printer or so that you can create a text file, the steps are the same once you have created a text file printer.

1. In the app in which you are printing, select the **File** menu (or the **File** tab in Microsoft Office 2013) and select **Print**.

2. Select the **Printer** down arrow, and select the ultimate printer or the **Generic/Text File** printer. Select the print range, number of copies, and other settings; and select **OK** or **Print** depending on your app. Select the folder, type the filename to use, and select **OK**.

Printer
Generic / Text Only
Ready
Printer Properties

Print Webpages

Printing webpages is not much different from printing any other document.

1. On the desktop, select the **Internet Explorer** icon on the taskbar to open your browser (assumed to be Internet Explorer).

2. Browse to the page you want to print, open the context menu for the page, and select **Print** or **Print Target**, as shown in Figure 6-13. The Print dialog box will open. Select the printer and other options, and select **Print** again.

3. Close your Internet browser.

Configure a Printer

Configuring a printer is usually done for special purposes and often isn't required. Nevertheless, all configuring is done from the printer's Properties dialog box.

1. Open the **System** menu and select **Control Panel | Hardware And Sound | Devices And Printers**. The Devices And Printers window will open.

2. Open the context menu for the printer you want to configure, select **Printer Properties**, and, if needed, select your printer. The printer's Properties dialog box will appear (you cannot change most settings for networked printers).

Open
Open in new window
See what's printing
Set as default printer
Printing preferences
Printer properties
Create shortcut
Remove device
Troubleshoot
Properties

In the General tab (shown in Figure 6-14), you can change the printer name, its location, and enter a comment. In the Ports tab, you can specify the port used by the printer, configure ports, and set up printer pooling. In the Device Settings tab, you can set what is loaded in each paper tray, how to handle font substitution, and what printer options are available (your printer may be different). Though most printer configurations are

Figure 6-13: **You can print from Internet Explorer, but many webpages also have a "Print" button for the same purpose, and often it is better at printing their material.**

self-explanatory, several items are worthy of further discussion and are explained in the following sections.

Enable Printer Pooling

Printer pooling allows you to have two or more physical printing devices with the same print driver assigned to one printer. When print jobs are sent to the printer, Windows determines which of the physical devices is available and routes the job to that device.

1. In the Properties dialog box for the printer to which all work will be directed, select the **Ports** tab and select **Enable Printer Pooling**.

2. Select each of the ports with a printing device that is to be in the pool. When all the ports are selected, select **OK** to close the Properties dialog box.

3. If the printer that contains the pool isn't already selected as the default printer, open the context menu for the printer and select **Set As Default Printer**.

Set Printer Priority

Assigning several printers to one printing device allows you to have two or more settings used with one device. If you want to have two or more priorities automatically assigned to jobs going to a printer, create two or more printers that all point to the same printer port but that have different priorities. Then have high-priority print jobs printed to a printer with a priority of 99 and low-priority jobs printed to a printer with a priority of 1.

1. Install all printers as previously described in "Install a Printer," all with the same port. Name each printer to indicate its priority, such as "High-Priority Printer" and "Low-Priority Printer."

2. In the Devices And Printers window, open the context menu for the high-priority printer, and select **Printer Properties**.

3. Select the **Advanced** tab, type a priority of <u>99</u>, and select **OK**.

4. Similarly, open the context menu for the other printers, open their Properties dialog boxes, select the **Advanced** tab, and set the priority, from 1 for the lowest priority to 98 for the second-highest priority.

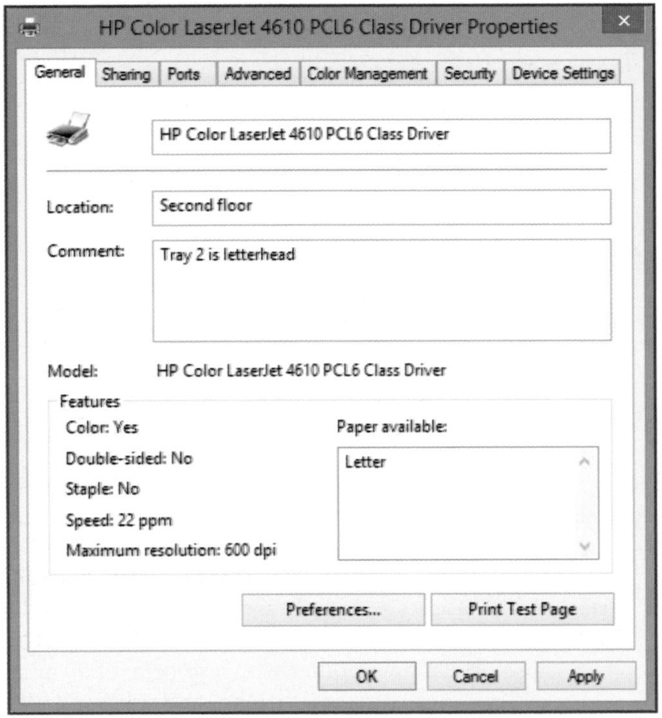

specific type and size of paper when printing, Windows 8 automatically designates the correct paper tray for the print job.

1. In the printer Properties dialog box for the printer whose trays you want to assign, select the **Device Settings** tab.

2. Select a tray, open the drop-down list, and select the type or size of paper in that tray.

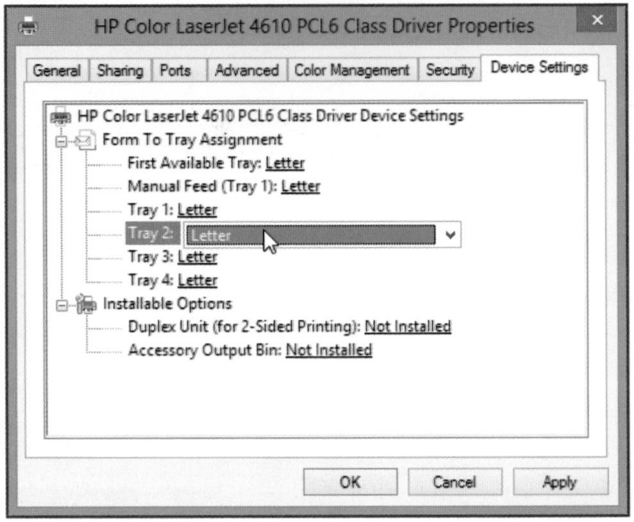

*Figure 6-14: **Printers, while having many settings, are often run without ever changing the default settings.***

Jobs with the highest priority will print before jobs with a lower priority if they are in the *queue* (waiting to be printed) at the same time.

Tip If you have an app that automatically prints certain tasks, such as incoming orders, you might want to assign that automatic task a lower priority than a word-processing task, such as a new proposal.

Assign Paper Trays

Some printers have more than one paper tray, and each tray can have different types or sizes of paper. If you assign types and sizes of paper to trays in the printer's Properties dialog box and a user requests a

3. When you have set the paper type or size in each tray, select **OK**.

Configure Spool Settings

The time it takes to print a document is normally longer than the time it takes to transfer the information to the printer. *Printer spooling* temporarily stores information on disk, allowing Windows to feed it to the printer as it can be handled. Under most circumstances, you want to use printer spooling and not tie up the app waiting for the printer. The printer's Properties Advanced tab lets you choose to spool or not, and gives you two options if you spool:

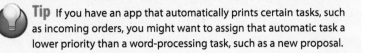

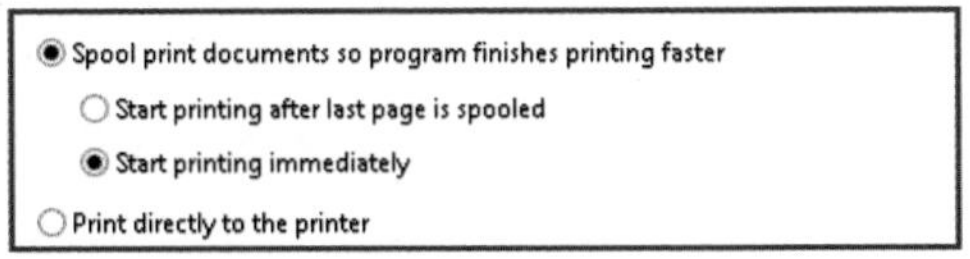

- **Start Printing After Last Page Is Spooled** waits to print until the last page is spooled, allowing the app to finish faster and the user to get back to the app faster, but it takes longer to finish printing.

- **Start Printing Immediately** allows printing to be done sooner, but the app will be tied up a little longer.

The default, Start Printing Immediately, provides a middle ground between getting the printing done and getting back to the app.

 Note The Print Spooled Documents First check box, located below the spool options, is selected by default. Normally, you want to keep it that way.

Use Separator Pages

If you have several jobs on a printer, it might be helpful to have a separator page between them. A separator page can also be used to switch a printer between PostScript (a printer language) and PCL (Printer Control Language) on Hewlett-Packard (HP) and compatible printers. Four sample SEP separation files come with Windows 8 and are located in the \Windows\System32\ folder:

- **Pcl.sep** prints a separation page before the start of each print job on PCL-compatible printers. If the printer handles both PostScript and PCL, it will be switched to PCL.

- **Pscript.sep** does *not* print a separation page, but printers with both PostScript and PCL will be switched to PostScript.

- **Sysprint.sep** prints a separation page before the start of each print job on PostScript-compatible printers.

- **Sysprtj.sep** is the same as Sysprint.sep, but in the Japanese language.

You can choose to have a separator page added at the beginning of each print job by selecting **Separator Page** on the Advanced tab of the Printer

Properties dialog box, browsing for and selecting the page you want, selecting **Open** and clicking **OK** twice.

 Note The separation files work with HP and PostScript or compatible printers. They will not work with all printers.

Tip If you know or have a guide to either the PCL or PostScript language (or both), you can open and modify the separator page files (or copies of them) with any text editor, such as Notepad, to suit your particular purpose.

▷▷ Control Printing

To control printing means to control the process as it is taking place, whether with one print job or with several in line. If several print jobs are spooled at close to the same time, they form a *print queue,* waiting for earlier jobs to finish. You may control printing in several ways, as described next. These tasks are handled in the printer's window, which is similar to that shown in Figure 6-15, and is shown by opening a printer's context menu and selecting **See What's Printing** in the Devices And Printers window, or by opening the printer icon in the notification area of the taskbar and then selecting **See What's Printing**.

HP Color LaserJet 4610 PCL6 Class Driver						– □ ×
Printer Document View						
Document Name	Status	Owner	Pages	Size	Submitted	
📄 Microsoft Word - 84605a		Marty	24	3.00 MB	9:53:11 PM 9/17/2012	
📄 Microsoft Word - 84606a		Marty	24	3.07 MB	9:52:58 PM 9/17/2012	
📄 Microsoft Word - 84606a		Marty	24	3.07 MB	9:52:51 PM 9/17/2012	
3 document(s) in queue						

*Figure 6-15: **Controlling printing takes place in the printer's window and allows you to pause, resume, restart, and cancel printing.***

Pause, Resume, and Restart Printing

While printing, a situation may occur (such as needing to add ink) where you want to pause and then resume printing, either for one or all documents:

- **Pause all documents**   In the printer's window, select **Printer | Pause Printing**. "Paused" will appear in the title bar, and, if you look in the Printer menu, you will see a check mark in front of Pause Printing.

Printer   Document   View
Connect
Set As Default Printer
Printing Preferences...
Update Driver
Pause Printing
Cancel All Documents
Sharing...
Use Printer Offline
Properties
Close

- **Resume printing all documents**   In the printer's window, select **Printer** and select **Pause Printing**. "Paused" disappears from the title bar and the check mark disappears from the Pause Printing option in the Printer menu.

- **Pause a document**   In the printer's window, select the document or documents to pause and then select **Document | Pause**. "Paused" will appear in the Status column of the document(s) you selected.

- **Resume printing a paused document where it left off**   In the printer's window, select the document and then select **Document | Resume**. "Printing" will appear in the Status column of the document selected.

- **Restart printing at the beginning of a document**   In the printer's window, select the document and then select **Document | Restart**. "Restarting" and then "Printing" will appear in the Status column.

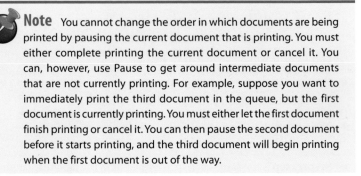

Printer   Document
Pause
Resume
Restart
Cancel
Properties

Note   You cannot change the order in which documents are being printed by pausing the current document that is printing. You must either complete printing the current document or cancel it. You can, however, use Pause to get around intermediate documents that are not currently printing. For example, suppose you want to immediately print the third document in the queue, but the first document is currently printing. You must either let the first document finish printing or cancel it. You can then pause the second document before it starts printing, and the third document will begin printing when the first document is out of the way.

Cancel Printing

Canceling printing can be done either at the printer level for all the jobs in the printer queue or at the document level for selected documents.

A canceled job is deleted from the print queue and must be restarted by the original app.

- **Cancel a job**   In the printer's window, select the job or jobs that you want canceled. Select **Document** and select **Cancel**. Select **Yes** to confirm the cancellation. The job or jobs will disappear from the window and the queue.

- **Cancel all the jobs in the queue**   In the printer's window, select **Printer** and select **Cancel All Documents**. You are asked whether you are sure you want to cancel all documents. Select **Yes**. All jobs will disappear from the queue and the printer window.

Redirect Documents

If you have two printers with the same print driver, you can redirect all the print jobs that are in the queue for one printer to the other, where they will be printed without having to be resubmitted. You do this by changing the port to which the queue is directed.

1. In the printer's window, select **Printer | Properties** and then select the **Ports** tab.

2. If the second printer is in the list of ports, select it. Otherwise, select **Add Port** to open the Printer Ports dialog box. Select **Local Port** and select **New Port**, which opens the Port Name dialog box.

3. Enter the UNC (Uniform Naming Convention) name for the printer (for example, \\Server3\HPLJ9050 for an HP printer to the Server3 computer), and select **OK**.

4. Select **Close** and then select **OK**. The print queue will be redirected to the other printer.

Change a Document's Properties

A document in a print queue has a Properties dialog box, shown in Figure 6-16, which is shown by opening the context menu for the document and selecting **Properties**. The General tab allows you to change a number of things:

- **Priority**   To change a document's default priority of 1, the lowest priority, so that the document can be printed before another that hasn't started printing yet, set the document's priority in the document's Properties dialog box to anything higher than the other document by dragging the **Priority** slider to the right.

- **Who to notify**   To change who is optionally notified of any special situations occurring during printing, as well as when a document has finished printing, put the name of another person (the individual's user name on a shared computer or network) in the Notify text box of the document's Properties dialog box.

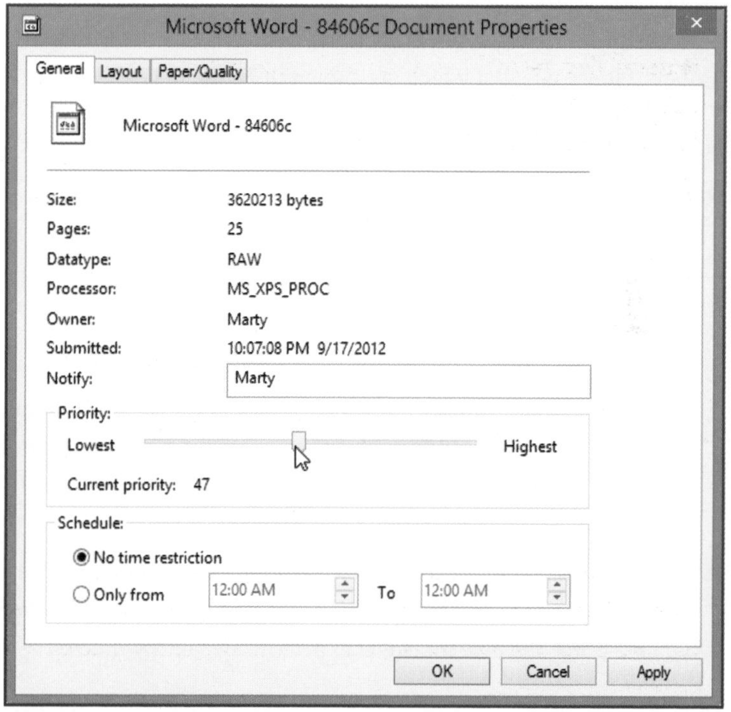

*Figure 6-16: **Setting the properties of a document in the print queue can change its priority and when it prints.***

- **Set print time** To change when a job is printed, open a document's Properties dialog box, select **Only From** at the bottom under Schedule, and then enter the time range within which you want the job printed. This allows you to print large jobs, which might otherwise clog the print queue, at a time when there is little or no load.

Schedule:
- No time restriction
- Only from 2:00 AM To 4:00 AM

▷▷ Handle Fonts

A *font* is a set of characters with the same design, size, weight, and style. A font is a member of a *typeface* family, all with the same design. The font 12-point Arial bold italic is a member of the Arial typeface with a 12-point size, bold weight, and italic style. Windows 8 comes with a large number of fonts, a few of which are shown in Figure 6-17.

Add Fonts

To add fonts to those that are automatically installed by Windows 8:

1. Open the **System** menu and select **Control Panel | Appearance And Personalization | Fonts**. The Fonts window opens as shown in Figure 6-17.

2. Either use File Explorer to locate a font (or fonts) on your computer (this can be a flash drive, a CD/DVD, or a hard disk) or on your network; or use Internet Explorer to download a font to your computer and then, with File Explorer, locate it so you can see and then select the new font(s) you want to install.

3. Open the context menu for the selected new font(s), and then select **Install**. A message will tell you the fonts are being installed. When you are done, the new fonts will appear in the Fonts window.

Delete Fonts

Remove fonts simply by selecting them in the Fonts window and pressing **DELETE** or by opening the context menu for the font(s) and selecting **Delete**. In either case, you are told that if the font is deleted some text might not appear as you intended and asked whether you are sure you want to do that. Select **Yes** if you are. The fonts will be deleted *permanently* and *cannot* be retrieved from the Recycle Bin.

Use Fonts

Fonts are used or specified from within an app. In Microsoft Word, for example, you can select a character, word, line, or more of text and then open the Font drop-down list on the Formatting toolbar (in versions prior to Office 2007) or in the Font group (in Office 2007 and later). Every app is a little different. One nice feature in recent versions of Word is that the list shows what the fonts look like.

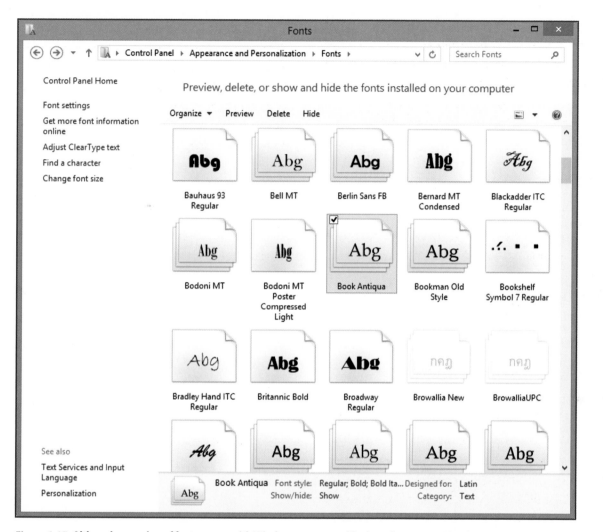

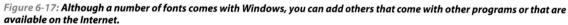

Figure 6-17: **Although a number of fonts comes with Windows, you can add others that come with other programs or that are available on the Internet.**

Chapter 7

Enjoying Multimedia

Multimedia is the combination of audio and video, with the term *media* referring to either audio or video. As an operating system, Windows 8 has to handle audio and video files and accept their input from a number of different devices. It has three default apps—Music, Video, and Windows Media Player—that enable you to work with multimedia files and read and write them onto CDs, DVDs, flash drives, and music players, as well as *stream* them to other computers (streaming sends audio or video files to another computer in such a way that the other computer can display the files as they are being sent). We'll look first at sound by itself, then at video with sound.

WORK WITH AUDIO

Audio is sound. Windows 8 works with and uses sound in several ways, the simplest being to alert you of various events, like an incoming email message or closing down the system. Chapter 2 shows you how to customize the use of sounds for these purposes. The other use of sound is to entertain or inform you—be it listening to music or lectures from CDs, Internet radio, or another Internet site. It is this use of sound that is the subject of this section.

▷▷ Play CDs

Playing a CD is as easy as inserting a disc in the drive. When you first do that Windows asks you to choose what happens with audio CDs. If you select that message, you will be asked if you want Windows Media Player to play the disc. In that case, if you select **Play**

Audio CD Windows Media Player, you are asked if you want Windows Media Player to be your default player. Select **Recommended Settings | Finish**. Media Player will open and begin playing the disc. Initially, the on-screen view, called "Now Playing," is a small window, as shown in Figure 7-1. If you select **Switch To Library** ▦ in the upper-right corner under the Close button, a larger, more comprehensive window will open, as you can see in Figure 7-2 (depending on the size of the window, there are some differences in what is displayed). The Media Player library window has a variety of controls that enable you to determine how it functions and looks. These controls are located either in the functional controls and option menus at the top of the window or in the playback controls at the bottom.

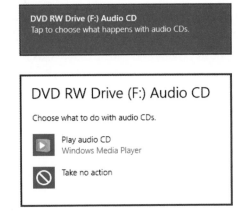

- **Menu options** include facilities to
  - **Organize** the Media Player window.
  - **Stream** media from your computer.
  - **Create a playlist** of selected tracks.
- **Functional controls** allow selection of the primary Media Player functions:
  - **Rip CD** copies audio CDs to the Media Library.
  - **Rip settings** determines how audio is copied from a CD.

Figure 7-1: *Windows Media Player Now Playing view shows you its controls when you move the mouse over it.*

- **Play** plays selected tracks and creates a playlist.
- **Burn** copies playlists from the library to writable CDs and DVDs.
- **Sync** synchronizes content between portable music devices and your PC.
- **Playback controls** provide CD player–like controls to play/pause, stop, go to a previous track, go to the next track, and adjust volume, as well as randomly play tracks (shuffle) and repeat a specific track.

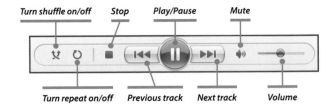

Menu options

Functional controls

Playback controls

Switch to Now Playing

Figure 7-2: Windows Media Player Library view gives you access to a wide range of audio and video entertainment.

When you select any of the three tabs for the functional controls in the upper-right area, the list pane opens. The Play tab initially lists what is currently being played, but can be cleared and used to build your own playlist. The parts of the Media Player in Play mode are shown in Figure 7-3, and include the following:

- **List options** hide (close) the list pane and manipulate the list.

- **Play to** starts an audio or video stream to a media device.

- **Clear list** stops what is being played and prepares the pane for creating a playlist.

- **Save list** saves the current playlist to your media library.

- **Shop CD/DVD** enables you to buy the item you are listening to or watching.

- **Previous** and **Next** let you cycle through the playlists in your library.

- **Switch to Now Playing** collapses the window to just the small window shown in Figure 7-1.

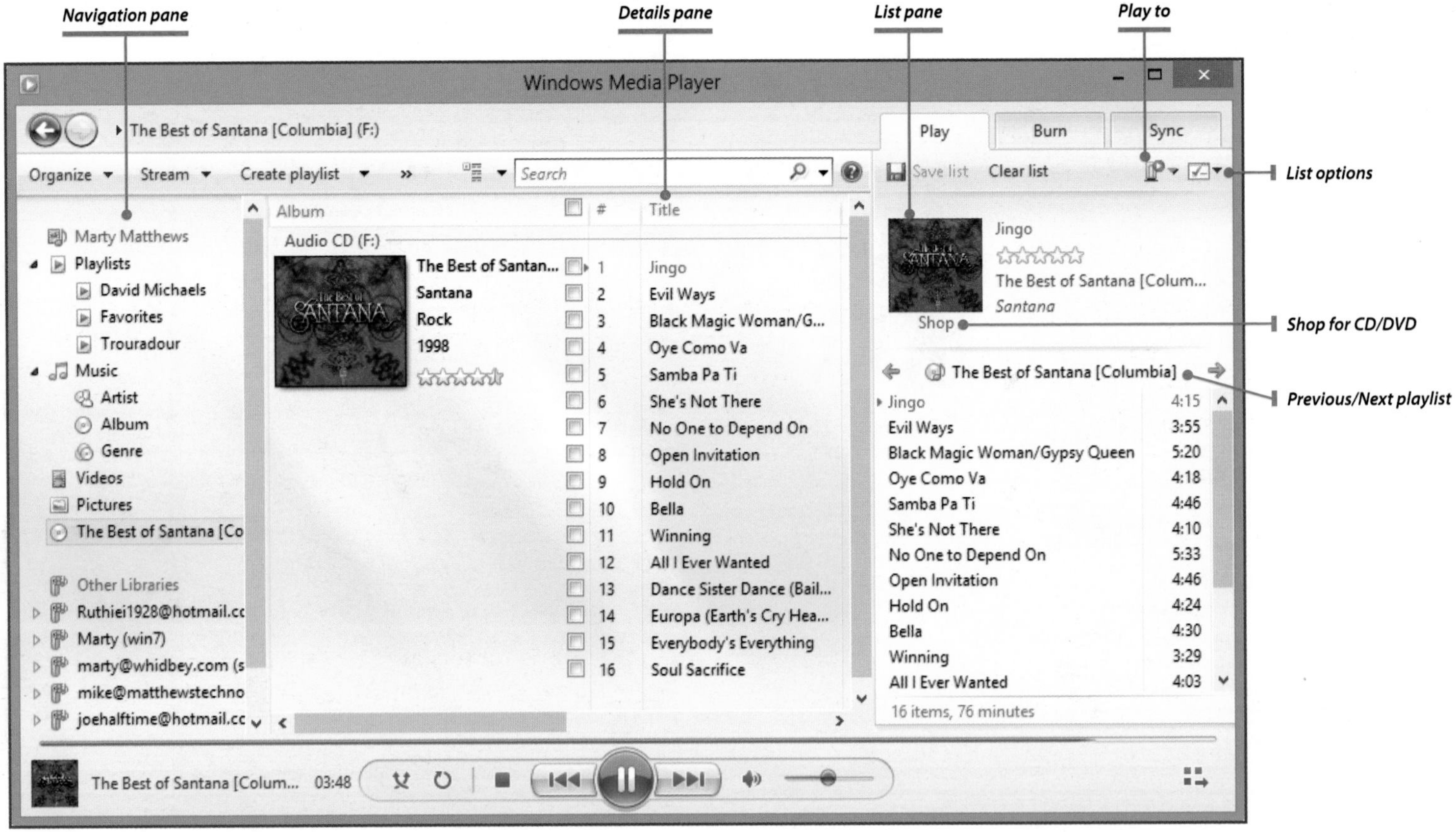

Navigation pane
Details pane
List pane
Play to

Windows Media Player

▸ The Best of Santana [Columbia] (F:)

Play | Burn | Sync

Organize ▾ | Stream ▾ | Create playlist ▾ | » | Search | 🔍 ▾ | ❓

Save list   Clear list — List options

Album		#	Title		Jingo
Audio CD (F:)					☆☆☆☆☆
	The Best of Santan...	▸ 1	Jingo		The Best of Santana [Colum...
	Santana	2	Evil Ways		*Santana*
	Rock	3	Black Magic Woman/G...		Shop ● — Shop for CD/DVD
	1998	4	Oye Como Va		
	☆☆☆☆☆	5	Samba Pa Ti		← 🔘 The Best of Santana [Columbia] ● → — Previous/Next playlist

Marty Matthews
▴ ▸ Playlists
   ▸ David Michaels
   ▸ Favorites
   ▸ Trouradour
▴ ♫ Music
   Artist
   Album
   Genre
Videos
Pictures
The Best of Santana [Co

Other Libraries
▸ Ruthiei1928@hotmail.cc
▸ Marty (win7)
▸ marty@whidbey.com (s
▸ mike@matthewstechno
▸ joehalftime@hotmail.cc

6	She's Not There		
7	No One to Depend On		
8	Open Invitation		
9	Hold On		
10	Bella		
11	Winning		
12	All I Ever Wanted		
13	Dance Sister Dance (Bail...		
14	Europa (Earth's Cry Hea...		
15	Everybody's Everything		
16	Soul Sacrifice		

▸ Jingo	4:15
Evil Ways	3:55
Black Magic Woman/Gypsy Queen	5:20
Oye Como Va	4:18
Samba Pa Ti	4:46
She's Not There	4:10
No One to Depend On	5:33
Open Invitation	4:46
Hold On	4:24
Bella	4:30
Winning	3:29
All I Ever Wanted	4:03

16 items, 76 minutes

The Best of Santana [Colum...   03:48   ⤨ ↻ | ◼ | ◀◀ ⏸ ▶▶ | 🔊 ━●━━━

*Figure 7-3: **The list pane shows what is currently playing and is where playlists are created.***

⟩⟩ Control the Volume

You can control your computer's audio volume from several places, including the physical volume control on your speakers or on your laptop computer, the volume control on the bottom-right of the playback controls of the Media Player, and the volume icon in the notification area on the right of the taskbar 🔊.

Selecting the **Speakers** or **Volume** icon in the notification area, which displays the percentage of full volume when pointed to, opens a small volume slider that you can drag for louder or softer sound, or you can select **Mute** (the blue speaker at the bottom of the slider) to do just that. Select anywhere on the desktop to close the volume slider.

Access Online Media

If you have a broadband Internet connection (as described in Chapter 4) of at least 512 Kbps (more will improve your experience) and sound capability, you can find a large amount of media, including music, movies, and TV. Windows 8 facilitates that through the Xbox Music app, and you can access online content directly through Internet Explorer.

Windows 8's new Xbox Music app allows you to search for, preview, and purchase music online, as well as play music in your library. When you first open Music, if you haven't started building your music library, you will be shown currently popular music, as you can see in Figure 7-4 (you might have to swipe/scroll to the right). You can preview and purchase this music.

1. On the Start screen, select the **Music** tile. Music will open and display new releases and popular music.

2. Preview some of this music by selecting one of the tiles and then selecting **Preview Top Songs** to preview all the top songs on the album album, or select a particular song and then select **Preview**.

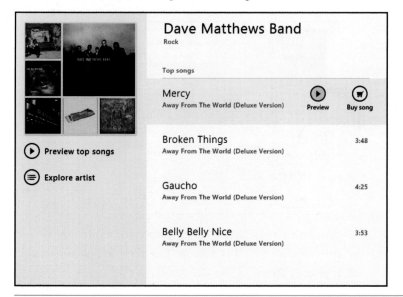

See the following sections to search Music and to purchase pieces from it.

 Tip Doing direct searches from your Internet browser may help you find what you want.

Find Your Music Online

Having spent my adolescent youth in the late 1950s, some of my favorite songs from that era are by The Platters and include *Unchained Melody, Smoke Gets in Your Eyes,* and *Twilight Time.* You can easily find and listen to your favorite music by searching Music or in a general online search engine such as Google or Bing.

Search Music

Music provides the ability to search the music industry and display the music related to your search. In my case, I want to search for the Platters.

1. With the Xbox Music app open on your computer (see "Access Online Media" previously), open **Charms** and select **Search**.

2. In the Search text box, type the artist's name, album name, group name, or composer name, and press **ENTER**. The results will be displayed on a full screen, as you see in Figure 7-5 for the Platters.

3. Select any of the albums and then select **Preview**, or select a song and then select **Preview**. We'll talk about purchasing music later in this chapter.

Search Google or Bing

You can find most other popular songs by simply typing a song's name into either the Google or Bing search text box. For example, I might type Platters – Smoke Gets In Your Eyes. This produces a list of links to sites where you can listen to, download, and buy the song, as you can see on

*Figure 7-4: **Music lets you preview the latest releases and popular music.***

the left of Figure 7-6. Many of the links that are found are on YouTube. Selecting one of these links opens YouTube and begins playing the song. On the page that opens there are links to either other songs by the same artist or other artists performing the same song, as you can see on the right of Figure 7-6.

Buy Media Online

There are many sources of media on the Internet. Buying media in Windows 8 is done through the Online Store in Music.

To buy music with the Xbox Music app:

1. Select the album you want to buy, either in total or a single song. The album list of songs will open.

2. To buy a single song, select the song and then select **Buy Song**. To buy the entire album, select **Buy Album.** The confirmation information will appear, as shown in Figure 7-7.

Figure 7-5: *Music provides a clean presentation of a full collection of many composers and artists.*

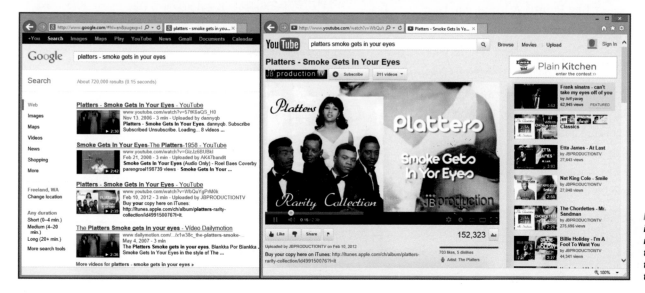

Figure 7-6: *Finding music online is simply a matter of typing the name of the performer and/or the song in a search text box and then selecting the one you want to hear.*

Figure 7-7: *You buy music using Microsoft points, which, at the time this was written, were worth approximately 1.25 cents U.S. each.*

3. If you need to buy points, select **Buy Points**. A list of purchase options will be presented.

4. Select the desired option you want, and select **Next**. Fill in your address and other information, and select **Save**.

5. Select **Add Credit Card** and fill in the credit card information. Then select **Save | Confirm Purchase | Done | Confirm**. You will get a message that your purchase is being automatically downloaded to your My Music folder. If you return to the Music home screen you should see the album under My Music. You will also get an email confirmation of the purchase.

> Thanks for buying *The Platters*!
>
> Your album is downloading. It will appear in My Music when the download is complete.

Tip You can get information about your point balance, payment options, billing history, and other information related to your purchases through Music by opening **Charms** and selecting **Settings | Account** while Music is open.

CAUTION! The Xbox Music app and many other online stores make it *very easy to buy from them,* and you can quickly run up a sizable bill. You need to create an account with the store and provide your name, address, email, and credit card info. Once you do this, it is almost too easy to buy in the future!

Copy (Rip) CDs to Your Computer

Media Player gives you the ability to copy (or "rip") CD tracks that you like to your hard disk so that you can build and manage a library of your favorite music and copy this material to a recordable CD or DVD, or to a music player. To copy from a CD (see Figure 7-8):

Note Where it makes sense, consider that when I say "CD" I mean "CD or DVD."

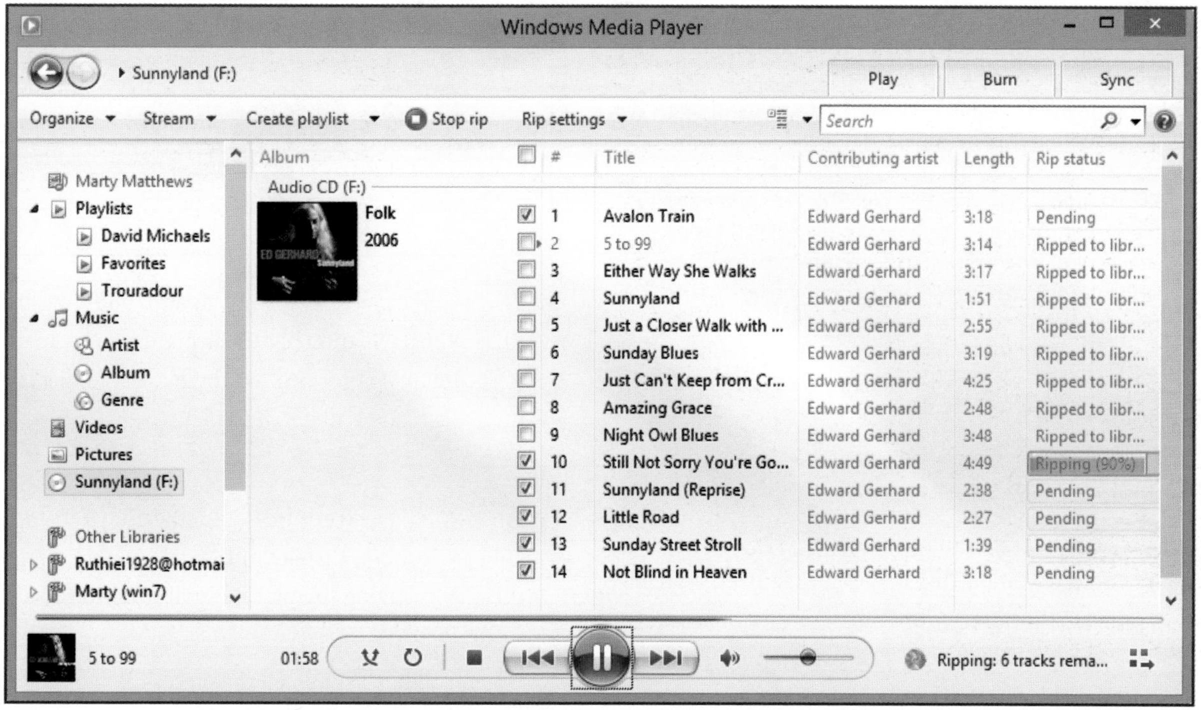

Figure 7-8: ***Media Player can be used to build a music library from your CDs.***

> **Note** Copying a music track from a CD to a digital file on your hard disk is time-consuming, even on a relatively fast computer. It also produces large files. To see the copying progress, look at the Rip Status column of the Media Player window, as well as the message in the bottom-right corner (see Figure 7-8).

1. Insert the CD from which you want to copy tracks. If it doesn't automatically start playing, click **Play Audio CD Using Windows Media Player** to open Windows Media Player.
2. Select **Switch To Library** in the upper-right corner. In the details pane, select the tracks you want to copy to your hard disk by selecting the check boxes to the left of each track. Select **Play** in the playback controls to listen to the tracks and to make sure your choices are correct.
3. If you wish, select **Rip Settings** and review the settings that are available to you. For the most part, the default settings provide the best middle ground between high quality and file size.

> **Tip** One setting worth mentioning—Rip Settings/Format—lets you change the default WMA format to MP3 for playing on many of the handheld music players.

4. When you are satisfied that you have selected the correct tracks and settings, select **Rip CD**. The selected tracks will be copied to your hard disk. When you are done, remove the CD and close Media Player.

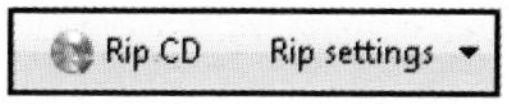

1 2 3 4 5 6 7 8 9 10

Note The material on most CDs and DVDs is owned and copyrighted by some combination of the composer, the artist, the producer, and/or the publisher. Copyright law prohibits using the copyrighted material in ways that are not beneficial to the owners, including giving or selling the content without giving or selling the original CD or DVD itself. To enforce this, most CDs and DVDs are protected to make copying difficult. Media Player provides the ability to copy copyrighted material to your hard disk and then to a recordable CD or a Universal Serial Bus (USB) flash drive with the understanding that the copy is solely for your own personal use and you will not sell or give away copies. This is both a great gift and a responsibility. As one who makes his living on copyrighted material, I urge you not to abuse it.

Organize Music

Once you have copied several CDs and have downloaded other music to your hard disk, you will likely want this material organized. When music and videos are copied to the library, the contents are automatically indexed alphabetically by album, artist, and genre. You may want to combine selected tracks into a *playlist* that allows you to play pieces from several albums. To build a new playlist:

Note You cannot add music to playlists directly from a CD in your drive even though it appears in Media Player. You must first add the music to your library and then select it from there.

1. Open Media Player and select **Create Playlist** in the menu options area. Type the name you want for the new playlist, and press **ENTER**. A new playlist will appear in the list of playlists in the navigation pane.

2. Open an album, artist, or genre; and select a piece or the pieces (hold down **CTRL** as you select multiple pieces that you want in the new playlist). Drag the piece(s) to the playlist title in the navigation pane.

3. Select other pieces you want to add, and drag them to the playlist title in the navigation pane. Select the playlist to display the contents in the details pane, or open the playlist to display it in the Play tab in the list pane and begin to play it.

–Or–

1. Open Media Player and select the **Play** tab to open it in the list pane. Select and display in the details pane the music you want in the playlist. Drag the piece(s) you want to the list pane, as you can see in Figure 7-9.

2. When you have added all the pieces that you initially want (you can always add more later), select **Save List**, type a name, and press **ENTER**.

3. Listen to the playlist by selecting the **Play** button in the playback controls. When you are done, select **Clear List** and then select the **Play** tab to close the list pane, and close Media Player.

Tip When listening to a playlist, you can randomize the order in which the pieces will play by selecting **Turn Shuffle On** in the playback controls, which is the first button on the left. Select it a second time to return to normal play.

Figure 7-9: *Media Player provides a way to manage the media you store on your computer, including building playlists.*

⏩ Make (Burn) a Music CD

Once you have created a playlist (see "Organize Music" earlier in this chapter), you can write (or "burn") it to a writable CD using Media Player's Burn feature. This creates an "audio" CD that works in a portable or car CD player. This is not the same as simply making a copy of the digital files as explained in step 4 of this procedure.

1. Put a blank recordable disc in the CD recording drive. A dialog box will appear and ask what you want to do. Select **Burn An Audio CD** to open Windows Media Player with the Burn functional area displayed.

2. Open your playlists in the navigation pane, and drag a playlist (or individual songs from an open playlist) that you want on the CD

to the Burn List on the right. Do this in the order you want the songs played. You can see how much of the CD is being used and the amount of time remaining just above the Burn List, as shown in Figure 7-10.

3. You can make corrections to the Burn List by dragging additional songs there until you use up the remaining time, or by opening the context menu for a song on the Burn List and selecting **Remove From List** in the context menu that opens. You can also clear the Burn List and start over.

4. When you are sure you have the list of pieces you want to burn, select **Start Burn**. The digital files will first be converted to analog music

files and then written to a CD or DVD. You can see the progress in the thermometer bar near the top of the list pane (it is not very fast!). When the burn is complete and if no one has changed the default settings, the disc will be ejected from the drive. Write the title on the disc with a soft felt-tip marker, or use a LightScribe drive to burn a label on the special discs you use for this purpose.

The resulting CD should be playable in most CD players.

*Figure 7-10: **Burning a playlist to a writable CD allows you to create a disc that has just your favorite songs.***

▷▷ Display Visualizations in Windows Media Player

The Media Player's Now Playing window, shown in Figure 7-1, can display a graphic visualization of the music that is playing instead of the album cover. Several visualizations come with Media Player, and you can download more. To display a visualization:

1. Open the context menu for the Now Playing window, select **Visualizations**, select one of the three types of visualizations (Album Art and Info Center View are static displays), and then select the visualization you want to use.

2. If you want to download additional visualizations, open the context menu for the Now Playing window and select **Visualizations | Download Visualizations**. Then follow the instructions on the websites you will visit.

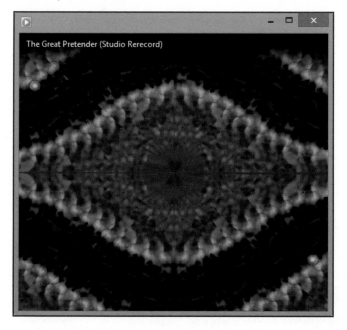

The Great Pretender (Studio Rerecord)

▷▷ Copy to (Sync with) Music Players

Windows Media Player allows you to plug in a digital music device, such as an iPod or MP3 player, and transfer music to and from (sync with) the device.

1. Start Windows Media Player, and select **Sync** in the Windows Media Player functional controls. You will be told to connect your device.

2. Start your device and then plug it into your computer. The first time you do that, Windows will install a driver for it, and then the AutoPlay dialog box will appear.

3. In the Devices Setup dialog box, select **Finish** or **Cancel**, depending on your situation. If you select **Cancel**, drag the playlists and/or songs you want on the device to the Sync List on the right. If you wish, you can play the Sync List by opening the first playlist or song.

4. When you are certain that you have all the music in the Sync List that you want on your device, select **Start Sync**, as shown in Figure 7-11. The music will be copied to the device.

5. When you see that the sync is complete, select **Click Here** to see the results on the player. When you are ready, disconnect your player.

 Note If you choose to sync your entire library, consider the Shuffle Music option. With this option selected, Windows will put the music on the device such that songs will randomly play. Each time you plug your device into your computer, a new random order will be established and copied to the device.

*Figure 7-11: **A digital music device can mirror your Media Player library if it has enough room and that is what you want.***

WORK WITH VIDEO

Windows 8 lets you watch videos from a DVD or downloaded from the Internet using the Windows 8 Video app or the Windows Media Player. It also allows you to capture videos and still images from a digital camcorder or digital camera.

Play DVDs

Playing DVDs is as easy as playing CDs: Simply insert a DVD into its drive. When you do that, the AutoPlay dialog box will appear, and you will be asked if you want to play the DVD using Windows Live Media Player. If you select **Play DVD Movie** using Windows Media Player, the player will open and play the disc. The Media Player controls are virtually the same for DVDs as they are for CDs, as you can see in Figure 7-12, except the

View Full Screen option enlarges the movie or video you are watching to fit the full screen, and the DVD menu has options for viewing menus and special features on the DVD.

Note After the first time you play a movie, the AutoPlay may not pop up; the movie may just start playing.

Figure 7-12: *Watching movies, or in this case a concert, is increasingly popular, especially with a laptop on a trip.*

 Import Video from a Camcorder

You can import or copy video directly from your camcorder to your hard drive, and then view the resulting file with the new Windows 8 Video app or with Windows Media Player.

1. Using a cable connected to your camcorder, plug the other end of cable into a USB or FireWire (IEEE 1394) port on your computer, and turn the camera on. Alternatively, if your camera also has a removable memory card, you can remove it from the camera and plug it into the memory card slot on your computer.

2. In either case, Windows 8 will see the camcorder or the memory card as a removable disk, install any needed driver software, and open a message asking what to do. Your two options are:

Removable Disk (H:)

Choose what to do with memory cards.

Import photos and videos
Photos

Open folder to view files
Windows Explorer

Take no action

a. **Import Photos And Videos** opens the Photos app and displays the video segments on the screen, which you can click the arrow to preview, uncheck if you don't want to import them, enter the folder where you want the files, and select **Import** to finish the process.

Removable Disk (H:) 8 files   Clear selection

3 files will be imported to this folder

2012-07-20 pig roast   Import   Cancel

b. **Open Folder To View Files** opens the File Explorer displaying the video files on the camera, as shown in Figure 7-13. This allows you to move the files anywhere on your hard disk. It is recommended that you put the video files in a folder in the Library's My Videos folder so the programs on your computer can easily find them.

3. To view your video with the Video app, select the **Video** tile on the Start screen to open the app. On the left side of the app (you may have to use the horizontal scroll bar to get there), you should see the videos you have added. Select a video to view it.

video

my videos

0 min 53 sec
IMAG0003

1 min 16 sec
IMAG0002

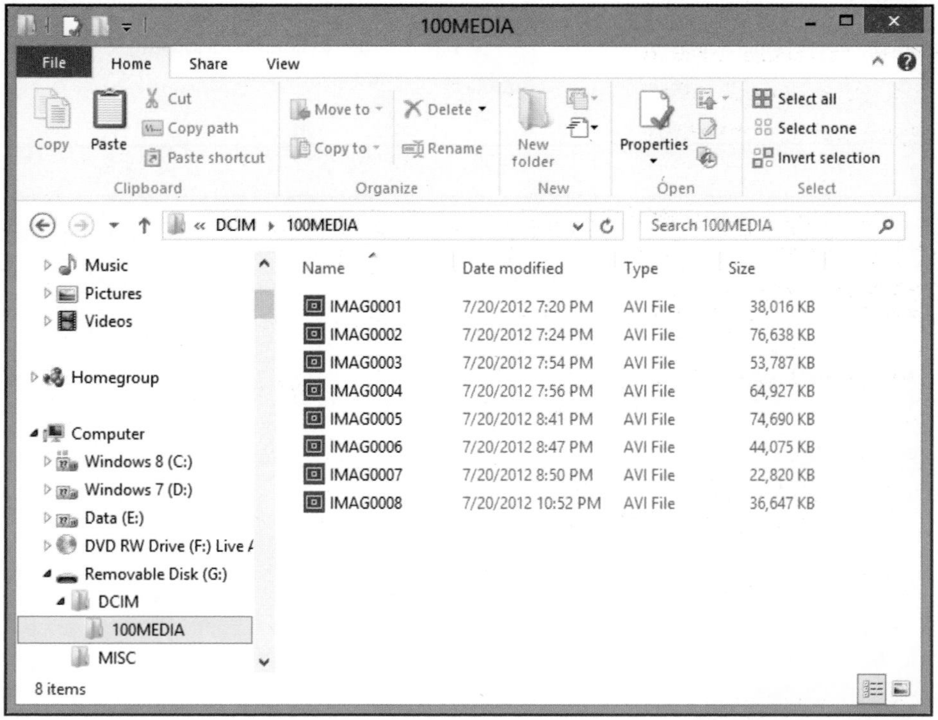

Figure 7-13: *Opening the folder to view the files gives you the greatest flexibility in storing your videos, but putting them in My Videos makes viewing them easier.*

4. To view your videos with Windows Media Player, in the Start screen, open the command bar and select **All Apps | Windows Media Player** under Windows Accessories. In the navigation pane, select **Videos** to display your files. Scroll down to find and select the one you want to play, as you can see in Figure 7-14. Double-select the file to play it in Media Player.

5. You can also use File Explorer to locate and play videos. On the desktop, select File Explorer, in the navigation pane open the drive and folders needed to locate your files, and double-select the file you want to play. The Video app will open and play the file.

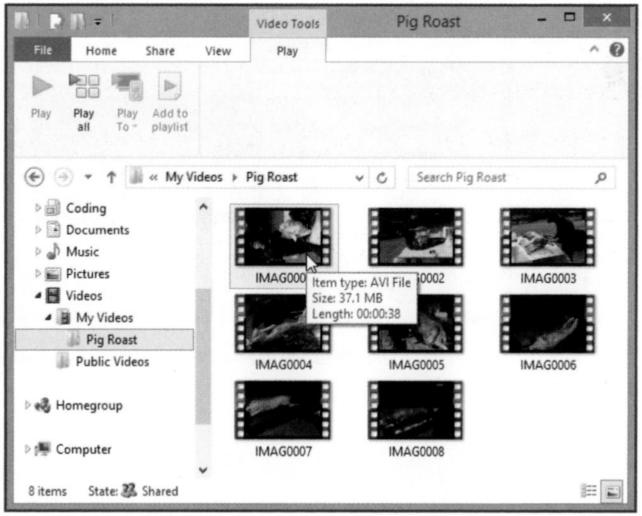

Note The File Explorer has a Video Tools Play contextual ribbon for playing videos and building a playlist of them.

 Tip The discussion about buying, organizing, and burning CDs applies equally to DVDs.

Figure 7-14: *The Windows Media Player gives you a better understanding than the Video app of where your files are located.*

Chapter 8

Controlling Security

Controlling computer security is a complex subject because of the many different aspects of computing that need protection. In this chapter you'll see how to control who uses a computer, control what users do, and protect data stored in the computer.

CONTROL WHO IS A USER

Controlling who uses a computer means identifying the users to the computer, giving them a secure way of signing on to the computer, and preventing everyone else from using it. This is achieved through the process of adding and managing users and passwords.

When you first use a new installation of Windows 8, on either a new computer or an upgrade of a prior Windows installation, you are asked to sign in with a Microsoft account such as Hotmail, Windows Live, or Xbox. If you do not have one of these accounts, you are encouraged to sign up for one of them, most likely Windows Live (live.com). I also encourage you to do that (see "Create a Microsoft Account" later in this chapter). Your email address and password for that account becomes your ID and password for Windows 8. You can sign in on any Windows 8 computer and many of your settings, preferences, and data will be synchronized across the computers.

Also in Windows 8, the first user of a computer is, by default, an administrator; however, the administrator operates like a standard user until there is a need to be an administrator. Then a Windows feature called *User Account Control* (UAC) pops up and asks if you want to allow a program to make changes to your computer. If so, select **Yes** to proceed.

A person who is not an administrator in the same circumstance would have to enter an administrator's password to continue.

> **Note** This book assumes that you are using a Microsoft account to sign on to Windows 8, which you can use across several computers on a local area network (LAN). If your computer is part of a domain (generally found in larger organizations—see Chapter 9 for a discussion of domains), you may be using domain user accounts. In that case you will need to work with your IT administrator to accomplish what is discussed here.

Set Up Users

If you have several people using your computer, each person should be set up as a separate user. To add users to your computer, or even to change your user characteristics (as well as to perform most other tasks in this chapter), you must be logged on as an administrator, so you first need to check on that. Then you may want to change the characteristics of your account, and, if you have multiple people using your computer, you may want to add user accounts and have each user sign in to his or her account.

Review Your PC Settings Account

Windows 8 has supplemented the Control Panel in several areas, including Users, with the PC Settings screen. Begin by looking at your information there and then review what is in Control Panel.

1. Open **Charms** and select **Settings | Change PC Settings** on the bottom right | **Users** on the left. Your account will appear in the PC Settings screen, as you can see in Figure 8-1.

2. If you would like an account and password that are independent of your Microsoft account and only valid on this computer, select **Switch To A Local Account**. Enter your current password with

which you signed in, select **Next**, use the existing user name or enter a new one, press **TAB**, enter and re-enter a password pressing **TAB** in between and at the end, and select **Next**. Make sure you've saved your work and select **Sign Out And Finish**. Your system will be restarted and you will need to sign back in with either your old account or your new one.

3. You can change your current password by selecting that option or, if you have a touch screen, create a picture password. In both cases you need to enter your current password and then either enter and re-enter a new password or select a picture and gesture for the picture password.

4. You can also create a four-digit PIN to use in place of your password by entering your current password, selecting **Next**, entering and confirming your PIN, and then selecting **Finish**.

5. If your computer is relatively safe when it is in Sleep mode, you can remove the requirement to enter a password or PIN when waking the computer after it has been put to sleep, but not when restarting it.

6. The Users screen also has the option to review and change the settings in your Microsoft account online. Select **More Account Settings Online**. Internet Explorer will open and ask for your password. Once you enter it, you can add to, change, and close your account by selecting the link, making the necessary changes, and selecting **OK**.

Review Your Settings in the Control Panel

The Control Panel provides additional user-related settings, but fewer than it did in previous versions of Windows. To open the User area of the Control Panel:

1. Open the **System** menu and select **Control Panel | User Accounts And Family Safety | User Accounts**. The User Accounts window opens.

PC settings

Personalize

Users

Notifications

Search

Share

General

Privacy

Devices

Wireless

Ease of Access

Sync your settings

HomeGroup

Your account

Marty Matthews

You can switch to a local account, but your settings won't sync between the PCs you use.

Switch to a local account

More account settings online

Sign-in options

Change your password

Create a picture password

Create a PIN

Any user who has a password must enter it when waking this PC.

Change

Other users

There are no other users on this PC.

+   Add a user

Figure 8-1: **Some but not all of the user settings are in the PC Settings Users screen, others are in the Control Panel's User Accounts.**

> **Note** As was mentioned in earlier chapters, this book assumes you are initially looking at the Control Panel's Category view.

2. You can see next to your picture the type of account you are using—"Administrator" in the previous illustration—and change it by selecting **Change Your Account Type** | a different type | **Change Account Type**.

3. Select **Change User Account Control Settings** to change when the User Account Control dialog box appears (see the following section). Move the slider up to have it appear more often; move it down to have it appear less.

4. Select the other options in the User Account window to familiarize yourself with them. Some of these will be discussed in later sections of this chapter.

Understand User Account Control

Windows 8 has a feature called User Account Control, or UAC. UAC monitors what is happening on the computer, and if it sees something that could cause a problem, like installing an app, adding a new user, or changing a password, it interrupts that process and asks for physical verification. It also freezes all activity on the computer so that nothing can happen until verification is provided. If the user has administrator privileges, he or she is asked if they want to allow changes to the computer and to confirm this action. If the user doesn't have administrator privileges, he or she is asked for the administrator's password. By requiring a physical action, UAC ensures that an actual person is sitting at the computer and that malware is not attempting to modify it.

All operations that require administrative privileges have a little shield icon beside them, as shown in earlier illustrations.

If you are installing several apps, the UAC dialog boxes can be irritating. You can turn it off in the User Accounts Control Panel, but this is strongly discouraged. If you do turn it off while you are installing several apps, it is strongly recommended that you turn it back on when you are finished.

Set Up Another User

To set up another user account:

1. Open **Charms** and select **Settings | Change PC Settings** on the bottom right | **Users** on the left. The User's account screen opens.

2. Select **Add A User** to open the Add A User panel, shown in Figure 8-2.

Other users

There are no other users on this PC.

╋ Add a user

Add a user

What email address would this person like to use to sign in to Windows? (If you know the email address they use to sign in to Microsoft services, enter it here.)

Email address

When you sign in to Windows with a Microsoft account, you can:
- Download apps from Windows Store.
- Get your online content in Microsoft apps automatically.
- Sync settings online to make PCs look and feel the same–this includes settings like browser favorites and history.

Privacy statement

Sign up for a new email address

Sign in without a Microsoft account

Next   Cancel

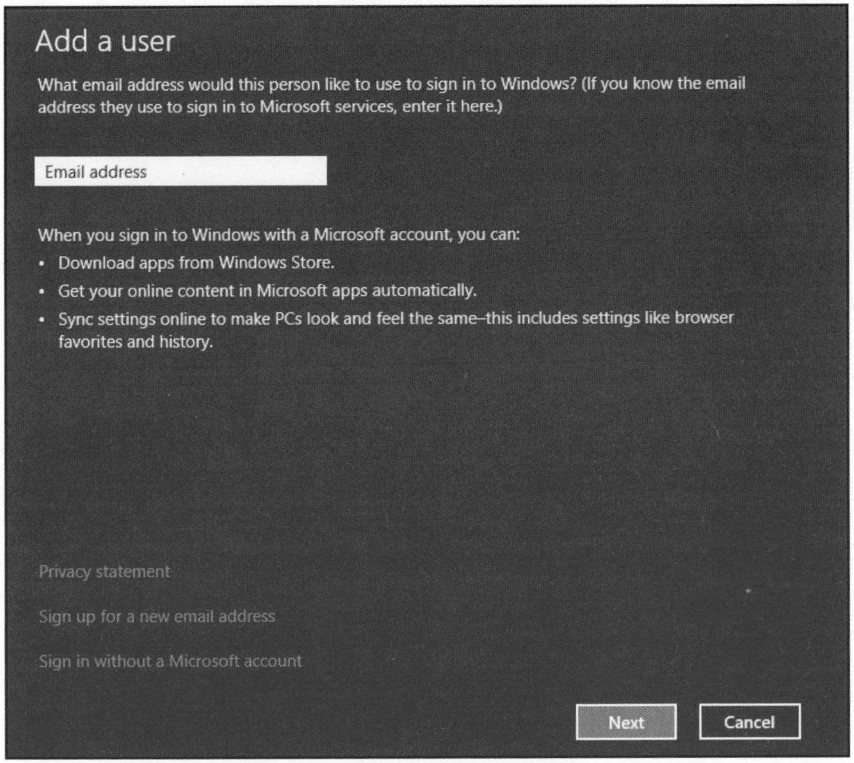

*Figure 8-2: **The Add A User panel starts the process of adding a new user.***

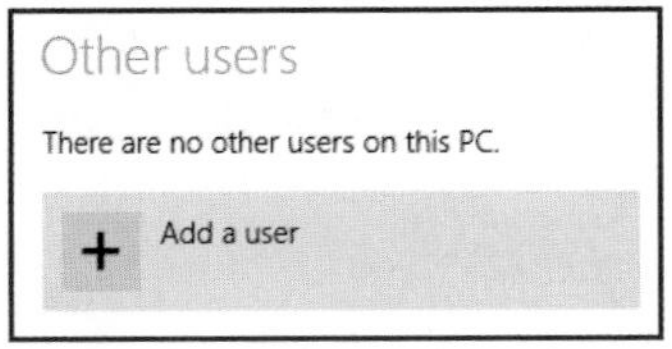

3. Type an email address for the new user tied to an account recognized by Microsoft. The email address can be with any Internet service provider (ISP), but it should be registered with one of the Microsoft services (live.com, Outlook.com, or Hotmail.com). If the new user does not have a Microsoft account, see "Create a Microsoft Account".

4. Select **Next | Finish**.

⊳⊳ Establish Passwords

Passwords are the primary keys used to allow some people to use a computer and to keep others away. In Windows 8, passwords originate in the Microsoft accounts used when setting up a new Windows 8 user, so the first step is to create a Microsoft account.

Create a Microsoft Account

While you can use Windows 8 without a Microsoft account (see the bottom option in the Add A User panel shown in Figure 8-2), you miss a lot if you do that. With a Microsoft account, you can sync your settings across several computers so when you go from computer to computer the look and feel will be the same. You can automatically get online content from Microsoft, and you can download free apps from the Microsoft Store without doing anything more than saying you want it. It is strongly recommended that new Windows 8 users get a Microsoft account. To create a Microsoft account and a password for Windows 8:

1. Follow the steps in "Set Up Another User" to open the Add A User pane. Select **Sign Up For A New Email Address** to open the sign-up panel.

2. Enter a name to be used as the first part of the email address, as you can see in Figure 8-3. Press **TAB** and select the Microsoft domain you want to use.

3. Press **TAB** and enter a password that is at least eight characters long and has any combination of at least two of the following: uppercase or lowercase letters, numbers, or symbols. For example, *seattle1962* works because it is over eight characters long and it has both lowercase letters and numbers. *Dogitdan* also works because it also has eight characters and both uppercase and lowercase letters. *12345678* does not work, although it is eight characters long, because it is just numbers.

4. Using **TAB** to go from field to field and **Next** to go from panel to panel, enter the requested information.

5. When you are told that your new user can now sign in to your computer, select the question if this is a child's account to turn on Family Safety (see "Set Up Family Safety" later in this chapter), and then select **Finish**.

Change a Password

When the new user signs on, they may want to set their own password. Also, it is a good idea to change a password periodically in case it has been compromised.

1. Open **Charms** and select **Settings | Change PC Settings | Users**. The User's account screen opens.

2. The first time a new user signs on to a computer they are asked if they want to trust the computer with their passwords and to sync with the other computers they use. If so, select **Trust This PC**.

3. Select **Change Your Password**, type the old password, type a new password, type it again to confirm it, and select **Next**.

Sign-in options
Change your password

Sign up for a new email address

You can use your Microsoft account to sign in to Xbox LIVE, Windows Phone, and other Microsoft services.

Email address: ruthie ✕ @ hotmail.com

New password

Reenter password

First name

Last name

Country/region: United States

ZIP code

Next   Cancel

*Figure 8-3: **Setting up a Microsoft account allows you to sync your settings over several computers.***

4. When you are told your password has changed, select **Finish**.

Tip You can see the actual characters in your password by selecting the icon on the right of the password text box.

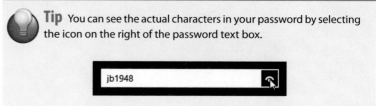
jb1948

Tip For a password to be *strong,* it must be eight or more characters long; use both upper- and lowercase letters; and use a mixture of letters, numbers, and symbols, which include ! # $ % ^ & * and spaces. It also should *not* be a recognizable word, name, or date. Instead of a password such as "mymoney23," consider using something like this: "my$Money23."

Cancel Using a Password

If you move a computer to a location that doesn't need a password—for example, if it is not accessible to anyone else, or if you want to cancel using a password for some other reason—you can do so, but only when you wake the computer from sleep. You will still need to use the password when you start the computer. To do this, you must be signed in as an administrator.

1. Open **Charms** and select **Settings | Change PC Settings | Users**. The User's account screen opens.

2. Select **Change** under Any User Who Has A Password Must Enter It When Waking This PC.

> Any user who has a password must enter it when waking this PC.
>
> Change

3. Read the warning that appears. If you want to go ahead, select **OK**. The message noted in step 2 changes to Any User Who Has A Password Doesn't Need To Enter It When Waking This PC.

> If you change this setting, anyone can wake this PC and access the currently signed-in account without entering a password. This affects all accounts on this PC and isn't recommended if you use your PC in a public place.
>
> OK

Remove a User Account

To remove a user account from a computer:

1. Open the **System** menu and select **Control Panel | User Accounts And Family Safety | Remove User Accounts**. The Manage Accounts window opens.

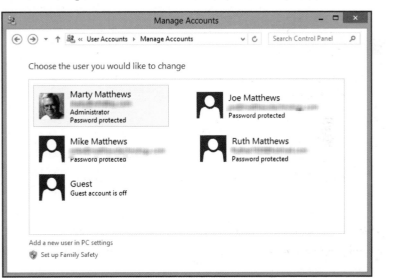

2. Select the account you want to remove | **Delete The Account**. Choose whether to delete the user's files or not, and select either **Delete Files** or **Keep Files**.

3. Confirm you really want to delete the account by selecting **Delete Account**. It takes a bit of time to do this. When it has finished, the Manage Accounts window will reopen.

4. Close the Manage Accounts window.

▷▷ Customize a User Account

Each user account can be unique, with a custom Start menu, desktop, color scheme, and screen saver. When apps are installed, you can choose whether they are for just the current user or for all users. When you set up a new user, it is as though you are setting up a new computer. The previous chapters of this book talk about the steps to set up a computer.

As you may have seen earlier in this chapter, a number of elements of the account itself can be changed, including the name, password, display picture, and account type. You can change the name and password in a manner almost identical to what you used to create them, as described in the "Set Up Users" and "Establish Passwords" sections earlier in this chapter.

CONTROL WHAT A USER DOES

User accounts identify people and allow them to log on to your computer. What they can do after that depends on the permissions they have. Windows 8 has two features that help you control what other users do on your computer: Family Safety and the ability to turn Windows features on and off for a given user. In addition, Windows 8's New Technology File System (NTFS) allows the sharing of folders and drives as well as the assignment of permissions to use a file, a folder, a disk, a printer, and other devices. The permissions are given to individuals and to groups to which individuals can belong. So far, you've seen two groups: Administrators and Standard Users (also called just "Users"), but there are others, and you can create more.

You can limit the sharing of files and folders to the *Public folder* within the Users folder on your computer. To do so, you must create or move the files and folders you want to share into the Public folder. The other option is to share directly the other folders on your computer. This is made easier by the *inheritance* attribute, where subfolders automatically inherit (take on) the permissions of their parent folder. Every object in Windows 8 NTFS, however, has its own set of *security descriptors* that are attached to it when it is created; with the proper permission, these security descriptors can be individually changed. When permissions are appropriately set, other users on your computer can access and optionally change your files and folders.

CAUTION! File sharing can be a valuable and useful capability, but it can also open up your computer to significant harm. It is important to think through what your needs are and how you want to do the file sharing to get the value without the harm.

 ## Set Up Family Safety

If you have a child or grandchild as one of the users on your computer and you are an administrator with a password, you can control what your child can do on your computer, including hours of usage, apps he or she can run, and access to the Internet. When your child encounters a blocked app, game, or website, a notice is displayed, including a link the child can select to request access. You, as an administrator, can allow one-time access by entering your user ID and password.

 Note A child for whom you want to set up Family Safety must have a Standard User account. To set up Family Safety, you must have an Administrator account with a password.

Note For Family Safety to work, the disk drives on which you want to control the use of games must use the NTFS file system. Family Safety will not work with the older File Allocation Table (FAT) file system. While you are installing Family Safety, if a drive with the FAT file system is detected, you will be told this. You can go ahead and install Family Safety, but content on the FAT drive will not be controlled.

1. Open the **System** menu and select **Control Panel | Set Up Family Safety**.

2. Select the user for whom you want to set up Family Safety to open the individual User Controls window.

3. Select **On** under Family Safety, as shown in Figure 8-4.

4. Select **Time Limits | Set Time Allowance | Can Only Use The PC For The Amount Of Time I Allow | Weekdays Hours And Minutes |**

Figure 8-4: *Family Safety allows you to determine what a child can do and see on your computer.*

Weekend Hours And Minutes. If you want to set the time allowed by individual day of the week, select the down arrow on the left of Weekdays and Weekend.

5. Select **Curfew | Can Only Use The PC During The Time Ranges I Allow**. Drag across the hours to block or allow (you can drag across multiple hours and days), as you can see in Figure 8-5.

6. Select **User Settings | Windows Store And Game Restriction | Can Only Use Games And Windows Store Apps I Allow | Set Game And Windows Store Ratings**. The game rating selection will open.

7. Choose whether to block games with no ratings and then select the highest level rating that is allowed.

8. Select **Allow Or Block Games |** whether to block or allow specific games installed on the computer.

9. Select **User Settings | App Restrictions | Can Only Use The Apps I Allow**. A list of all the apps on the computer is presented. Select those for which you want to allow access.

10. Select **User Settings | Web Filtering | Can Only Use The Websites I Allow | Set Web Filtering Level**. A list of web restriction levels is presented. Select the highest level you want to allow and whether to block file downloads.

11. Select **Allow Or Block Websites**. Enter websites and select **Allow** or **Block**. Repeat this for all the sites you want to allow or block.

12. Close the Allow Or Block Websites window.

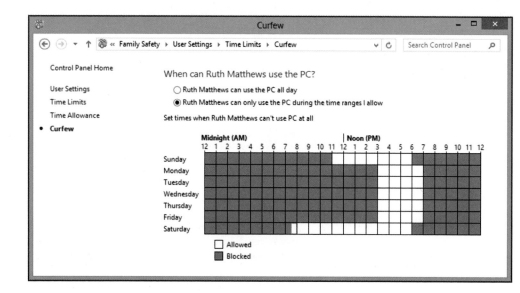

*Figure 8-5: **Family Safety allows you to tightly control your children or grandchildren's computer usage.***

Control What Parts of Windows Can Be Used

As an administrator, you can control what parts of Windows 8 each user can access.

1. Log on as the user for whom you want to set Windows feature usage.

2. Open the **System** menu and select **Control Panel | Programs | Programs And Features**.

3. Select **Turn Windows Features On Or Off** in the left column. If needed, type a password and select **Yes**. The Windows Features dialog box appears.

4. Select an unselected check box to turn a feature on, or select a selected check box to turn a feature off. Select the plus sign (+) where applicable to open subfeatures and turn them on or off.

5. When you have selected the features the user will be allowed to use, select **OK**.

6. Close the Programs And Features window.

Set File and Folder Sharing

Files are shared by being in a shared folder or drive. Folders and drives are shared by their creator or owner or by an administrator. To share folders and drives, as well as printers and other devices, both locally and over a network, you must address three components of Windows 8 that allow you to control access to your computer and its components (see Figure 8-6):

- **The Windows Firewall**, which protects your computer and its contents from network access

- **The Network And Sharing Center**, which is the primary means of controlling sharing in Windows

- **Sharing individual drives and folders**, which lets you determine if a drive, folder, or other device is shared; who has permission to access it; and what they can do with the contents

Set Up the Windows Firewall

Windows 8 includes the Windows Firewall, whose objective is to slow down and hopefully prevent anybody from accessing your computer without your permission, while at the same time allowing those who you want to use your computer to do so. The Windows Firewall is turned on by default. Check to see if it is; if it isn't, turn it on.

1. Open the **System** menu and select **Control Panel | System And Security | Windows Firewall**. The Windows Firewall window opens and shows your firewall status.

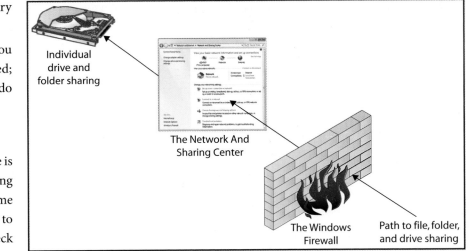

Individual drive and folder sharing

The Network And Sharing Center

The Windows Firewall

Path to file, folder, and drive sharing

*Figure 8-6: **Sharing your computer requires that you set up your firewall, the Network And Sharing Center, and the individual drives and folders to accomplish that.***

2. If your firewall is not turned on, or if you want to turn it off, select **Turn Windows Firewall On Or Off** in the pane on the left. If needed, type a password and select **Yes**. The Windows Firewall Customize Settings window opens. Select the respective option button to turn on your firewall (highly recommended) or to turn it off (not recommended). You can do this for both your local network and for a public network to which you may be connected. Select **OK**.

3. To change the settings for what the firewall will and won't let through, select **Allow An App Or Feature Through Windows Firewall** at the top of the left column. The Allowed Apps window opens, shown in Figure 8-7.

Windows Firewall

Control Panel ▶ System and Security ▶ Windows Firewall

Search Control Panel

Control Panel Home

Allow an app or feature through Windows Firewall

Change notification settings

Turn Windows Firewall on or off

Restore defaults

Advanced settings

Troubleshoot my network

See also

Action Center

Network and Sharing Center

Help protect your PC with Windows Firewall

Windows Firewall can help prevent hackers or malicious software from gaining access to your PC through the Internet or a network.

Private networks — Connected

Networks at home or work where you know and trust the people and devices on the network

Windows Firewall state: On

Incoming connections: Block all connections to apps that are not on the list of allowed apps

Active private networks: Matthews

Notification state: Notify me when Windows Firewall blocks a new app

Guest or public networks — Not connected

4. In the Allowed Apps And Features list, select the services running on your computer that you want to allow sites on the Internet to use. To share information across a LAN, select the following items:

- Core Networking (set by default)

- File And Printer Sharing (set by default)

- HomeGroup (set by default)

- Network Discovery (set by default)

- Windows Collaboration Computer Name Registration Service (optional, not set by default)

- Windows Peer To Peer Collaboration Foundation (optional, not set by default)

Tip In the Windows Firewall Allowed Apps window, you can determine what each option does by highlighting it and selecting **Details** at the bottom of the dialog box.

Note You will probably have other apps selected, such as Internet Explorer and Windows Live Messenger, that can be used on the Internet.

5. Select each app or feature you want to allow through the firewall. Select **OK** to close the Windows Firewall Allowed Apps window, and then select **Close** to close the Windows Firewall Control Panel.

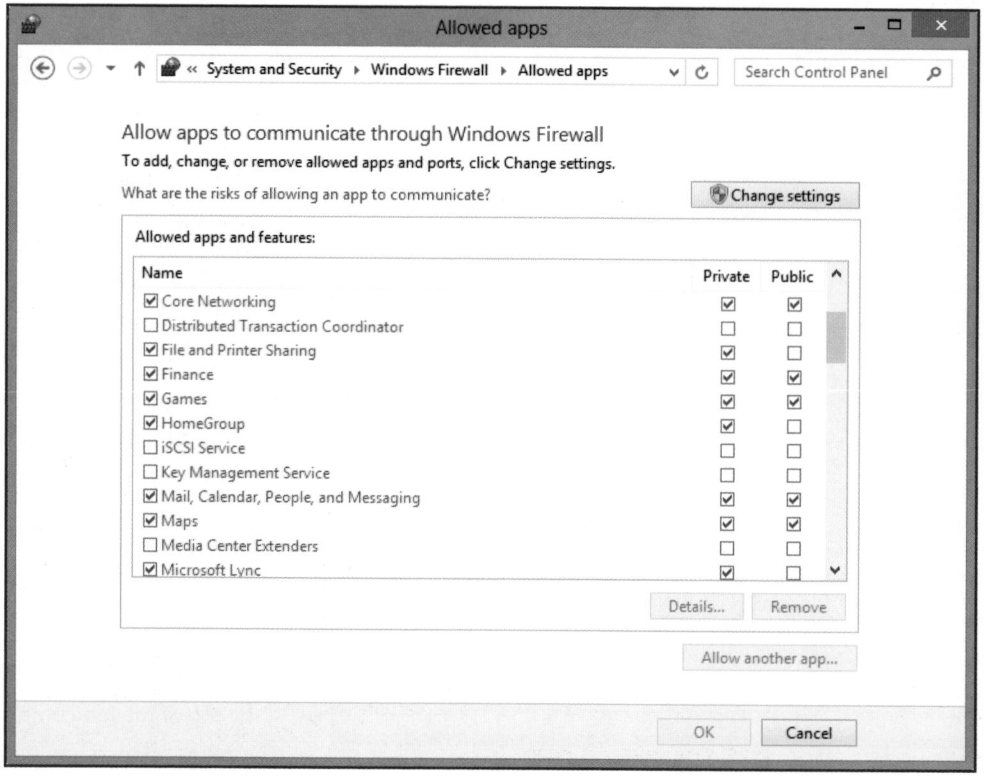

*Figure 8-7: **The Windows 8 Firewall can be configured to allow certain apps and features to come through.***

Tip If you have a specific app not on the Windows Firewall Allowed Apps And Features list, you can include that app by selecting **Allow Another App** at the bottom of the Windows Firewall Allowed Apps window. Select the app from the list or browse to its location | **Add**.

Use the Network And Sharing Center

The second layer of file-sharing protection in Windows 8 is controlled with the Network And Sharing Center, shown in Figure 8-8, which allows you to turn on or off the primary components of sharing information among users on a computer and across a network.

When Windows was initially set up, a choice was made between a public and private network. The Network And Sharing Center allows you to change that. If you are primarily sharing your computer with other computers within an organization or a residence, you should select Private Network, where network sharing is relatively simple. If you are primarily using public wireless or cable Internet connections and very little sharing of your computer, select Public, which makes it more difficult for someone to get into your computer.

1. Open the **System** menu and select **Control Panel | Network And Internet | Network And Sharing Center**. The Network And Sharing Center window opens, as shown in Figure 8-8.

2. If you want to change the type of network (private or public) you are connected to and the settings within each, select **Change Advanced Sharing Settings**. The Advanced Sharing Settings window will open.

3. Review the settings that are shown. In a private network, you probably want and will have already set the following:

   - Turn On Network Discovery
   - Turn On Automatic Setup Of Network Connected Devices
   - Turn On File And Printer Sharing
   - Allow Windows To Manage HomeGroup Connections (With A Home Network)

   For a public network, you probably want the opposite settings.

4. Make any changes that you feel you need, and then, if you made changes, select **Save Changes**. If needed, enter the password and select **Yes**. Otherwise, select **Cancel**.

5. When you have finished with the Network And Sharing Center, select **Close**.

Use HomeGroup Library Folder Sharing

The final layer of sharing settings is the determination of the disks and folders you want to share. Windows 8's HomeGroup makes sharing files and folders within the homegroup much easier. When Windows 8 is first installed or started, you are asked if you want to set up or

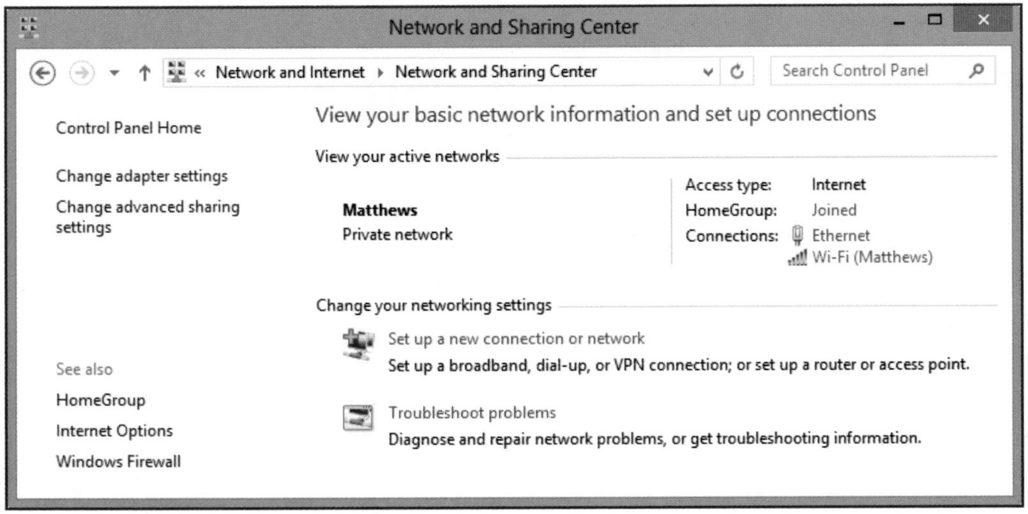

*Figure 8-8: **The Network And Sharing Center is the primary means of sharing your computer.***

join a homegroup, depending on whether a homegroup already exists on your network. By default, your pictures, music, printers, videos, and documents are shared for anyone in the homegroup to read, view, and change. You can make these changes at the library level or at the disk and folder level. To do this at the library level:

> **Note** A *homegroup* is a group of networking computer users who want to easily share information and resources on their computers. Such a group can be in a residence or in a smaller organization. Only Windows 7 (original Windows 7 or SP1) or Windows 8 computers can join a homegroup.

1. Open the **System** menu and select **Control Panel | Network And Internet | HomeGroup**. The HomeGroup window opens.

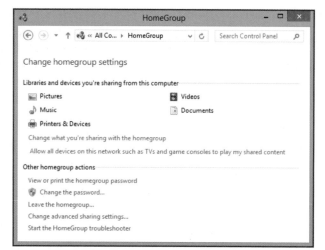

2. Select **Change What You're Sharing With The Homegroup**. The Change Homegroup Sharing Settings will open. Make any changes that you feel you need, and then, if you made changes, select **Save Changes**. If needed, enter the password and select **Yes**. Otherwise, select **Cancel**.

Use HomeGroup Extended Sharing

You can go beyond the sharing of libraries and share devices such as TVs and game consoles.

1. In the HomeGroup window, opened in the previous section, select **Allow All Devices On This Network** to open the Media Streaming Options window.

2. Enter a name for your library, select the devices you want to share with | **Next**.

3. Close the HomeGroup window.

Share Standard Folders with Specific People

Standard folders are shared differently than disk drives and the Users folders, but are similar to sharing libraries, where you can share them with specific people. To share standard folders with specific people:

1. Open the **System** menu and select **File Explorer**. In the folders pane on the left, open the disk and folders necessary to see in the right pane the folder you want to share.

2. Open the context menu for the folder and select **Share With**. The file-sharing menu will appear.

3. Select **Specific People** to open the File Sharing dialog box. This shows you the current sharing of the folder.

4. Select the down arrow on the right of the top text box to open a list of users and groups known to your computer. Select the user or group you want to give permission to use this disk or folder, possibly the Everyone group, and select **Add**. The user or group is added to the list in the lower part of the dialog box with the minimal permission level of Read.

5. Select the **Permission Level** down arrow for your new user or group to open the alternative permission levels. Select the level you want for the addition:

   - **Read** allows the user to view the files in the shared folder.

   - **Read/Write** allows the user to view, add, change, and delete any of the files in the shared folder.

Name	Permission Level
Everyone	Read ▼ ✔ Read
Marty Matthews	Owner Read/Write
	Remove

6. Select **Share** and, if needed, type a password and select **Yes**. Select **Done** to complete the process.

> **Note** When you share a folder, all folders and files within it are given the same sharing status due to inheritance. If that is not what you want for a particular folder, you must individually change the sharing status of the folders within it.

Share Drives and Special Folders

Disk drives and special folders—like the Users, Program Files, and Windows folders—have a more detailed sharing process.

1. Open the **System** menu and select **File Explorer**. In the folders pane on the left, open the disk and folders necessary to see in the right pane the drive or folder you want to share.

2. Open the context menu for the drive or folder you want to share, select **Share With | Advanced Sharing**. The Properties dialog box will appear with the Sharing tab displayed, as shown in Figure 8-9.

3. Select **Advanced Sharing** and, if needed, type a password and select **Yes**.

4. Select **Share This Folder**, change the share name if desired, and select **Permissions**.

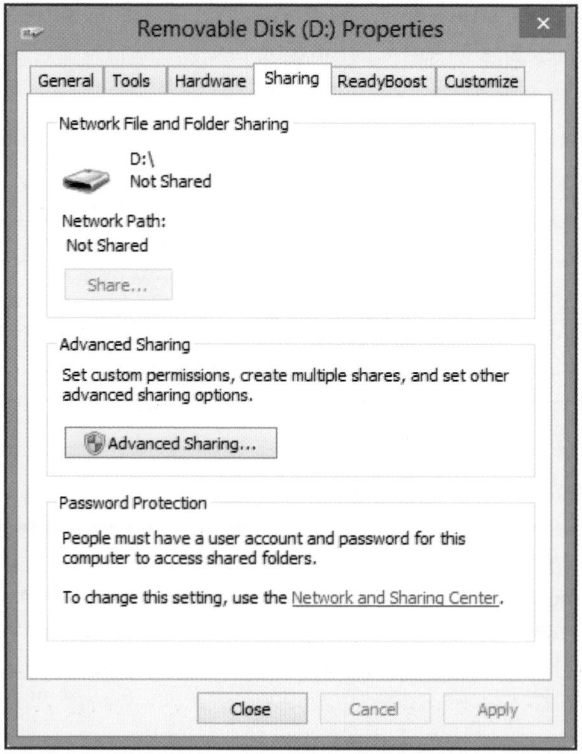

Figure 8-9: *Drives and special folders use a different sharing procedure.*

- **Full Control** allows the user or group to read, change, or delete a file or folder.

5. Select a listed user or group; or, if the one you want is not listed, select **Add** | **Advanced** | **Find Now**, double-select a user or group, and select **OK**.

6. With the user or group selected, select the permission level you want for that entity. The levels of permission are as follows:

   - **Read** allows the user or group to read but not change or delete a file or folder.

   - **Change** allows the user or group to read and change but not delete a file or folder.

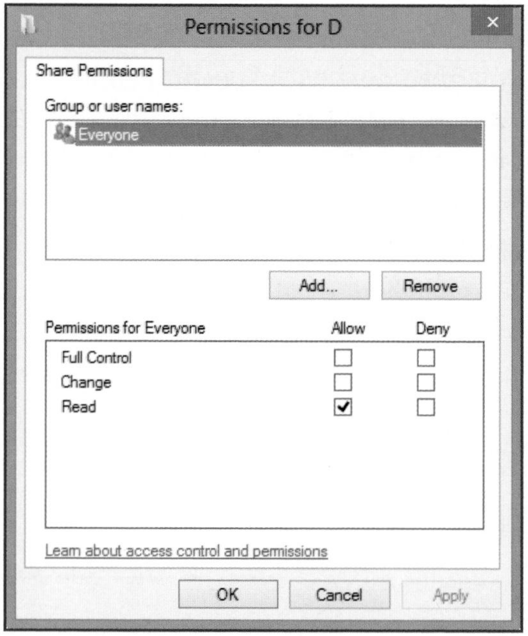

7. Select **OK** twice and close the Properties dialog box and File Explorer.

Use and Add Groups

Groups, or *group accounts,* are collections of user accounts that can have permissions, such as file sharing, granted to them. Most permissions are granted to groups, not individuals, and then individuals are assigned to groups. You need a set of groups that handles both the mix of people and the mix of permissions that you want to establish. A number of standard groups with pre-assigned permissions are built into Windows 8, but you can create your own groups, and you can assign users to any of these.

Open Existing Groups

You can open existing groups and see what permissions they contain.

1. Open the **System menu** and select **Control Panel | System And Security | Administrative Tools**.

2. In the right pane, open **Computer Management**. If needed, type a password and select **Yes**.

3. In the left pane, if it is not already open, select the triangle opposite **System Tools** to open it, select the triangle opposite **Local Users And Groups** to open that, and **select Groups**. The list of built-in groups is displayed, as shown in Figure 8-10.

4. Open a few groups to open the Properties dialog box for each and see the members they contain.

 Note "Standard Users" are called just "Users" in the list of groups.

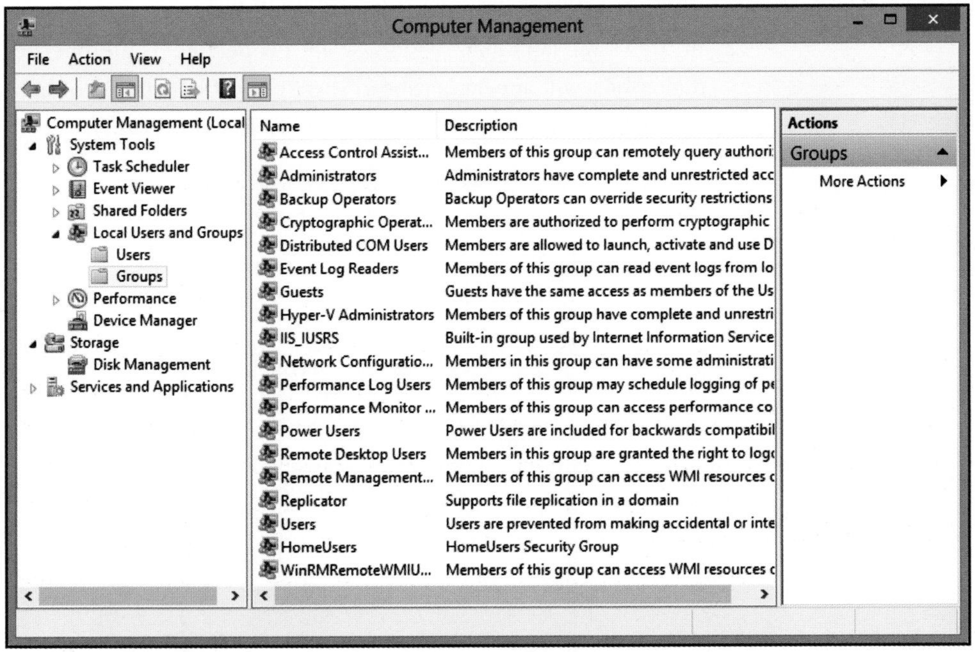

Add Users to Groups

1. Open the context menu for a group to which you want to add a user, and select **Add To Group | Add**. The Select Users dialog box will appear.

2. Either type a name in the text box and select **Check Names**, or select **Advanced | Find Now**. A list of users on that computer will be displayed. Select the user that you want to add (hold down **CTRL** to select several), and select **OK**.

3. When you are done, select **OK** twice.

Add a Group

1. In the Computer Management window, in the list of groups in the middle (subject) pane, open the context menu in a white area so that no group is selected, and then select **New Group**. The New Group dialog box appears.

2. Enter a group name. It cannot contain just numbers, periods, or spaces; it can't contain " / \ [ ] : ; | = ,+ * ? < >; and leading spaces or periods are dropped.

3. Enter the description of what the group can uniquely do, and select **Add**. Then follow the instructions in "Add Users to Groups" except for selecting OK the final time in step 3.

4. When your group is the way you want it (see Figure 8-11), select **Create** and then select **Close**. The new group will appear in the list in the middle of the Computer Management window. Close the Computer Management window.

*Figure 8-10: **There are a number of built-in groups to which users can be assigned.***

Figure 8-11: *Creating your own group lets you give it your own set of permissions.*

Understand Permissions

Permissions authorize a user or a group to perform some function on an object, such as files, folders, disks, and printers. Objects have sets of permissions associated with them that can be assigned to users and groups. The specific permissions depend on the object, but all objects have at least two permissions: Read and either Modify or Change. Permissions are initially set in one of three ways:

- The app or process that creates an object can set its permissions upon creation.

- If the object allows the inheritance of permissions and they were not set upon creation, a parent object can propagate permissions to the object. For example, a parent folder can propagate its permissions to a subfolder that it contains.

- If neither the creator nor the parent sets the permissions for an object, the Windows 8 system default settings will do it.

Once an object is created, its permissions can be changed by its owner, an administrator, or anyone else who has been given authority to do this.

PROTECT STORED DATA

Protecting stored data is another layer of protection. It works to make unusable whatever is found on the computer by someone who managed to break through the other layers of protection.

▷▷ Protect Files and Folders

You can protect files and folders by hiding them and encrypting them. The easiest way is to hide them. Start by opening the Properties dialog box for the file or folder.

1. On the desktop, select the **File Explorer** icon on the toolbar. In the navigation pane, open the disk and folders necessary to locate in the right pane the file or folder you want to protect.

2. In the Home tab Open section, select **Properties**. The Properties dialog box will appear, as shown here for a file (there are slight differences among file and folder Properties dialog boxes).

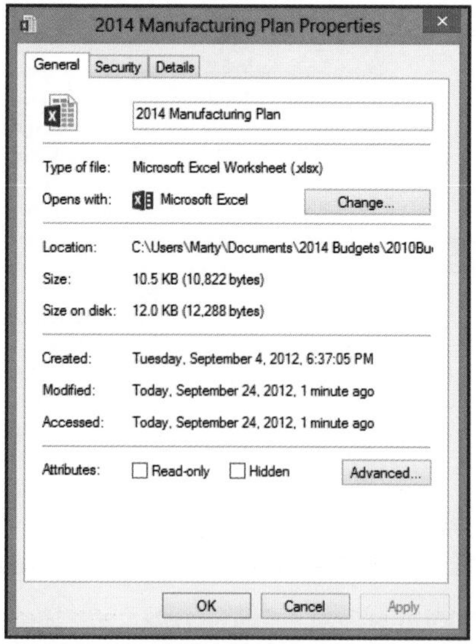

Hide Files and Folders

Hiding files and folders lets you prevent them from being displayed by File Explorer. This assumes the person from whom you want to hide them does not know how to display hidden files or how to turn off the hidden attribute. To hide a file or folder, you must both turn on its hidden attribute and turn off the Display Hidden Files feature.

1. In the file or folder Properties dialog box, on the General tab, select **Hidden | OK**. If needed, type a password and select **Yes** (the

object's icon becomes dimmed or disappears). Select **OK** to close the Properties dialog box.

–Or–

In the File Explorer window, select the **View** tab | **Hide Selected Items**, as you can see in Figure 8-12.

2. In the File Explorer window, select the **View** tab | **Options** | **Change Folder And Search Options** | the **View** tab | **Don't Show Hidden Files, Folders, Or Drives**. Select **OK** to close the Folder Options

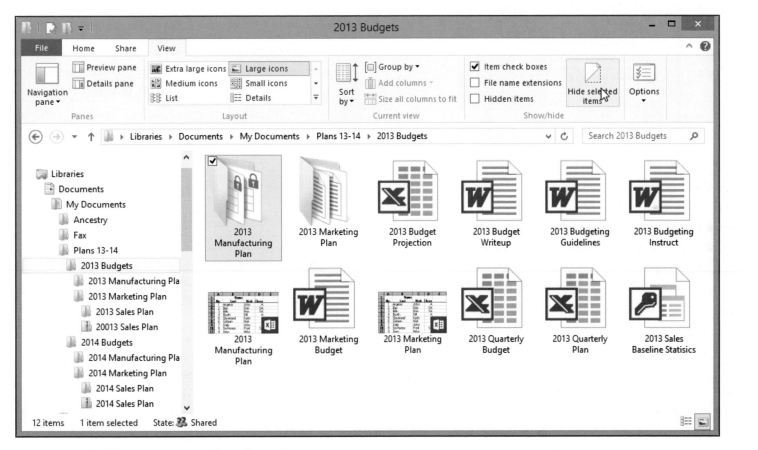

*Figure 8-12: **Hiding files is not a very secure form of protection.***

dialog box. Close and reopen the parent folder, and the file or folder you hid will disappear.

–Or–

In the File Explorer window, select the **View** tab | **Hidden Items** to unselect (uncheck) it.

Note If you hide a folder you will get a message asking if you want to hide only the folder or additionally its contents.

3. To restore hidden files and/or folders to view, in the File Explorer **View** tab select **Hidden Items** to check it.

Encrypt Files and Folders

File and folder encryption, called the *Encrypting File System (EFS),* is built into Windows 8 using NTFS. Once EFS is turned on for a file or a folder, only the person who encrypted the file or folder will be able to read it. However, you can back up the encryption key and use that to access the file or folder. For the person who encrypted the file, accessing it requires no additional steps, and the file is re-encrypted every time it is saved.

To encrypt a file or folder from File Explorer, starting with files:

1. On the desktop, select the **File Explorer** icon on the toolbar. In the navigation pane, open the disk and folders necessary to locate in the right pane the file or folder you want to encrypt.

2. In the Home tab Open section, select **Properties** | **Advanced**. The Advanced Attributes dialog box appears.

3. Select **Encrypt Contents To Secure Data** | **OK** twice.

4. If you are encrypting a file, you will see an encryption warning that the file is not in an encrypted folder, which means that when you edit the file, temporary or backup files might be created that are not encrypted. Choose whether to encrypt only the file or to encrypt both the file and its parent folder, and then select **OK**. The filename will turn green.

Encryption Warning [×]

⚠ You are encrypting a file that is in an unencrypted folder. If this file is modified, the editing software might store a temporary, unencrypted, copy of the file. To ensure that files created in the parent folder are encrypted, encrypt the parent folder.

What do you want to do?

◉ Encrypt the file and its parent folder (recommended)
○ Encrypt the file only

☐ Always encrypt only the file   [OK]   [Cancel]

5. If you are encrypting a folder, the Confirm Attribute Changes dialog box that you saw earlier appears, asking if you want to apply the encryption to this folder only or to both the folder and its contents. If you select **This Folder Only**, *existing* files and folders in the folder will *not* be encrypted, while files and folders later created in or copied to the encrypted folder will be. If you select **This Folder, Subfolders, And Files**, all files and folders will be encrypted. Choose the setting that is correct for you, and select **OK**. If needed, type a password and select **Yes**.

6. Restart your computer, and log on as another user. Select **Start | Computer**, and open the drive and folders necessary to display in the right pane the file or folder you encrypted. You can see that the file exists, but when you try to open it, edit it, print it, or move it, you will get a message that access is denied.

7. To decrypt a file or folder, log on as yourself (given you're the person who encrypted it), reopen the file or folder Properties dialog box, select **Advanced**, deselect **Encrypt Contents To Secure Data**, and select **OK** twice (three times with folders).

 Tip Because many apps save temporary and secondary files during normal execution, it is recommended that folders rather than files be the encrypting container. If an app is then told to store all files in that folder, where all files are automatically encrypted upon saving, security is improved.

CAUTION! If you encrypt a shared folder and select This Folder, Subfolders, And Files, any files or subfolders belonging to others will be encrypted with your key and the owners will not be able to use what they created.

Back Up Your Encryption Key

If you use file encryption, it is important to back up your file encryption key so that you do not lose the information you have, and you may be reminded of this. It is also important, of course, to keep the media that you back up on safe so that it can't be used. The key is part of a digital certificate, so this section refers to backing up the certificate.

1. Open the **System** menu and select **Control Panel | User Accounts And Family Safety | User Accounts**. Your User Account window opens.

2. Select **Manage Your File Encryption Certificates** in the left column. If needed, type a password and select **Yes** to open the Encrypting File System dialog box.

3. Read about what you can do with this wizard, and select **Next**. By default, a certificate was automatically created when Windows was installed—that certificate or a more recent one will appear in the Certificate Details area, as shown in Figure 8-13. Select **Next**.

Encrypting File System

Select or create a file encryption certificate

Select an existing file encryption certificate or create a new one. If you have already encrypted files, you can update them to use this certificate.

◉ Use this certificate
If you are using a smart card, select the certificate on the smart card.

Certificate details:

Issued to: Marty
Issued by: Marty
Expires: 8/15/2112

[View certificate]
[Select certificate]

○ Create a new certificate

Why do I need a certificate for file encryption?

[Next] [Cancel]

*Figure 8-13: **A security certificate is required to use file encryption.***

4. Select **Browse** and navigate to the removable disk and folder you want to hold the certificate (it is not recommended to save the key on the same machine where the encryption is located). Type a filename and select **Save**.

5. Type a password and confirm it, and then select **Next**. Select **All Logical Drives** or select the plus sign and then select the individual drives and/or the folders with encrypted files that you want the new certificate and key applied to, and select **Next**. Your files will be updated with the new key.

6. When you are told the files have been updated and where the key is stored, select **Close** and close the User Accounts window.

7. Store the removable disc or USB flash drive in a safe place.

Tip To use a backed-up encryption key, insert the removable media with the key, open the drive in File Explorer, and browse to and open the file with the key. In the Certificate Import Wizard that opens, select **Next**, confirm that you have the right file, and select **Next**. Type the password used to back up the key, select how you want to use the key | **Next**. Select the certificate store you want, and then select **Next** | **Finish**.

▷▷ Use Encrypted Files and Folders

If you are the person who encrypted a file or folder and you log on as yourself, you can use the file or folder exactly as you would if it hadn't been encrypted. The only way you know the files or folders are encrypted is that File Explorer shows them in green, as shown in Figure 8-14. If you log on as someone else, or if someone else logs on as anyone other than you, they will not be able to use the files or folders. Copying and moving encrypted files and folders, however, has a special set of rules:

- If you copy or move a file or folder into an encrypted folder, the item copied or moved will be encrypted.

- If you copy or move a file or folder to an unencrypted folder, the item moved remains as it was prior to being moved. If it was unencrypted, it remains so. If it was encrypted, it is still encrypted after being moved.

- Someone other than the owner who tries to copy or move encrypted files or folders to a different computer sees an error message that access is denied.

- If the owner copies or moves an encrypted file or folder to another file system, such as Windows NT 4 NTFS or Windows 98 FAT32, the encryption is removed, but a warning message is generated before the copy or move is complete.

- Backing up encrypted files or folders with Windows 8 File History leaves the items encrypted.

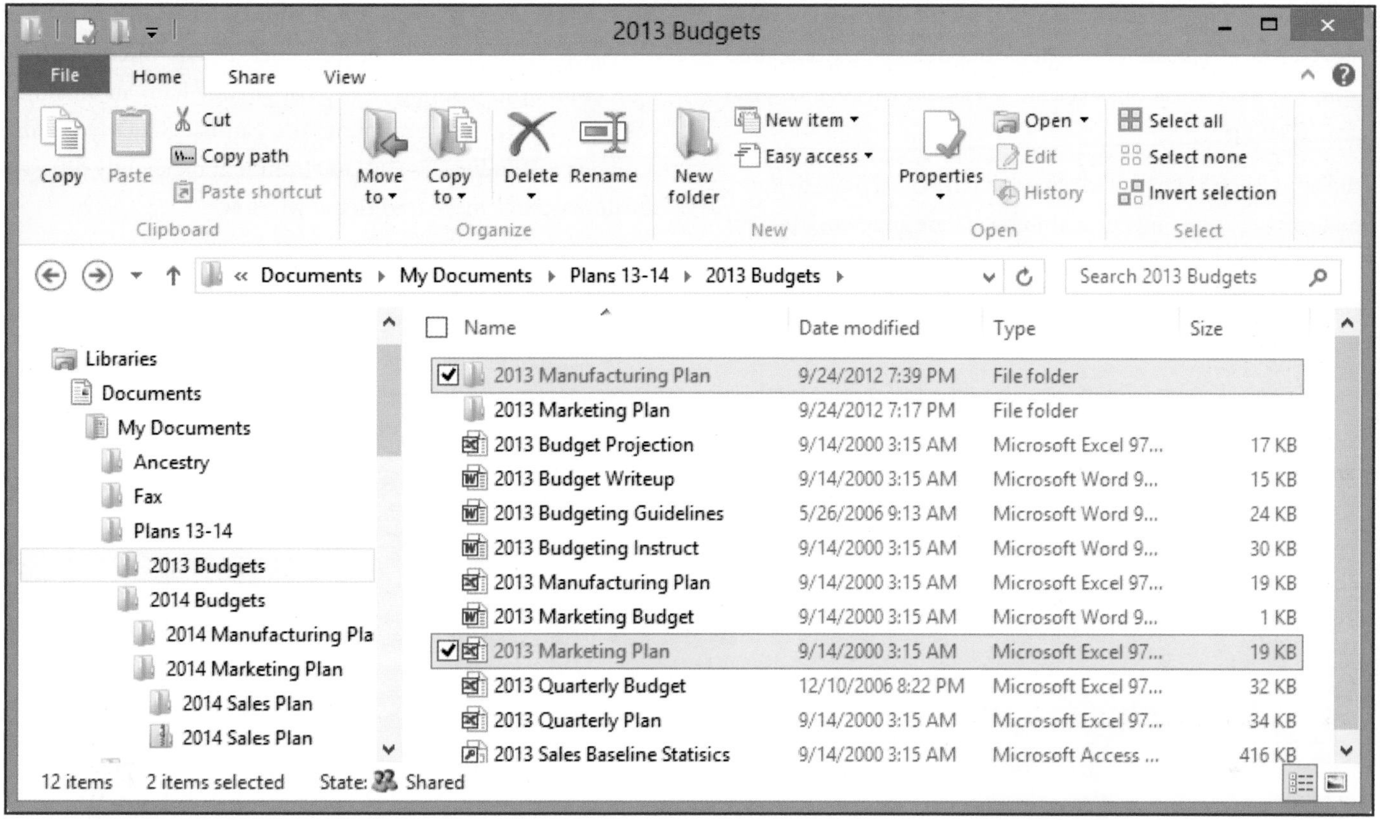

*Figure 8-14: **File Explorer shows the information for encrypted files in green.***

Back Up Your Information

Computers are a great asset, but like any machine, they are prone to failures of many kinds. Once you have started using your computer regularly, it becomes important to make a copy of your information and store it in another location should your hard drive fail or something else happen to your computer.

There are several solutions to copying and saving your information. The term normally used for this is *backup* (or to back up—the verb form).

This means storing a copy of your information in a location other than on your computer. You can back up both on your computer and on the Internet. In Chapter 3 we discussed using Windows 8's File History app to automatically back up files and folders on your computer as well copying files and folders to CDs and DVDs. Here we will look at backing up on the Internet.

Back Up to the Internet

Recently, many people are choosing to save their information to the *cloud,* meaning that they back up the data on their computer to a location (a server) accessed through the Internet. This method makes it easy to access your data from any location, as well as your new computer, should your old computer fail. These services are reasonable in cost, or even free, and easy to set up.

Some backup apps, such as Dropbox, once you have subscribed to them, install a small software app on your computer. These apps work behind the scenes, copying new photos, data files, deposits, or letters to a secure, encrypted location. Should your old computer break down, you can restore your files and data to your new computer.

Some personal financial management apps also offer this service for their data. For example, Quicken's Online Backup service charges a nominal fee per month to protect your financial information.

An example of a currently free cloud service is Microsoft's SkyDrive. Microsoft gives you 7GB of free storage. The Microsoft account you signed up for to use Windows 8 (or already had) automatically signed you up for a SkyDrive account. You can use SkyDrive from the Start screen in a Windows 8–style environment or, slightly differently, from the desktop in a more traditional window.

Use SkyDrive from the Start Screen

1. On the Start screen select the **SkyDrive** tile to open the Windows 8–style SkyDrive screen, and open the command bar, as shown in Figure 8-15.

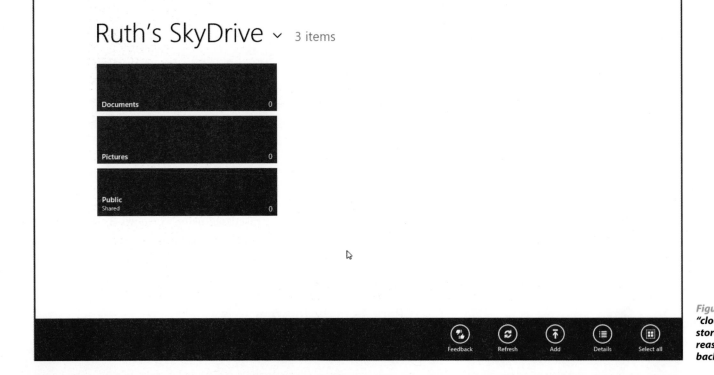

Figure 8-15: **Online "cloud" Internet storage is a good and reasonably safe way to back up important files.**

2. Open a folder you want to use, and then select **Upload** in the command bar. If you see the folder on your computer with the files you want to move to SkyDrive, select it. Otherwise, select **Go Up** until you see the folder you want or its parent and select that folder. Select additional folders as needed until you see the files you want.

3. Select the individual files or select **Select All | Add To SkyDrive** as you see in Figure 8-16. When the files have been added, they will appear in the SkyDrive folder you selected.

4. To work with the files on SkyDrive, select the file or files you want to work with and open the command bar and

   ■ Select **Clear** to clear the selection of the items.

   ■ Select **Manage | Delete** to delete the items.

*Figure 8-16: **Moving files to SkyDrive is as easy as moving them to another folder on your hard drive.***

- Select **Save Local**, select the folder you want to save the items in | **Choose This Folder** | **OK**. The files will saved in the selected folder in addition to being left on SkyDrive.

5. When you have done all you want to do in SkyDrive, close it.

Use SkyDrive from the Desktop

1. Select the **Internet Explorer** icon on the taskbar to open it. In the address bar, type skydrive. com and press **ENTER**. Assuming you have signed on to Windows with your Microsoft account, your SkyDrive page will open, where you can use existing folders or set up your own, as you can see in Figure 8-17.

2. Select a SkyDrive folder you want to use to open it, and then select **Upload**. A File Explorer window will open titled "Choose File To Upload." Use the navigation pane to open the correct drives and folders and then, in the subject pane, select the file (or files using **SHIFT** to select contiguous files or **CTRL** to select several individual files), and select **Open**. A message box will open and show you the progress of the files being added, and the files will appear in the SkyDrive folder when it is done.

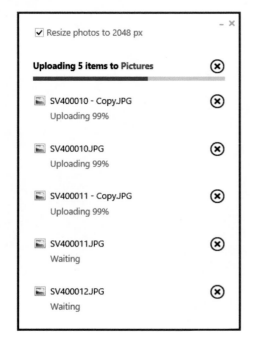

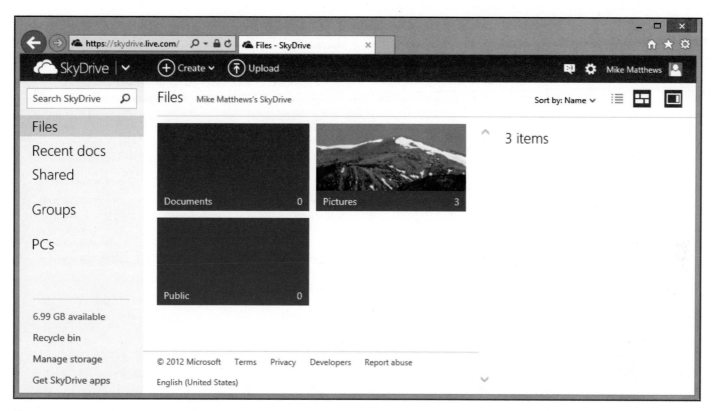

*Figure 8-17: **Microsoft has integrated SkyDrive into Microsoft Office as well as other Microsoft products.***

3. You can select **New Folder**, enter a name for the folder, and then select the new folder to open it. When the folder is open, you are invited to drag and drop documents there or to create a new document using one of the Microsoft Office Web Apps.

4. To drag and drop a file or files from your computer to the SkyDrive window, open File Explorer, select the files as in step 2, and then drag the files from File Explorer to the SkyDrive folder in Internet Explorer, as you can see in Figure 8-18. Again, a message box will show you the progress.

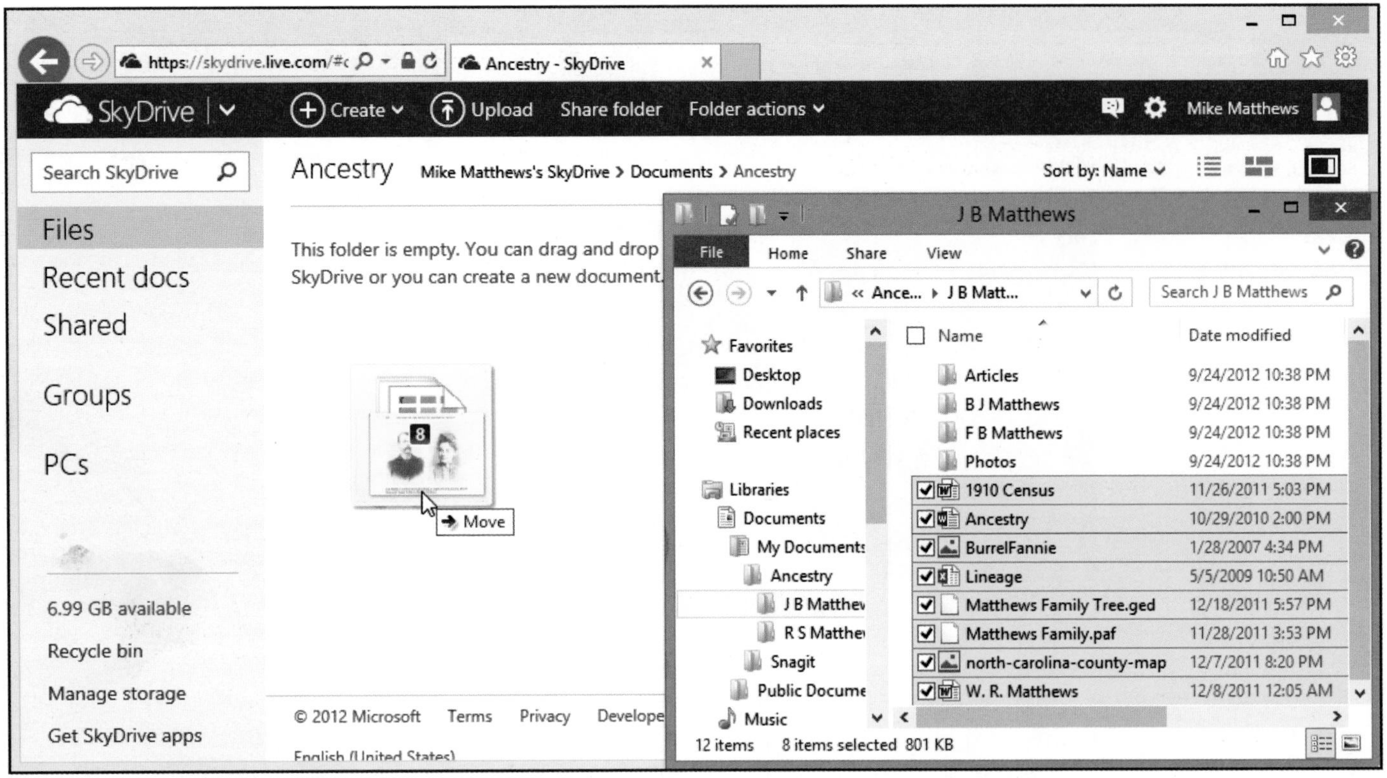

Figure 8-18: *Dragging files to SkyDrive is very intuitive.*

Note You cannot drag a folder from your computer to the SkyDrive. You must create a new folder in SkyDrive and drag the individual files to it.

5. When the files have been added, you can work with them by selecting the file and selecting a command in the right column. If the file is for Microsoft Word, Excel, PowerPoint, or OneNote, you can edit it directly in your browser (Internet Explorer) using either the Microsoft Office Web Apps in SkyDrive (shown in Figure 8-19) or the app on your computer if you have it.

6. When you are done, close the SkyDrive website and if desired, Internet Explorer.

Tip SkyDrive on the desktop offers several advantages over SkyDrive from the Start screen, including the online office applications and more comprehensive file management.

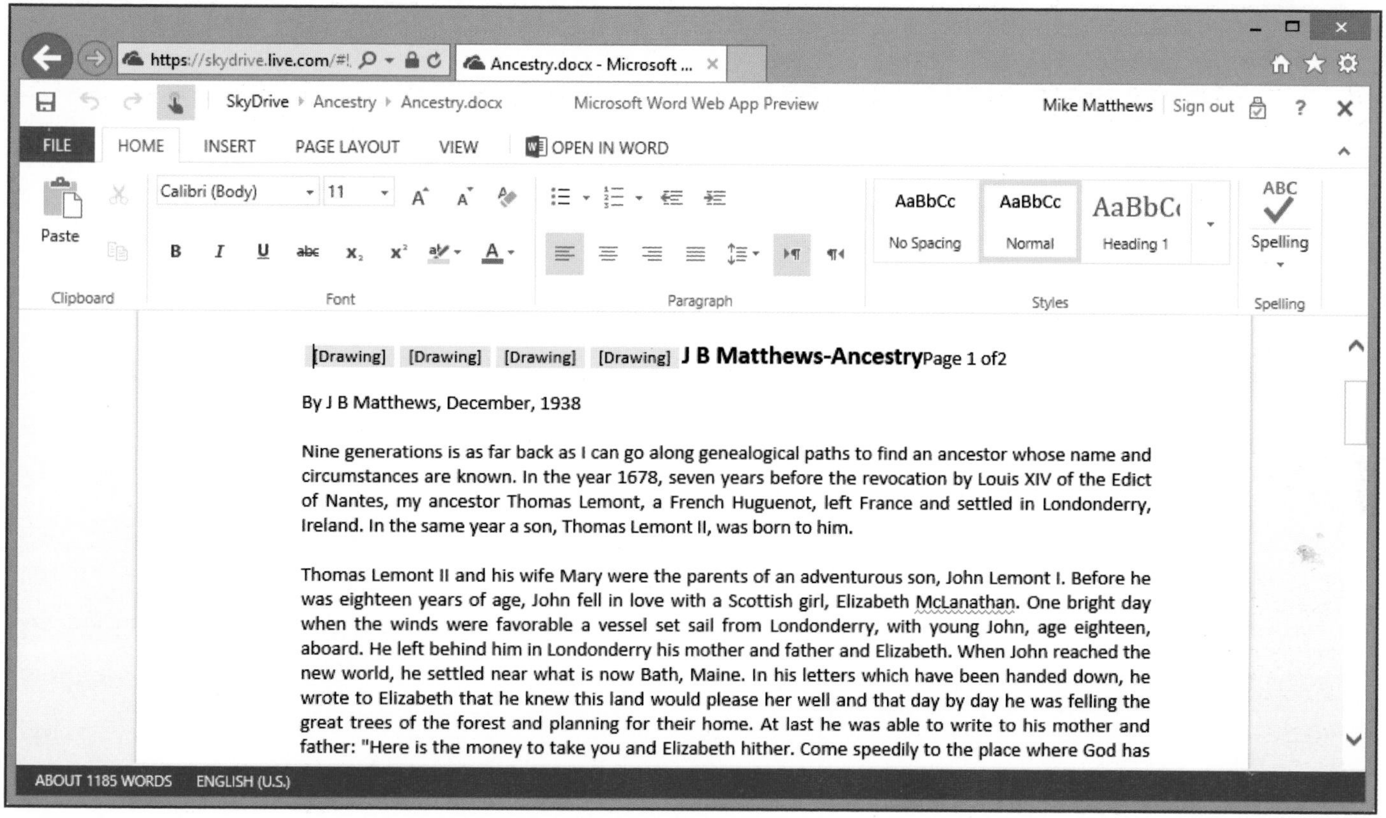

Browser window showing SkyDrive Word Web App:

Address bar: https://skydrive.live.com/#! — Ancestry.docx - Microsoft ...

SkyDrive ▸ Ancestry ▸ Ancestry.docx   Microsoft Word Web App Preview   Mike Matthews | Sign out

FILE   HOME   INSERT   PAGE LAYOUT   VIEW   OPEN IN WORD

Ribbon: Calibri (Body) 11 — Clipboard, Font, Paragraph, Styles (No Spacing, Normal, Heading 1), Spelling

[Drawing] [Drawing] [Drawing] [Drawing] **J B Matthews-Ancestry**Page 1 of2

By J B Matthews, December, 1938

Nine generations is as far back as I can go along genealogical paths to find an ancestor whose name and circumstances are known. In the year 1678, seven years before the revocation by Louis XIV of the Edict of Nantes, my ancestor Thomas Lemont, a French Huguenot, left France and settled in Londonderry, Ireland. In the same year a son, Thomas Lemont II, was born to him.

Thomas Lemont II and his wife Mary were the parents of an adventurous son, John Lemont I. Before he was eighteen years of age, John fell in love with a Scottish girl, Elizabeth McLanathan. One bright day when the winds were favorable a vessel set sail from Londonderry, with young John, age eighteen, aboard. He left behind him in Londonderry his mother and father and Elizabeth. When John reached the new world, he settled near what is now Bath, Maine. In his letters which have been handed down, he wrote to Elizabeth that he knew this land would please her well and that day by day he was felling the great trees of the forest and planning for their home. At last he was able to write to his mother and father: "Here is the money to take you and Elizabeth hither. Come speedily to the place where God has

ABOUT 1185 WORDS   ENGLISH (U.S.)

*Figure 8-19: **SkyDrive on the desktop provides access to the Microsoft Office Web Apps.***

Chapter 9

Setting Up Networking

Networking is the ability to connect two or more computers and allow them to share information and resources, whether at home, in an organization, or around the world. The Internet, as was discussed in Chapter 4, is a form of networking. This chapter discusses a *local area network,* or *LAN,* which is generally confined to a single residence or building, or perhaps just a section of a building. (The Internet is a *wide area network,* or *WAN.*) You'll see what comprises a LAN, how to set it up, and how to use it.

PLAN A NETWORK

Windows 8 is a *network operating system.* This allows the interconnection of multiple computers for many purposes:

- **Exchanging information**, such as transferring a file from one computer to another
- **Communicating**, for example, sending email among network users
- **Sharing information** by having common files accessed by network users
- **Sharing network resources**, such as printers and Internet connections

Networking is a system that includes the connection between computers that facilitates the transfer of information, as well as the scheme for controlling that transfer. The scheme makes sure that the information is transferred correctly and accurately. This is the function of the networking hardware and software in your computer and the protocols, or standards, they use.

Select a Network Architecture

Your network *architecture* is the combination of hardware, software, and standards that is used to perform networking. Today, the majority of LANs use the *Ethernet* standard, which determines the type of network hardware and software needed by the network, and *TCP/IP* (Transmission Control Protocol/Internet Protocol), which determines how information is exchanged over the network. With this foundation, you can then choose between using a peer-to-peer LAN or a client-server LAN.

Peer-to-Peer LANs

All computers in a *peer-to-peer LAN* are both servers and clients and, therefore, share in both providing and using resources. Any computer in the network may store information and provide resources, such as a printer, for the use of any other computer in the network. Peer-to-peer networking is an easy first step to networking, accomplished simply by joining computers together, as shown in Figure 9-1. It does not require the purchase of new computers or significant changes to the way an organization is using computers, yet resources can be shared (as is the printer in Figure 9-1), files and communications can be transferred, and common information can be accessed by all.

Peer-to-peer LANs tend to be used in smaller organizations that do not need to share a large central resource, such as a database, or to have a high degree of security or central control. Each computer in a peer-to-peer LAN is autonomous and often networked with other computers simply to transfer files and share expensive equipment. Putting together a peer-to-peer LAN with existing computers is easy, and can be inexpensive (less than $40 per station).

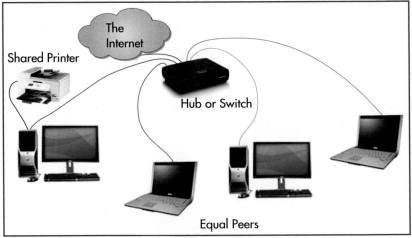

Figure 9-1: *In a peer-to-peer LAN, all computers are both servers and clients.*
Computer equipment photos are courtesy of Dell, Inc., and are used by permission. Network equipment photos are courtesy of LinkSys by Cisco and are used by permission.

> **Note** Figures 9-1 through 9-3 show the Internet being connected to the networks directly into hubs or switches. In most cases, the Internet will come into a network through some form of router that may be part of a hub or switch, or separately plug into a hub or switch. Because the nature of the router can take various forms, and may not even be a separate element, it is omitted in these figures.

Client-Server LANs

The computers in a *client-server LAN* perform one of two functions: they are either servers or clients. *Servers* manage the network, centrally store information to be shared on the network, and provide the shared resources to the network. *Clients,* or *workstations,* are the users of the network and are standard desktop or laptop computers. To create a network, the clients and server(s) are connected together, with the possible addition of stand-alone network resources, such as printers, as shown in Figure 9-2.

The management functions provided by the server include network security, managing the permissions needed to implement security, communications among network users, and management of shared files on the network. Servers generally are more capable than clients in terms of having more memory, faster (and possibly more) processors, larger (and maybe more) disks, and more special peripherals, such as large, central back-up devices. In general, servers are dedicated to their function and are infrequently used for normal computer tasks, such as word processing.

Clients generally are less capable than servers are and, infrequently, may not even have a disk. Clients usually are standard desktop and laptop computers that perform the normal functions of those types of machines in addition to being part of a network. Clients can also be "mini-servers" by sharing some or all of their disk drives or other resources. So the principal difference between peer-to-peer networks and client-server networks is the presence of a dedicated server.

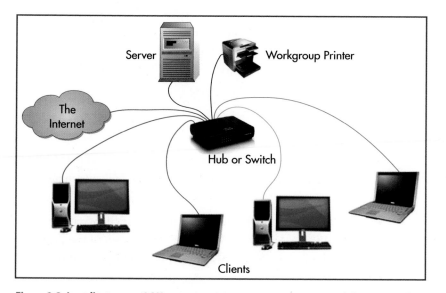

Figure 9-2: *In a client-server LAN, one or more computers are servers and the rest are clients.*
Computer equipment photos are courtesy of Dell, Inc., and are used by permission.
Network equipment photos are courtesy of LinkSys by Cisco and are used by permission.

Windows 8 and Windows Server 2012 work together to form a client-server network operating environment, with Windows Server performing its function and Windows 8 acting as the client. Several Windows 8 computers (as well as computers using other versions of Windows, or even other operating systems) can operate in a client-server network.

> **Tip** If you are using all Windows 8 or Windows 7 computers in a peer-to-peer network, the Windows 8 HomeGroup (as described in Chapter 8) provides an easy setup and a number of file-sharing features that could be beneficial even to smaller organizations.

There are simple client-server networks, and there are client-server networks where one or more servers are set up as *domain controllers* and the entire network is considered a *domain*. In a large organization, a domain provides many benefits—most importantly, a central registry for all users so that one registration provides access to all the computers and resources in the domain. Domains, however, are complex and require significant expertise to set up and manage. This book, therefore, focuses on setting up and using a peer-to-peer network and on connecting to a client-server network.

▶▶ Select a Network Standard

Windows 8 supports the two predominant networking standards: wired Ethernet and wireless. These, in turn, determine the type of hardware you need.

Use Wired Ethernet

The wired Ethernet standard comes in several forms based on speed and cable type. The most common, called 10/100/1000BaseT, provides a network that operates at the regular Ethernet speed of 10 Mbps, at the Fast Ethernet speed of 100 Mbps, or at the Gigabit Ethernet speed of 1000 Mbps.

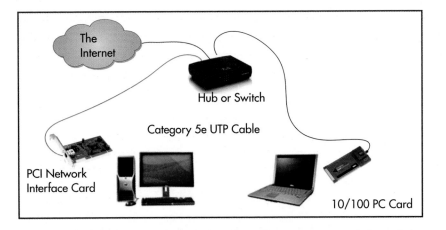

Figure 9-3: *A wired Ethernet network consists of a card in your computer, a hub or switch into which other computers are connected, and a cable connecting the two.*
Computer equipment photos are courtesy of Dell, Inc., and are used by permission.
Network equipment photos are courtesy of LinkSys by Cisco and are used by permission.

Note In the name for the Ethernet standard, 10/100/1000BaseT, the "10/100/1000" indicates the alternative operating speeds in Mbps; the "Base" is for baseband, a type of transmission; and the "T" stands for the type of cabling (twisted-pair).

A wired Ethernet 10/100/1000BaseT system, shown in Figure 9-3, has three major components:

- The **network interface card (NIC)** plugs into your computer or is built into it and connects it to the network.
- A **hub**, **switch**, or **router** joins several computers together to form the network:
  - A **hub**, the simplest and oldest device, is where all computers are on the equivalent of a telephone party line (everybody can hear everybody else).
  - A **switch** is a newer device, about the same price as a hub and has virtually made them obsolete, where all computers are on the equivalent of a private telephone line.

- A **router** joins two different networks, for example, the Internet to a local area network. Often, a router is combined with a hub or a switch, either in one device or in two devices, to join the Internet to several computers.
- An **unshielded twisted-pair (UTP)** telephone-like cable with a simple RJ-45 connector (similar to that for a telephone but larger) joins the NIC to the hub, switch, or router. This cable is called Category 5, enhanced Category 5, or Category 6 ("Cat 5," "Cat 5e," or "Cat 6," respectively).

Ethernet networks are easy to set up (see "Set Up a Network" later in this chapter), have become pervasive throughout organizations, and have an average cost for all components of less than $40 per computer on the network.

Use a Wireless LAN

Wireless LANs (WLANs) replace the cable used in a wired network with small radio transceivers (transmitter and receiver) at the computer and at the switch and/or router. There are several wireless standards, but the most common are 802.11b, 802.11g, and 802.11n. All three are Wi-Fi compliant (Wi-Fi is a trademark for a set of wireless fidelity standards) and are compatible with one another:

- **802.11b** is the oldest and provides data transfer of *up to* 11 Mbps using a secure transmission scheme.
- **802.11g** came next, is *up to* five times faster than 802.11b (54 Mbps) but generally operates at 22 to 24 Mbps, and is built into many older computers.
- **802.11n** is currently the dominant standard, is between three and seven times faster than 802.11g, operating between 70 and 140 Mbps under normal conditions, and it can be as much as ten times faster (300 Mbps) under perfect conditions, which are difficult to achieve.

802.11n will operate proportionally faster at a longer distance than 802.11g will, but all three standards are range-sensitive (the greater the distance between the computer and the wireless access point, the slower the speed). 802.11n is built into most newer computers.

Almost all public Wi-Fi locations will handle 802.11b or g, and n is often available.

A WLAN has two components (see Figure 9-4):

- An **access point** is connected to the wired Ethernet network by being plugged into a hub, a switch, or a router. It uses a transceiver to communicate wirelessly with the computers using the WLAN.

- An **adapter** plugs into or is built into your computer, and has a transceiver to communicate wirelessly with an access point within its range. There are various adapters for use in both notebook and desktop computers.

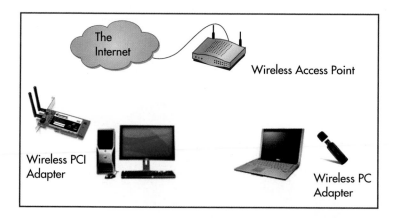

Figure 9-4: *A wireless network consists of an adapter that plugs into or is built into your computer and an access point that is connected to a wired network, the Internet, or both.*
Computer equipment photos are courtesy of Dell, Inc., and are used by permission. Network equipment photos are courtesy of LinkSys by Cisco and are used by permission.

If the access point is plugged into a hub or switch on a wired network, the wireless computers within the range of the access point operate on the network in exactly the same way as they would with a cable connection, except they are slower. A WLAN has some significant benefits over a normal wired LAN:

Note In addition to the WLAN standard, the Wi-Fi standard makes sure that the hardware from different manufacturers is compatible. Thus, you can walk into any office, airport, or coffee shop with a Wi-Fi standard wireless system and connect to the WLAN at that location if you have the appropriate permissions. In many airports, hotels, and coffee shops, you see signs for "Wi-Fi hotspots," meaning you can use a wireless connection to access the Internet at that location—sometimes free and sometimes at a cost.

- You do not have the expense of cabling and the even higher expense of installing and maintaining cabling.

- Adding and removing users from the network is extremely easy.

- Users can move easily from office to office.

- Users can roam within an area, say, carrying their laptops to a meeting.

- Visitors can easily get on the network.

The downsides are (potentially) cost, speed, and security, but all of these are manageable. The cost per computer of a wired network, as was said previously, is less than $40 per computer. The cost per computer of a wireless network may be the same or less, considering that a wireless adapter is built into almost all laptops. The speed difference is more significant, not just because of the difference between a 100-Mbps or higher "n" access point and a 1000-Mbps network, but because of the net rate of dividing the 100-Mbps access point by the number of people trying to use it. Despite these drawbacks, WLANs are becoming almost universal for both offices and homes, especially with tablets and smartphones being able to use them and not wired networks.

> **Note** Lessened security is also a potential downside with wireless if it isn't set up properly. For example, if you don't turn on encryption and the use of passwords, your neighbor (or hacker cruising your neighborhood) might be able to get on your network or look at your network traffic.

Select Wired Ethernet Hardware

Selecting networking hardware for wired Ethernet means selecting a NIC, a hub or switch, and cabling. For all hardware, a brand-name product giving you a company that stands behind what you are buying can be beneficial. Respected brands of networking gear include 3Com, Cisco and its subsidiary Linksys, D-Link, Netgear, and RealTek.

Select a Network Interface Card

Most new computers come with a built-in 10/100/1000 Ethernet NIC, so you may not need to add this. You already have a NIC if your computer has a telephone-style jack that is slightly larger than a normal telephone jack. This is the connection to the NIC.

If you don't have a NIC, you can generally add one to your computer. For a desktop computer, you want a 10/100/1000 NIC for either the PCI (Peripheral Component Interconnect) bus or the USB (Universal Serial Bus). If you use a NIC that plugs into the PCI bus, you will need to open the computer case and plug it in. If you are uncomfortable doing that, most computer stores will do it for little more than the cost of the card ($25 to $50). You need to carry in only the computer itself, not the monitor, keyboard, or mouse. If you choose to use a USB NIC, it will cost slightly more, but it plugs into a USB socket on the outside of the case.

For a laptop computer, the NIC plugs in from the outside, so it is easy to add. It uses one of three connections (in all cases, you want a 10/100/1000 NIC):

PC Card, short for PCMCIA (Personal Computer Memory Card International Association), which goes into a slot on the side of laptops

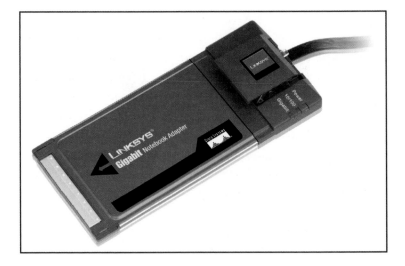

Express card, which also goes into a slot on the side of newer laptops

USB connector, which plugs into a USB port on the computer, either in laptops or desktops

Select Connecting Devices

As discussed in "Use Wired Ethernet," there are two common connecting devices: hubs, which are like a party-line telephone system where everybody hears all the traffic; and switches, which are like a private-line telephone system. Switches once cost a lot more, so hubs were used. Today, switches and hubs are virtually the same price. A simple switch runs from under $20 for a 10/100/1000 four-port one, to under $50 for an eight-port switch. You need a port for each user on the system, plus one for your broadband (DSL or cable) Internet connection. The largest switches have 48 ports, but you can stack switches by plugging them into one another. You want an Ethernet 10/100/1000 switch with the number of ports that meets your needs.

Select Cabling

For 10/100/100 Ethernet networking, you need either Category 5e or Category 6 cabling with RJ-45 male connectors on each end. Such cables come in various colors and lengths, up to 100 feet with the ends molded on, or in lengths up to 1,000 feet without the ends, where you need a crimping tool to add the ends (*not* a simple task!). Cat 5e cable, which provides better transmission capability, is almost the same price as Cat 5, so I recommend it, and Cat 6, while a little more expensive, is a good investment.

Tip If you want to network only two computers, you can do so without a hub or a switch, but you need a special *crossover* cable where the connections are reversed on each end. Most computer stores carry such a cable.

▷▷ Select Wireless Hardware

Selecting networking hardware for a wireless network means selecting a wireless adapter and a wireless access point. The same manufacturers that were listed for wired Ethernet hardware are recommended.

Select a Wireless Speed

If you are installing a new wireless network, the up-to-54-Mbps 802.11g standard is the minimum, and you probably want to consider the up-to-300-Mbps 802.11n, which is only a little more expensive.

Select a Wireless Adapter

Most tablet and laptop and many desktop computers come with a built-in wireless adapter, so you may not need to buy one. Otherwise, for a desktop computer, you will need a PCI or USB wireless adapter for the speed you have chosen, and, with PCI, you will need to open up the computer to plug it in or have a store do it. For a laptop computer without the built-in capability, you need a PC Card, Express Card, or USB wireless adapter of the appropriate speed, which you can easily plug in (you need to check whether your laptop uses a PC Card or Express Card adapter by looking at the information that came with your computer).

Select a Wireless Access Point

Wireless access points come in simple versions that plug into a wired Ethernet network, as well as more sophisticated versions, called "wireless broadband routers," that terminate a Digital Subscriber Line (DSL), FiOS (fiber optic), or cable Internet connection. You have that choice and a choice of speeds when you choose a wireless access point.

SET UP A NETWORK

When you installed Windows 8, a basic set of networking services was installed and configured using system defaults and what the installation software "saw" on your network. This setup may, but doesn't always, provide an operable networking system. Look at these three areas to set up *basic networking,* which means that your computer can communicate with other computers in the network:

- Be sure the NIC is properly set up.
- Review the networking functions that you want to perform.
- Review your network security settings.

 Note In many of the steps in the following sections of this chapter, you will be interrupted and asked by User Account Control (UAC) for permission to make changes to the computer. So long as it is something you started, select **Yes** and, if needed, enter an administrator's password. To keep the steps as simple as possible, we have left out the UAC instructions. Chapter 8 discusses UAC in more detail.

Set Up Network Interface Cards

If the computer you are setting up has a Windows-compatible NIC, then your NIC was installed by Windows Setup without incident and you don't need to read this section. Otherwise, this section examines how the NIC was installed and what you need to do to make it operational.

Assuming that a NIC *is* properly plugged into the computer, any of these things could be causing it to not operate:

- The NIC driver is not recognized by Windows 8; it is either missing or not properly installed.
- The NIC is not functioning properly.

Look at each of these possibilities in turn.

Check the NIC and Its Driver

Check the status of your NIC and whether you have a driver installed. If you don't, you can install one.

1. Open the **System** menu and select **Control Panel | Network And Internet | Network And Sharing Center**. The Network And Sharing Center window opens.

2. In the Network And Sharing Center, which is shown in Figure 9-5, you can see if you are connected to a network by looking in the upper-right area. If your Access Type is "Internet," you are connected to the Internet. In the middle-right area of the Network And Sharing Center, you can see if you have a wired connection (on the left of

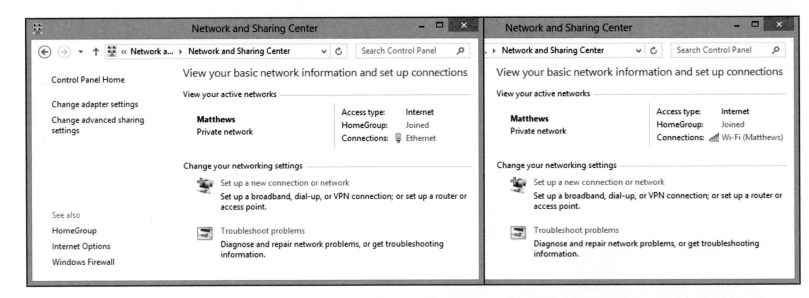

Figure 9-5: In the Network And Sharing Center you can tell if you are connected to a wired local area network (as on the left) or a wireless network (on the right) and to the Internet.

Figure 9-5) and/or a wireless connection (on the right). If your Network And Sharing Center looks like Figure 9-5, you have all these connections (either wired or wireless) and you can be assured your NIC is working, and you can skip to the next chapter.

3. If you do not see one of the connections shown in Figure 9-5, you need to start the process of figuring out why and getting it fixed. Select **Change Adapter Settings** in the left pane. The Network Connections window opens. If you have an icon in the window labeled "Ethernet" and/or "Wi-Fi," as shown next, you have the NIC driver properly installed and you can go on to the section "Enable Windows 8's Networking Functions."

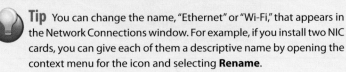

Tip You can change the name, "Ethernet" or "Wi-Fi," that appears in the Network Connections window. For example, if you install two NIC cards, you can give each of them a descriptive name by opening the context menu for the icon and selecting **Rename**.

4. If you do not have an icon for either connection, you must first install a Windows 8 driver for the NIC. Since a driver was not automatically installed by Windows 8, you will need to get one before proceeding. If a driver did not come with the NIC (most likely on a CD), you need to use another computer attached to the Internet to locate and download it.

5. On the other computer, bring up the manufacturer's website, locate and download the Windows 8 driver (you need to know the make and model of the NIC), copy it onto a disc or a USB flash drive, and then go back to your original computer.

Tip I went through the process of downloading a driver and found it painless. The hard part is figuring out what type of card you have, because often it is not written on the card. You may be able to see it in step 6 of "Check the NIC and Its Driver." If not, you need to locate purchase records or documentation—if you know which records go with the card.

6. Open the **System** menu and select **Control Panel | Hardware And Sound | Device Manager** under Devices And Printers. The Device Manager window opens.

7. Open **Network Adapters** to display the network adapter in your computer. If you see your NIC and it doesn't have a problem icon (an exclamation point), Windows thinks that the NIC is installed and running properly. If you open the device, you should see the device status, "This device is working properly." If so, you may need to only install a new driver. Skip to step 14.

> ▲ 🖳 Network adapters
>   🖳 802.11n Wireless LAN Card
>   🖳 Microsoft Kernel Debug Network Adapter
>   🖳 Realtek PCIe GBE Family Controller

> Device status
> This device is working properly.

8. If you see your NIC with a problem icon, open the NIC. You will most likely see a device status message telling you that a driver was not installed. Skip to step 14.

9. If you don't see your NIC in the Device Manager window, select the **Action** menu | **Add Legacy Hardware**. The Add Hardware Wizard will open. Select **Next**. Select **Install The Hardware That I Manually Select From A List**—you don't want Windows to search for new hardware; if it was going to find it, it would have—and select **Next**.

10. Scroll down and open **Network Adapters** in the Common Hardware Types list. A list of network adapters appears. If your NIC had been on the list, Windows Setup would have found it, so you need to insert and use either the disc that you made prior to step 3 or the disc that came with the NIC.

11. Select **Have Disk**. In the Install From Disk dialog, select **Browse**. In the Locate File dialog, if necessary, find and select the driver (.inf file extension), and select **Open**. In the Install From Disk dialog, select **OK**. When told that the device will be installed, select **Next** again.

12. You may see a message stating that the driver you are about to install does not have a Microsoft digital signature. Select **Yes** to go ahead and install it anyway. The driver and its necessary supporting software will be installed.

13. Select **Finish**. The Network Connections window should now show the Local Area Connection icon. If you see this icon, go to the section "Enable Windows 8's Networking Functions."

14. If you saw your NIC in the Device Manager window, with or without a problem icon, you can install or reinstall a driver from there. Place the disc with the driver software in the drive. Open the context menu for your NIC and select **Update Driver Software**, as shown in Figure 9-6.

15. Select **Browse My Computer For Driver Software | Browse**, locate the drive and folder with the driver, and select **Next**. You will be told when the driver is installed. Select **Close** to close the Update Driver Software dialog box.

If you still do not have a Local Area Connection icon, or if some other problem occurred in the preceding process that does not point to an obvious solution, continue through the next section to see if a solution is presented.

Determine If a NIC Is Functioning

If installing a NIC driver did not cause the Local Area Connection icon to appear, it is likely that the NIC itself is not functioning properly. The easiest way to test that is to replace the NIC with a known good one, ideally one that is both Windows 8 certified and Plug and Play compatible. It is wise to have a spare NIC; they are not expensive (as low as $25), and replacing a suspected bad one can quickly solve many problems.

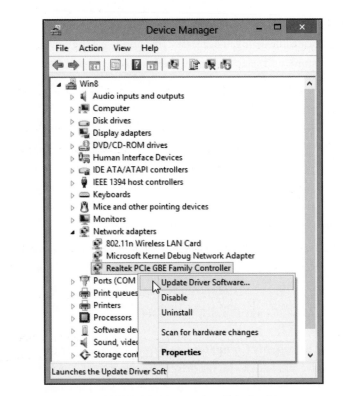

Figure 9-6: *It is common to have to install device driver software for older hardware.*

Tip If you suspect that your NIC is not working and it is built into the computer, you can still add another NIC and use it. Almost all systems allow you to have two or more NICs installed.

⟩⟩ Enable Windows 8's Networking Functions

Windows 8's networking functions provide the software for a computer to access other computers and, separately, for other computers to access the computer you are working on. In other words, the two primary functions allow the computer to be a client (it accesses other computers)

and to be a server (other computers access it). Make sure that these two services are enabled by following these steps (the steps are the same for both a wired and a wireless network—only the option and title names are different; the figures show a wired network).

1. Open the **System** menu and select **Control Panel | Network And Internet | Network And Sharing Center**. The Network And Sharing Center window opens.

2. Opposite Connections in the middle-right area, select **Ethernet** (or **Wi-Fi**). The Ethernet (or Wi-Fi) Status dialog box appears, as shown in Figure 9-7. In the particular case shown here, the computer indicates it is connected to the network and that it is sending and receiving information, which indicates it is correctly set up.

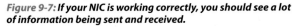

Figure 9-7: *If your NIC is working correctly, you should see a lot of information being sent and received.*

3. Select **Properties**. The Local Area Connection Properties dialog box, shown in Figure 9-8, appears and displays the services and protocols that have been installed automatically.

The minimum services needed for networking are Client For Microsoft Networks and File And Printer Sharing For Microsoft Networks, plus one protocol: Transmission Control Protocol/Internet Protocol Version 4 (TCP/IPv4). By default, Windows 8 installs additional services and protocols.

4. Select **Install**. The Select Network Feature Type dialog box appears, in which you can add clients, services, and protocols if they are not already installed.

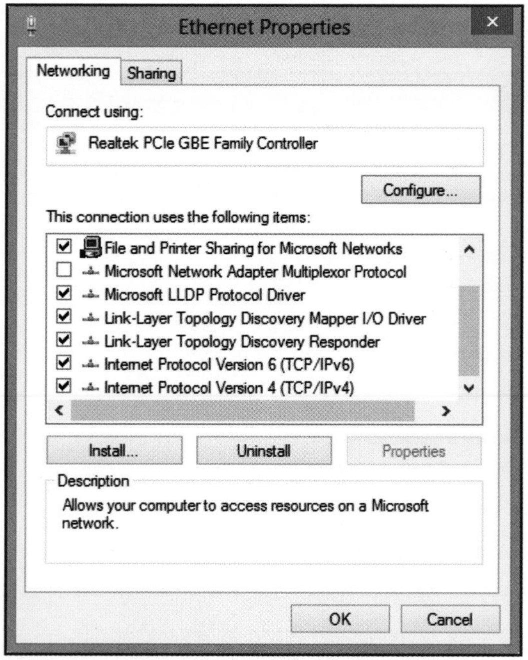

*Figure 9-8: **Windows 8 automatically installs the networking services and protocols shown here.***

Install a Client

1. Open **Client**. If you already have Client For Microsoft Networks installed, you will not have any services to install.

2. If Client For Microsoft Networks is not installed, select it and, in any case, select **OK**.

Note In this and the two following sections you can use the Have Disk button to install unique, non-Windows services for special purposes.

Install a Service

Windows 8 provides two services, both of which are automatically installed:

- **File And Printer Sharing For Microsoft Networks** handles the sharing of resources on your computer.

- **QoS (Quality of Service) Packet Scheduler** helps balance a network and alleviate bottlenecks when one part of the network is fast and another part is slow.

1. In the Select Network Feature Type dialog box, open **Service**. If you already have File And Printer Sharing For Microsoft Networks and QoS Packet Scheduler installed, you will not have any services to install.

2. If File And Printer Sharing For Microsoft Networks and QoS Packet Scheduler are not installed, select them and, in any case, click **OK**.

⬦⬦ Configure a Networking Protocol

Networking protocols are a set of standards used to package and transmit information over a network. The protocol determines how the information is divided into packets, how it is addressed, and what is done to assure it is reliably transferred. The protocol is, therefore, very important to the success of networking, and its choice is a major one.

Windows 8 offers three Internet protocols, one for connecting virtual machines, and two network-mapping protocols:

- **Internet Protocol Version 4 (TCP/IPv4)**, for use with the Internet and most LANs
- **Internet Protocol Version 6 (TCP/IPv6)**, the newest system for use with the widest variety of networks (almost all Internet service providers and the routers they use now handle IPv6 because the world is very close to running out of the over four billion IPv4 addresses)
- **Reliable Multicast Protocol**, which is a special one-to-many protocol used in conferencing
- **Hyper-V Extensible Virtual Switch** is used to manage and connect virtual machines
- **Link-Layer Topology Discovery Mapper I/O Driver** that goes out and finds devices on the network
- **Link-Layer Topology Discovery Responder** that responds when it is queried by a Discovery Mapper

All of these protocols, except Reliable Multicast Protocol and Hyper-V Extensible Virtual Switch, are installed by default. Unless you're having problems, you can leave things as is. If the computer you are working on is or will be connected to the Internet, it will require TCP/IPv6.

Check and Change Protocols

Check (and change if necessary) the protocols that have been installed and the settings that are being used.

> **Note** In the Local Area Connection Properties dialog box, you should see at least one protocol installed, as shown previously in Figure 9-7. In most cases, both TCP/IPv4 and TCP/IPv6 should already be installed.

1. In the Select Network Feature Type dialog box, open **Protocol**. The Select Network Protocol dialog box appears listing the available protocols.

2. If you see any protocol you want installed, open it. If you want to install another protocol, open it too. Otherwise, select **Cancel** twice to close the Select Network Protocol and Select Network Feature Type dialog boxes.

3. Select the **Internet Protocol Version 6 (TCP/IPv6)** protocol in the Ethernet (or Wi-Fi) Properties dialog box | **Properties**. The Internet Protocol (TCP/IP) Properties dialog box appears, shown in Figure 9-9. Here you can choose either to use a dynamic IP (Internet Protocol) address automatically assigned by a server or DSL router or to enter a static IP address.

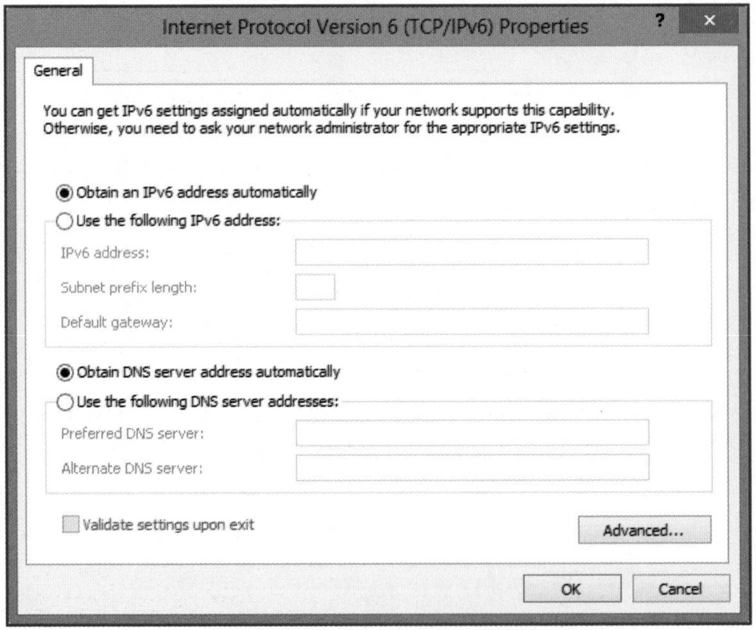

Figure 9-9: If you use dynamic IP addresses that are automatically assigned, you don't have to worry about having two devices or computers with the same IP address.

If you have a server or a DSL router that automatically assigns IP addresses, you need to leave the **Obtain An IP Address Automatically** option selected (it is selected by default).

Enter Your Own IP Address

1. If you are working on a computer that you know must have a static IP address, select **Use The Following IPv6 Address** and enter an IP address. The IP address that you use should be from the block of IP addresses that an ISP or other authority has assigned to your organization.

2. If you entered a static IP address, you must also enter a subnet mask. This mask tells the IP which part of an IP address to consider a network address and which part to consider a computer, or *host,* address. If your organization was assigned a block of IP addresses, it was also given a subnet mask. If you used the APIPA range of addresses, use 255.255.0.0 as the subnet mask.

Obtain an IP Address Automatically

1. If you don't have a specific reason to use a static IP address, select **Obtain An IP Address Automatically**.

2. Select **OK** to close the Internet Protocol Version 6 (TCP/IPv6) Properties dialog box | **Close** to close the Ethernet/Wi-Fi Properties dialog box | **Close** to close the Ethernet/Wi-Fi Status dialog box, and close all open dialog boxes and windows.

3. Open **Charms | Power | Restart**. This is required to utilize your new network settings.

Verify Your Connection

1. When the computer restarts, reopen the Local Area Connection Status dialog box (open the **System** menu and select **Control Panel | Network And Internet | Network And Sharing Center**). Select **Ethernet** (or **Wi-Fi**) in the middle-right area to open the Status dialog box. You should see activity on both the Sent and Received sides.

2. If you do not see both sending and receiving activity, in the Start screen, enter a computer name in your same subnet in the form *computername*\, and press **ENTER**. File Explorer will open and you should see the drives on the computer you entered, as shown in Figure 9-10. If you see this, the computer is networked. If this doesn't work, you need to double-check all the possible settings previously described:

- If you are using APIPA, make sure that the computer you are trying to contact is also using that range of numbers, either as a static assigned address or with automatic assignment.

- If all the settings are correct, check the cabling by making a simple connection of just several computers.

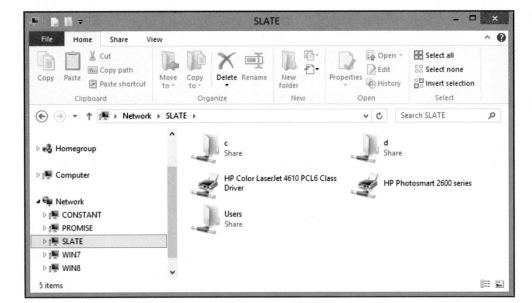

Figure 9-10: When networking is functioning properly, you'll be able to see shared resources on other computers in your network.

- If you do a direct connection between two computers, remember that you need a special crossover cable with the transmitting and receiving wires reversed.

- If all else fails, replace the NIC.

- It could also be that network security is getting in your way of seeing the drives and resources on the other computer. See "Review Network Security" later in this chapter.

With a good NIC, good cabling, the correct settings, and network security properly handled, you'll be able to network.

⧫⧫ Get a Block of IP Addresses

The block of IP addresses you use with the Internet Protocol depends on whether the computers to be assigned the addresses will be private or public.

Get Private IP Addresses

If the computers will be operating only on an internal network, where they are separated from the public network by a router or bridge, they are *private* and need only organizational uniqueness. Four blocks of IP addresses have been set aside and can be used by any organization for its private, internal needs without any coordination with any other organization, but these blocks should not be used for directly connecting to the Internet. These private-use blocks of IP addresses are

- 10.0.0.0 through 10.255.255.255

- 169.254.0.0 through 169.254.255.255 (the APIPA range)

- 172.16.0.0 through 172.31.255.255

- 192.168.0.0 through 192.168.255.255

Get Public IP Addresses

If your computer(s) will be interfacing directly with the Internet, they are *public* and thus need a globally unique IP number. If you want a block of public IP addresses, you must request it from one of several organizations, depending on the size of the block that you want. At the local level, for a moderate-sized block of IP addresses, your local ISP can assign it to you. For a larger block, a regional ISP may be able to handle the request. If not, you have to go to one of three regional Internet registries:

- American Registry for Internet Numbers (ARIN), at arin.net, which covers North and South America, the Caribbean, and sub-Saharan Africa

- Réseaux IP Européens (RIPE), at ripe.net, which covers Europe, the Middle East, and northern Africa

- Asia Pacific Network Information Centre (APNIC), at apnic.net, which covers Asia and the Pacific

> **CAUTION!** Remember that private ranges work only with other computers in their own subnets and with IP addresses from the same range. You can tell what the subnet is from the subnet mask. For example, with a subnet mask of 255.255.255.0, all computers in the network must have IP addresses with the same first three groups of numbers and vary only in the last group. Thus, computers with the numbers 192.168.104.001 and 192.168.104.002 are in the same subnet.

Test a Network Setup and Connection

You can use several command-line utilities to test a TCP/IP installation. The more useful of these commands are the following:

- **Ipconfig** is used to determine if a network configuration has been initialized and if an IP address is assigned. If an IP address and valid subnet mask are returned, the configuration is initialized and there are no duplicates for the IP address. If a subnet mask of 0.0.0.0 is returned, the IP address is a duplicate.

- **Hostname** is used to determine the computer name of the local computer.

- **Ping** is used to query either the local computer or another computer on the network to see whether it responds. If the local computer responds, you know that TCP/IP is bound to the local NIC and that both are operating correctly. If the other computer responds, you know that TCP/IP and the NICs in both computers are operating correctly and that the connection between the computers is operable. Figure 9-11 shows the testing results on my system.

> **Note** Figure 9-11 reflects that my computer has both wireless and wired networking ability, but the wireless is currently turned off.

1. Open the **System** menu and select **Command Prompt**. The Command Prompt window opens.

2. Type <u>ipconfig</u> and press **ENTER**. The IP address and subnet mask of the current computer should be returned. If this did not happen, there is a problem with the current configuration.

3. Type <u>hostname</u> and press **ENTER**. The computer name of the local computer should be returned.

4. Type <u>ping</u>, type a space, type the name of another computer on your network, and press **ENTER**. You should get four replies from the other computer.

```
Command Prompt

C:\>ipconfig

Windows IP Configuration

Wireless LAN adapter Local Area Connection* 11:

   Media State . . . . . . . . . . . : Media disconnected
   Connection-specific DNS Suffix  . :

Wireless LAN adapter Wi-Fi:

   Media State . . . . . . . . . . . : Media disconnected
   Connection-specific DNS Suffix  . :

Ethernet adapter Ethernet:

   Connection-specific DNS Suffix  . :
   Link-local IPv6 Address . . . . . : fe80::34d2:545d:257d:a04c%12
   IPv4 Address. . . . . . . . . . . : 192.168.2.8
   Subnet Mask . . . . . . . . . . . : 255.255.255.0
   Default Gateway . . . . . . . . . : 192.168.2.1

Tunnel adapter Teredo Tunneling Pseudo-Interface:

   Connection-specific DNS Suffix  . :
   IPv6 Address. . . . . . . . . . . : 2001:0:4137:9e76:14a1:267f:bc61:3474
   Link-local IPv6 Address . . . . . : fe80::14a1:267f:bc61:3474%16
   Default Gateway . . . . . . . . . : ::

Tunnel adapter isatap.{35E5E0B9-C2A8-40FE-A524-A28980B9B181}:

   Media State . . . . . . . . . . . : Media disconnected
   Connection-specific DNS Suffix  . :

C:\>hostname
Win8

C:\>ping slate

Pinging Slate [fe80::7d98:b345:4243:ecdf%12] with 32 bytes of data:
Reply from fe80::7d98:b345:4243:ecdf%12: time<1ms
Reply from fe80::7d98:b345:4243:ecdf%12: time<1ms
Reply from fe80::7d98:b345:4243:ecdf%12: time<1ms
Reply from fe80::7d98:b345:4243:ecdf%12: time<1ms

Ping statistics for fe80::7d98:b345:4243:ecdf%12:
    Packets: Sent = 4, Received = 4, Lost = 0 (0% loss),
Approximate round trip times in milli-seconds:
    Minimum = 0ms, Maximum = 0ms, Average = 0ms

C:\>_
```

*Figure 9-11: **You can test a network with TCP/IP utilities such as Ipconfig, Hostname, and Ping.***

5. If Ping did not work with a remote computer, try it on the current computer by typing ping <u>127.0.0.1</u> and pressing **ENTER**. Again, you should get four replies, this time from the current computer. If you didn't get a reply here, you have a problem with either the network setup or the NIC. If you did get a reply here but not in step 4, there is a problem either in the other computer or in the cable and devices connecting them.

6. Type <u>exit</u> and press **ENTER** to close the Command Prompt window.

> **Note** The 127.0.0.1 IP address is a special address set aside to refer to the computer on which it is entered.

If you do find a problem here, go on to the next section on network security, and then review earlier sections on setting up network hardware, functions, and protocols to isolate and fix the problem.

▷▷ Review Network Security

Chapter 8 discusses network security in depth. This section provides a brief synopsis of the specific steps you need to take to share your computer across a LAN so that other computers similarly set up can see your computer and access the drives, folders, and printers. You will be able to see and access other computers that do the same thing. The steps to take in the appropriate order are described next. The detailed explanation behind these steps, as well as the specific settings to use, are discussed in Chapter 8.

1. When you complete the installation of Windows 8, or the first time you turn on a new computer with Windows 8 already installed, you are asked if the network you want is to be a part of a private network either at home or at work, or a public network in some public location. You can change this as described in step 2.

2. If you want to share your computer's resources, such as files, folders, disk drives, and printers, you need to turn on that capability (it is turned off by default in a public network, but turned on with a homegroup in a private network). This is done in the Advanced Sharing Settings window, shown in Figure 9-12, for both the private and public aspects of this computer. (Open the **System** menu and select **Control Panel | Network And Internet | Network And Sharing Center | Change Advanced Sharing Settings**.)

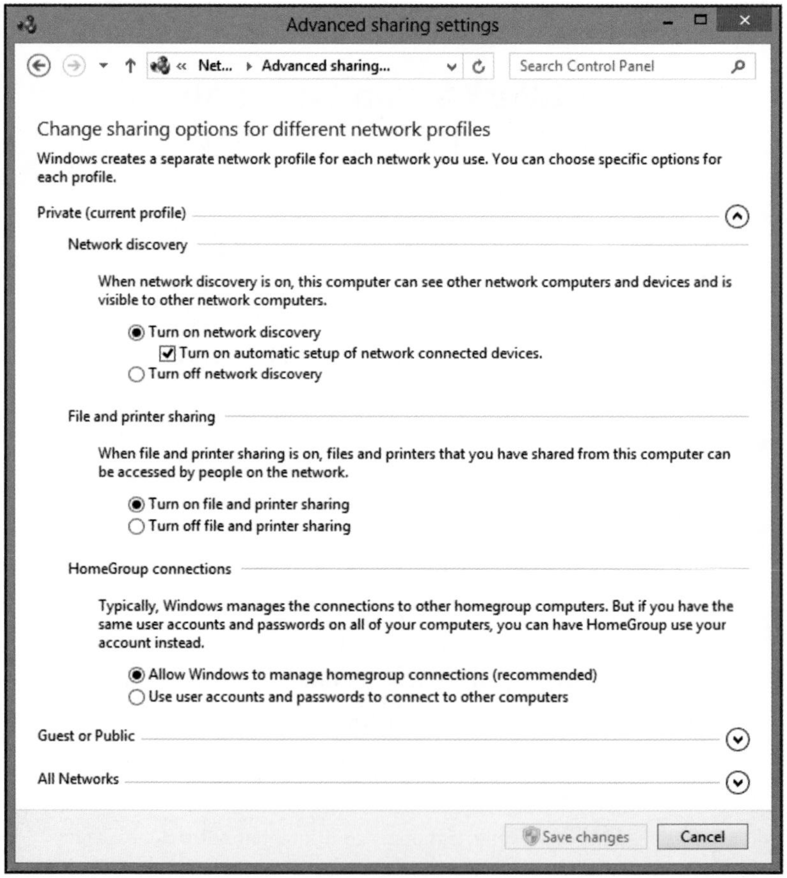

Figure 9-12: *Turn on the sharing of your computer.*

3. To share individual drives, folders, and printers, you must turn on that capability for the most senior drive or folder you want to share (also known as the parent). Subsidiary folders and the files within those folders will inherit the sharing aspect of the parent unless you individually change that sharing. Only in a homegroup can you share the full C: (or system) drive. Sharing a drive, folder, or printer is done through the object's Properties dialog box, shown in Figure 9-13. (On the desktop select **File Explorer**, open the context menu for the drive or folder you want to control, and select **Share With | Advanced Sharing**.)

4. Finally, you must set up Windows Firewall to allow the network and its sharing aspects to come through even though you have Windows Firewall turned on (which is highly recommended). Setting up the firewall to allow networking is done in the Windows Firewall Allowed Apps window, shown in Figure 9-14. (Open the **System** menu and select **Control Panel | System And Security | Windows Firewall | Allow An App Or Feature Through Windows Firewall**.)

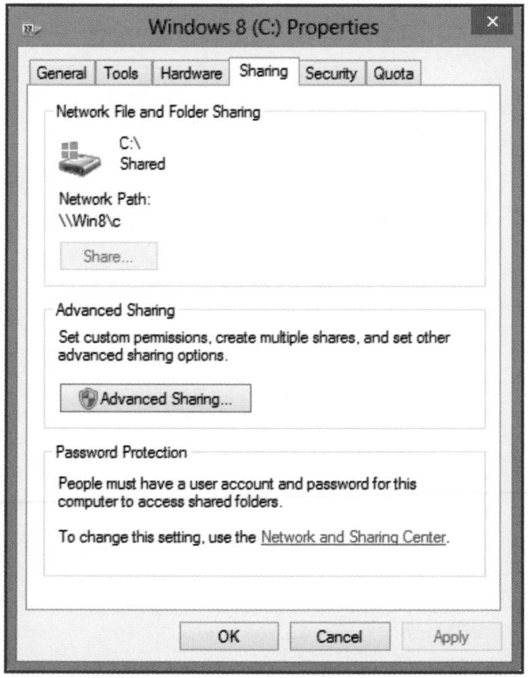

Figure 9-13: Share the specific objects you want others to be able to use.

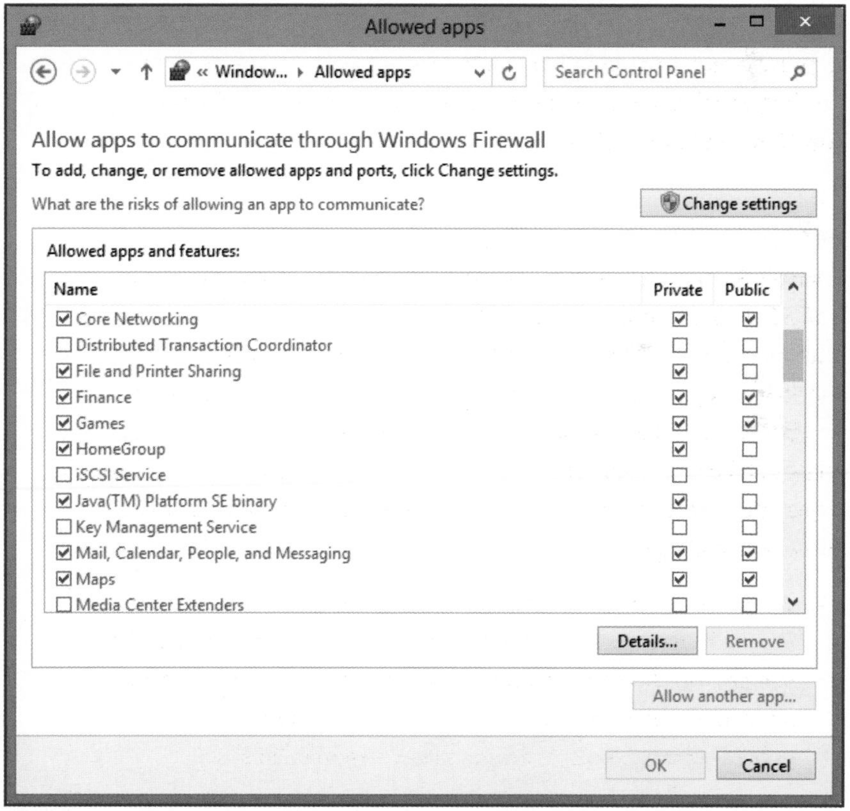

Figure 9-14: Make sure Windows Firewall allows networking.

Chapter 10

Using Networking

Networking brings a vastly enlarged world of computing to you, giving you access to all the computers, printers, and other devices to which you are connected and have permission to access. Using a network and its resources is no more difficult than accessing the hard disk or printer that is directly connected to your computer. Your network connection can be either wired or wireless, and you'll notice no difference, except for the hardware and the possibility that wireless is slower.

In this chapter you'll see how to access other computers and printers over a local area network (LAN), how to let others access your computer and resources, and how to access your computer remotely—across a LAN, through a telephone connection, or over the Internet.

 Note This chapter assumes that you have networking operating on your computer, as discussed in Chapter 9, and that you and others on your network have set up sharing and security parameters such that networking can take place, as described in Chapters 8 and 9.

 Note In many of the steps in this chapter, you may be interrupted and asked by User Account Control (UAC) for permission to change your computer. So long as it is something you started, you should select **Yes** and, if needed, enter an administrator's password. To keep the steps as simple as possible, I have left out the UAC instructions. Chapter 8 discusses UAC in more detail.

ACCESS NETWORK RESOURCES

Begin by looking at the network available to you through your computer. Then access a disk and retrieve files and folders from another computer, use a network printer, and access the Internet over the network.

Explore a Network

Whether you have just installed a small home network or have just plugged into a large company network, the first thing you'll probably want to do is explore it—see what you can see. You can do that from File Explorer.

1. On the desktop, select **File Explorer**, scroll down the navigation pane, and select **Network** to open it. The network resources will be displayed, as you see in Figure 10-1 for my network.

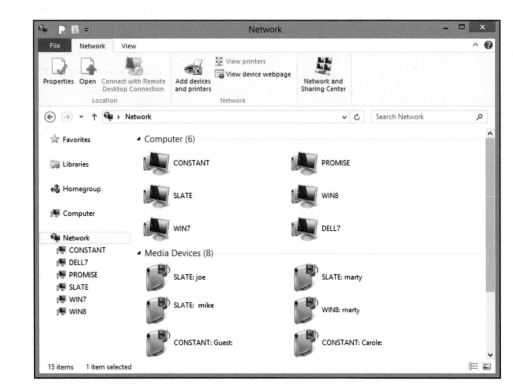

Figure 10-1: Opening your network displays the computers and media that are being shared.

2. Open one of the shared computers on your network. It will open and display the drives, printers, and other resources (such as memory cards, USB flash drives, and removable disks) on that computer.

3. In the navigation pane, select the triangle next to one of the drives to open it, and then select one or more of the folders to see the files available to you (see Figure 10-2).

4. Open other computers, drives, and folders to fully explore your network.

5. Select **Close** to close File Explorer.

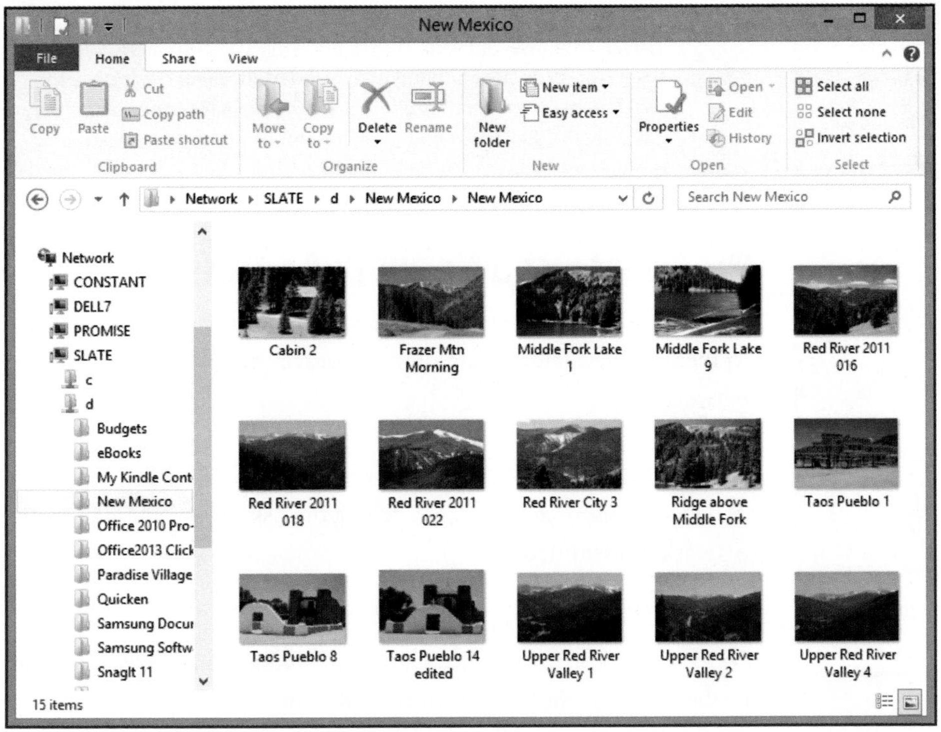

Figure 10-2: If the computers on your network have been shared, you should be able to see the folders, files, and other resources that are available to you. (Courtesy of Tom Beard.)

Tip The shared folders, disks, and other resources that appear when you open your network are the result of your computer having searched your workgroup or domain for shared resources. When you first set up networking, you won't see anything until resources have been shared by other computers and your computer has had time to find them.

Permanently Connect to a Network Resource

If you use a specific network drive or folder a lot, you may want to connect to it permanently so that you can use it as if it were a drive on your computer.

This permanent connection is called a "mapped network drive." Note that it is only "permanent" until you decide to disconnect from the drive. See "Disconnect a Mapped Drive" later in this chapter.

Connect to a Mapped Network Drive

To set up a mapped network drive:

1. On the desktop, select **File Explorer**, scroll down the navigation pane, and select **Network** to open it. The network resources will be displayed, as you saw in Figure 10-1.

   In the navigation pane, select the triangle opposite **Network |** the computer that contains the drive you want to connect to permanently. You should see the drive in the subject pane.

2. Open the context menu for the drive in the subject pane, and select **Map Network Drive** (see Figure 10-3). The Map Network Drive dialog box will appear.

3. Select the drive letter you want to use for the mapped drive or the specific folder, if that is applicable; choose whether you want to reconnect to the drive every time you log on to your computer; and choose whether you need to use different credentials—whether you want to log on to that resource using a different user name and password.

4. Select **Finish**. The drive will open in a separate window. Close that window.

5. In the navigation pane of the original File Explorer window, select the triangle to the left of **Network** to close it. Then, if it isn't already displayed, select **Computer** to open that view. Both in the navigation pane and in the subject pane, you should see the new network drive, as shown in the Network Location area of Figure 10-4.

Figure 10-3: Mapping a network drive gives you a permanent connection to that device.

Note The shared media sources described earlier that appeared when Network was opened also appear in the Network Location area along with mapped drives (as shown in Figure 10-4).

Disconnect a Mapped Drive

1. In File Explorer, scroll down the navigation pane so you can see your mapped drive(s).

> ◢ 💻 Computer
> ▷ 🖴 Local Disk (C:)
> ▷ 🖴 Removable Disk (D:)
> ▷ 🖳 c (\\Win7) (G:)
> ▷ 🖳 Carole (constant)
> ▷ 🖳 Guest (constant)

2. In the navigation pane, open the context menu for the mapped network drive, and select **Disconnect**. The drive will disappear from the navigation and subject panes.

Note If you see an error message saying you have files open on the mapped drive and that you may lose data if you don't close the files before disconnecting, check if you do have files open, and if so, close them. Then once you are sure nothing is open, select **Yes** to disconnect.

⏩ Construct a Network Address

Network addressing uses the *Uniform Naming Convention,* or UNC, to identify files, folders, and other resources on any computer on the network.

Identify a Network Resource

A network resource, which is a folder or disk on a computer on the network, is identified by:

\\computername\drivename\ folder name

For example, on a computer named "Win7," a folder named "2013 Budgets" on the D: drive in the Budgets folder would have the full network address of:

\\Win7\D\Budgets\2013 Budgets

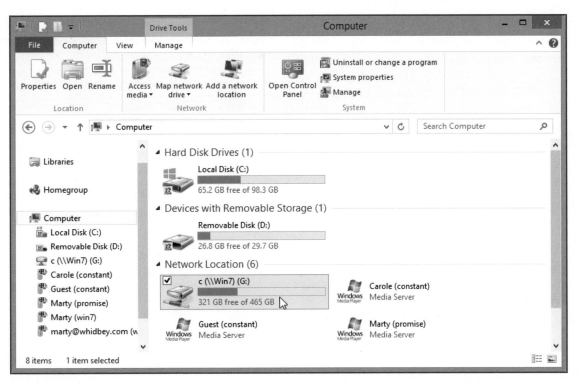

Figure 10-4: You have the same access to a mapped network drive across a network as you do to any drive on your computer.

Identify a Network Printer

Identifying a network printer is similar to identifying any other network resource. It takes the form of:

\\computername\printername

For example, a printer named HP4500 on Server 1 would have the UNC of:

\\Server1\HP4500.

▷▷ Copy Network Files and Information

Once you have opened a network resource, it is easy to copy information from the resource to your local hard disk.

Tip You can copy information between any computers on the network, not just from a network computer to your local computer, *if* you have the necessary permissions.

1. In File Explorer select the triangle opposite **Network** to open it. Then open the computer, drive, and folder(s) in order to see the files that you want to copy in the subject pane.

2. In the navigation pane on your local computer, select the triangle opposite the drive and, if needed, open any parent folder to display the folder you want to hold the information from the network.

3. In the subject pane, select the first file or folder you want to copy, and then hold down **CTRL**, selecting the remaining files and/or folders you want. When all are selected, drag them to the folder in the navigation pane in which you want them, as you can see in Figure 10-5.

4. Close File Explorer.

▷▷ Find or Add a Network Printer

There are two ways to locate a network printer: by using Find Printer in the Print dialog boxes of some apps and by using Add A Printer in the Printers And Faxes dialog box.

Use Find Printer

Recent versions of Microsoft Office products and other apps have included a Find Printer option to search for and locate network printers.

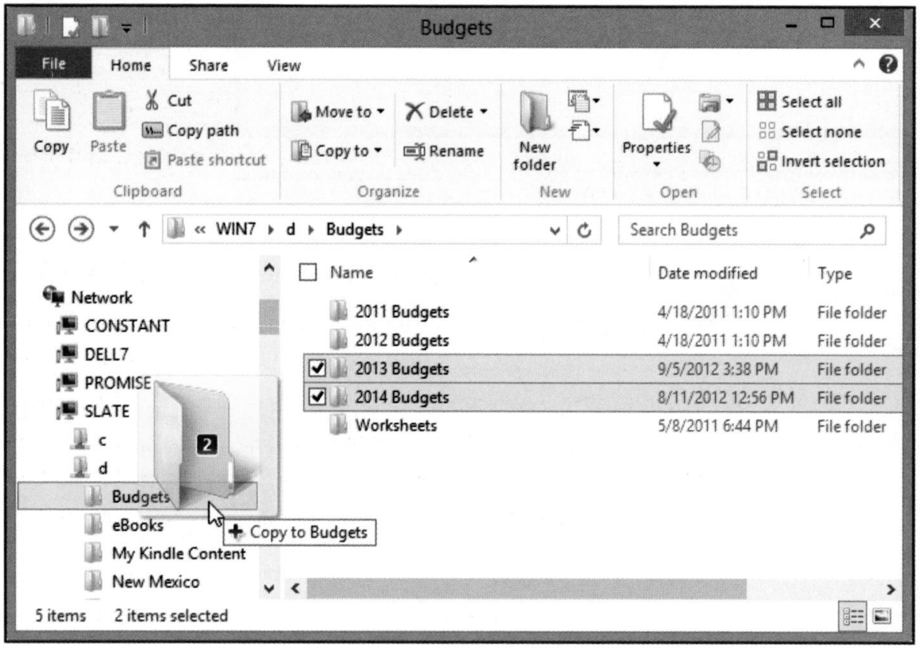

Figure 10-5: You can locate and move or copy files and folders across the network.

This is the same as the printer search capability, which uses the Windows domain's Active Directory service. To use this, you must be in a domain and not in a workgroup.

1. In an Office 2010 or 2013 app, select the **File** tab | **Print** | the **Printer** down arrow | **Add Printer**.

   If your network is not part of an Active Directory domain, you will get a message to that effect. Otherwise, the Find Printers dialog box will appear and begin a search for a printer.

2. A list of printers will be displayed. When you have located the printer you want, open the context menu for that printer and select **Connect**.

3. Close the Search Results window.

Use Add A Printer

Add A Printer is the most common way to locate a network printer, and is available to both workgroup and domain users.

1. Open the **System** menu and select **Control Panel** | **Hardware And Sound** | **Devices And Printers**. The Devices And Printers window opens.

2. Select **Add A Printer**. A list of printers will be presented to you (see Figure 10-6). Select one and skip to step 4.

3. If you don't see a list of printers, select **The Printer That I Want Isn't Listed**. Select **Select A Shared Printer By Name** | **Browse**, open the computer that has the printer you want, and then open the printer. You should see the printer you want in the Add Printer dialog box, as shown in Figure 10-7.

4. Select **Next**. A permanent connection will be made to the printer. Select **Install Driver** if you are asked to do so. Select **Next**.

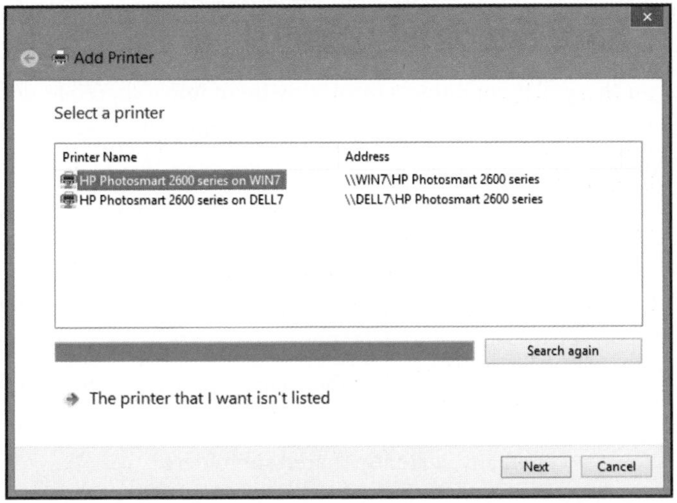
Add Printer
Select a printer
Printer Name
Address
HP Photosmart 2600 series on WIN7
\\WIN7\HP Photosmart 2600 series
HP Photosmart 2600 series on DELL7
\\DELL7\HP Photosmart 2600 series
Search again
The printer that I want isn't listed
Next
Cancel

Figure 10-6: The automatic search for a printer may not find the printer you are looking for if you are not on an Active Directory domain.

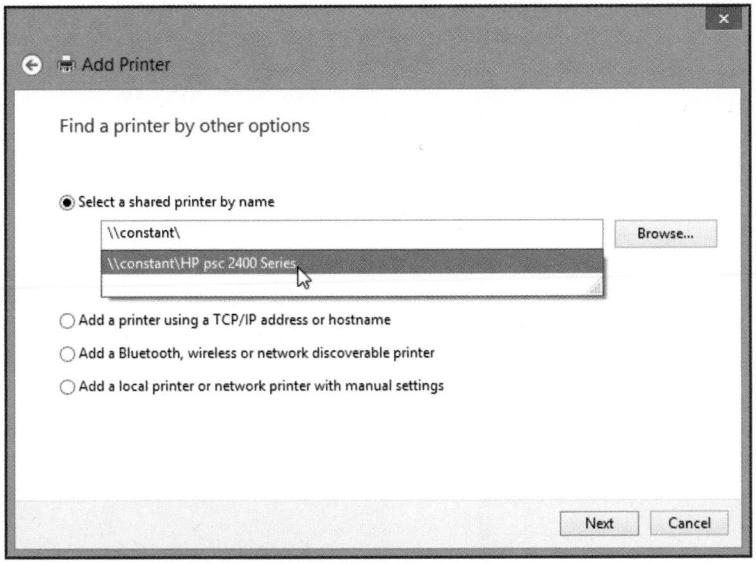
Add Printer
Find a printer by other options
Select a shared printer by name
\\constant\
\\constant\HP psc 2400 Series
Browse...
Add a printer using a TCP/IP address or hostname
Add a Bluetooth, wireless or network discoverable printer
Add a local printer or network printer with manual settings
Next
Cancel

Figure 10-7: If you know of a network computer to which a printer has been attached and it has been shared, you can connect to it easily.

5. If desired, select the **Set As The Default Printer** check box. Select **Print A Test Page**. When a test page prints, select **Close** and then select **Finish**. If a test page does not print, select **Get Help With Printing**, and follow the suggestions.
6. Close Control Panel.

Print on Network Printers

Like using other network resources, using a network printer is not much different from using a local printer. To locate a network printer, see "Find or Add a Network Printer."

To use a network printer that has been previously found, either automatically or manually—from Microsoft Word 2010 or 2013—for example:

1. Select the **File** tab | **Print** to open the Print screen.
2. Under Printer, select the down arrow, and choose the network printer you want to use.

Printer
HP Photosmart 2600 series on Wi...
Ready
HP psc 2400 Series on CONSTANT
Ready

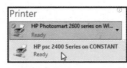

3. Make any needed adjustments to the printer settings, and select **Print** to complete the printing.

Access a Network Internet Connection

If the network you are on has an Internet connection, you are automatically connected to it and can use it directly, unless it requires a user name and password. In most instances, you simply have to open your browser (select the **Internet Explorer** tile on the Start screen or the icon on the desktop's taskbar) or your email app (select the **Mail** tile on the **Start** screen), and you are using the Internet. See Chapter 4 for more information.

Let Others Access Your Resources

The other side of the networking equation is sharing the resources on your computer to allow others to use them. This includes sharing your files, folders, and disks, as well as sharing your printers. The mechanics of setting up your computer to share its resources are discussed in Chapters 8 and 9 (in particular, see Chapter 8). Here we'll look at how that is used once it is turned on.

> **Note** By default, Windows 8 does not share its resources, except in a homegroup, and further protects them with a strong firewall. To share resources, you must set up file and folder sharing and enable the appropriate exceptions in the Windows Firewall, as described in Chapters 8 and 9.

Share Files and Folders

You can share files and folders by putting them into a shared folder. By default, your computer has a series of folders within Libraries beginning with the word "Public" that can be shared; however, these folders aren't shared by default unless you are in a homegroup. You can also create more shared folders (see Chapters 8 and 9).

1. In File Explorer, open the disk and folder(s) needed to locate and display the files and/or folders you want to share in the subject pane.

2. In the navigation pane, select the triangle opposite **Libraries And Pictures** to display the Public Pictures folder. Select its triangle, if shown, to open any currently shared subfolders.

3. Drag the files and/or folders you want to share from the subject pane to one of the Libraries folders in the navigation pane, as shown in Figure 10-8.

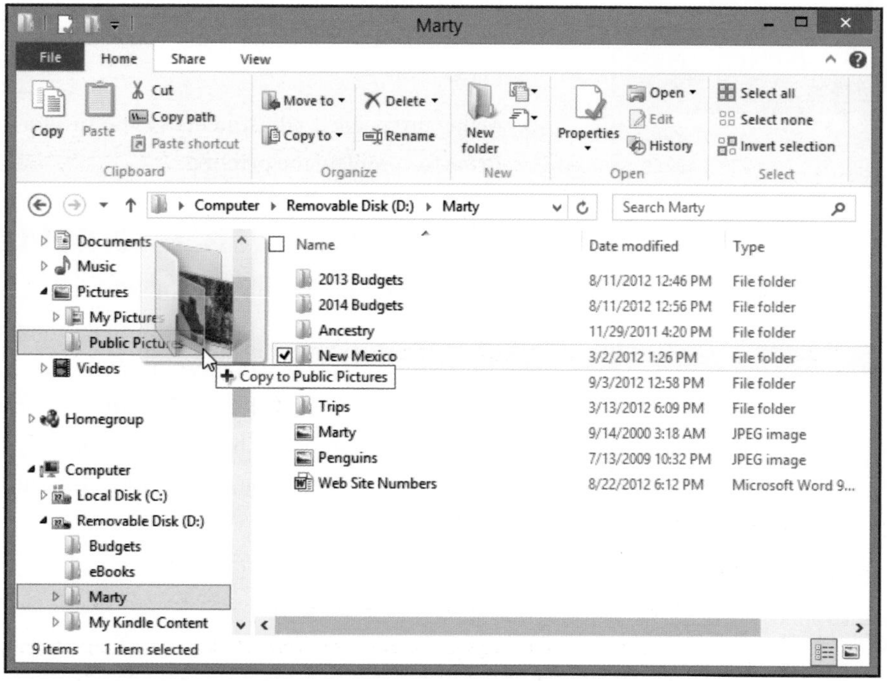

Figure 10-8: You can share a file by putting it into one of the Libraries folders.

> **Note** To share a folder effectively, you may need to provide the user who will be accessing it with the appropriate permissions (see Chapter 8).

WORK REMOTELY

Windows 8 allows you to work remotely from another computer—for example, from a remote computer (like your laptop) to a computer or server in your office—using Windows 8's Remote Desktop Connection. The objective is to transfer information and utilize resources from a distance using a LAN connection. Using Remote Desktop Connection requires both a Remote Desktop host and a Remote Desktop client.

> **Note** Only Windows 7 Professional, Enterprise, and Ultimate editions or Windows 8 Professional and Enterprise editions can be a Remote Desktop host. All versions of Windows 7 and 8 can be a Remote Desktop client, as can Windows Vista and Windows XP.

▷▷ Set Up a Remote Desktop Connection

Remote Desktop Connection enables you to literally take control of another computer and do everything on it as if you were sitting in front of that computer. Remote Desktop Connection is run over a LAN, where the computer you are sitting at is the *client* and the computer you are accessing is the *host*. To set up the host, you must first establish user accounts and then enable a LAN-based host.

Set Up Remote Desktop Users

To use Remote Desktop Connection, a user registered on the host must be a member of the Remote Desktop Users group. Therefore, the first step is to set up one or more users in that group on the host.

1. Open the **System** menu and select **Control Panel | System And Security | Administrative Tools**.

2. In the subject pane, open **Computer Management**. In the Computer Management window that opens, in the left column, if it isn't already open, select the triangle opposite **System Tools** to open it | the triangle opposite **Local Users And Groups** to open it | **Users**. In the list of users in the subject pane, shown in Figure 10-9, open the remote user and select **Properties**.

3. In the user's Properties dialog box that appears, select the **Member Of** tab | **Add**. In the Select Groups dialog box, select **Advanced** and then select **Find Now** to search for groups. Select **Remote Desktop Users**, select **OK** three times, and close the Computer Management and Administrative Tools windows.

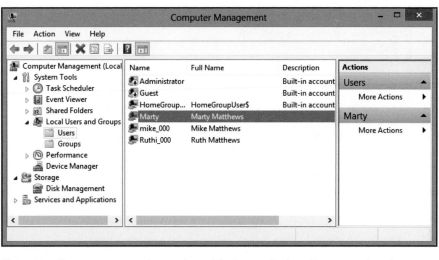

Figure 10-9: User accounts must be members of the Remote Desktop Users group in order to use Remote Desktop Connection.

Set Up a LAN-Based Host

Set up the host for using Remote Desktop Connection within a LAN.

1. In the Control Panel System And Security window, select **System | Remote Settings** on the left. The System Properties dialog box will appear with the Remote tab displayed.

2. In the bottom Remote Desktop panel, select **Allow Remote Connections To This Computer | Allow Connections Only From Computers Running Remote Desktop**, as shown in Figure 10-10.

3. Select **Select Users**. Users that you added to the Remote Desktop Users group are displayed.

4. If you want to add more users, select **Add | Advanced | Find Now**. Select the users you want to include by holding down CTRL while selecting them, and then select **OK** four times to close all open dialog boxes. Close the Control Panel.

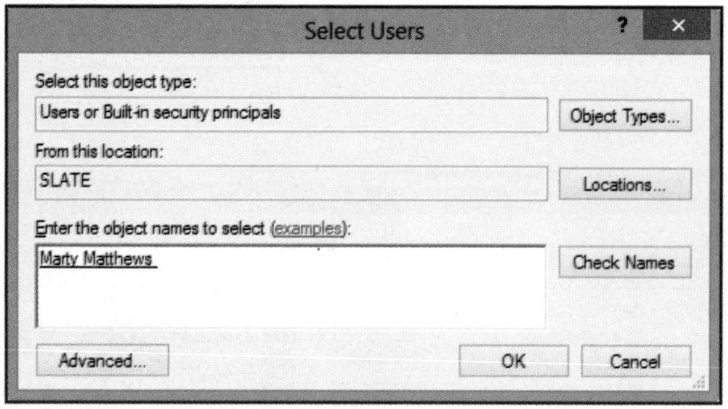

Set Up a Remote Desktop Client

The Remote Desktop Connection client is probably already installed on the computer you will be using for the client, since it is part of the default Windows 8 installation. Verify this, and, if it is not installed, do so.

In the Start screen, begin typing <u>Remote Desktop</u> (you probably do not have to type more than "rem") and press ENTER.

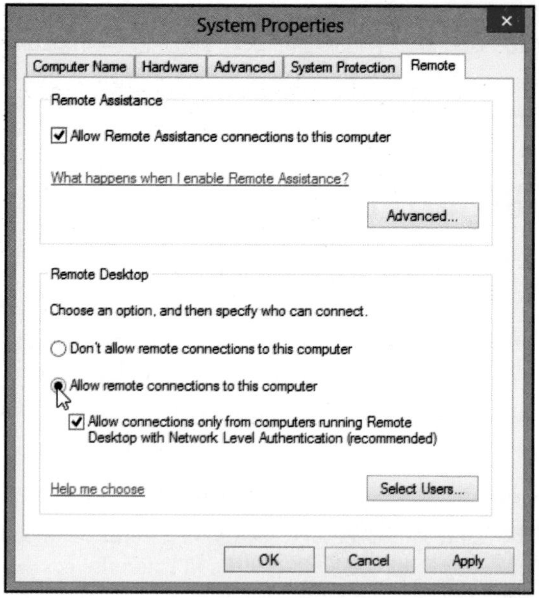

Figure 10-10: Remote Desktop Connection is not turned on by default.

If you see the Remote Desktop Connection dialog box, you need to do nothing further here.

If you do not see Remote Desktop Connection, you'll need to reinstall Windows 8.

Connect to a Remote Desktop over a LAN

When you are sitting at the client computer connected to a LAN to which the host is also connected, you can connect to the Remote Desktop host.

1. In the Remote Desktop Connection dialog box, enter the name or IP address of the computer to which you want to connect in the form *computer name*.

2. After you have entered the computer name, select **Connect**. The Windows Security dialog box appears. Enter the user name and the password you registered for the Remote Desktop Users group on the host computer, and select **OK**.

If you see a message that someone is currently logged on to the remote host, decide if you can disconnect them, and select the appropriate choice. (See "Use a Remote Desktop Connection.")

If you see a message that the remote computer does not have a security certificate from a trusted certifying authority, select **Yes** to go ahead and connect. (You may have created your own certificate in Chapter 8.)

The Remote Desktop toolbar appears in the top center of the screen with the name of the computer that is hosting you, as you can see in Figure 10-11.

Figure 10-11: The Remote Desktop is often used when you are away from your office and want to access your office computer.

▷▷ Use a Remote Desktop Connection

Once you are connected to the host computer, you can perform almost any action that you could if you were sitting in front of that computer—you can run apps, access data, and more. In addition, the Remote Desktop toolbar, called the Connection Bar, provides these controls from left to right:

- **Down arrow** opens a menu of commands for the remote (host) computer:

  - **App Commands** opens the host computer's command bar at the bottom of the window.

  - **Charms** opens Charms.

  - **Snap** snaps the open windows to the right side of the screen.

  - **Start** switches between the Start screen and the desktop.

- **Pushpin** switches between having the Connection Bar always on the desktop and having it only there when you move the mouse to the upper-center portion of the screen.

- **Connection** provides information on the quality of the connection between the client and the host.

- **Minimize** minimizes the remote window to the taskbar with its apps still running. Restore the Remote Desktop window by selecting the **Remote Desktop Connection** icon on the taskbar.

- **Restore** reduces the full-screen Remote Desktop to a smaller window so that you can see the computer you are sitting at (see Figure 10-12).

- **Close** allows you to close the Remote Desktop window without logging out so that your apps will keep running.

Remote Desktop Connection also gives you the ability to transfer information between the host computer and the client computer you are using. This means that you can

- Print to a local printer connected to the client (this is enabled by default)

- Work with files on both the remote host and the client computers in the same window (this is not enabled by default)

- Cut and paste between both computers and documents on either one (this is enabled by default)

The local client resources that are available in a Remote Desktop session are controlled by the Remote Desktop Connection dialog box options.

1. In the Remote Desktop Start screen, begin typing Remote Desktop and press **ENTER**. The Remote Desktop Connection dialog box appears.

2. Select **Show Options**, and the box expands to give you a number of controls for Remote Desktop.

3. Select the **Display** tab. The default for a LAN is to use Full Screen mode and up to the maximum color level your computer can use, as well as to display the Connection Bar.

 Tip If your LAN has particularly heavy traffic and is slow, you might want to lower the screen size and colors.

4. Select the **Local Resources** tab. As you can see in Figure 10-13, you can determine your audio settings, which include bringing sound to the client, and if you want the ability to use shortcut keys. Also

   - If you want to print on the printer attached to the local client, keep the default Printers selection.

   - If you want to transfer information using the Cut and Paste commands between the two computers, the Clipboard should be selected.

10

Figure 10-12: When the Remote Desktop is reduced from full-screen size, the Remote Desktop toolbar, the Connection Bar, disappears.

- If you want to transfer information by dragging between disk drives, select **More** and select **Drives** to select them all; or select the plus sign (+) next to **Drives**, and select individual drives.

- If you intend to use a Plug and Play device on the local client, select that option. Select **OK** when you are finished with Local Devices And Resources.

5. If you want to start an app when you open the Remote Desktop Connection, select the **Programs** tab | the relevant check box, and enter the path and filename of the program and the starting folder to use.

6. Select the **Experience** tab, and select the connection speed you are using. This will determine which of the items below the drop-down list box are selected. You can change the individual items if you want.

7. Select the **Advanced** tab. Look at the choices for authentication, and select the one that is correct for you. If you have to go through a Remote Desktop (RD) Gateway (generally in larger organizations), select **Settings**, select the option that is correct for you, type any needed information, and select **OK**.

Figure 10-13: You can control what client devices are available with Remote Desktop.

8. Select the **General** tab. If you will use several settings, save the ones you just made by selecting **Save As**, entering a name, and selecting **Save**.

9. If you are not already connected, enter your password and select **Connect**. Otherwise, close the Remote Desktop Connection dialog box.

10. When you are done using Remote Desktop, you may leave it in any of three ways:

   ■ Select **Close** on the Connection Bar. This leaves you logged on, and any apps you have will remain running. If you restart Remote Desktop Connection with the host computer and no one else has logged on locally, you will return to the same session you left.

   ■ Select the down arrow in the Connection Bar | **Charms** | **Settings** | **Power** | **Disconnect**. This terminates your Remote Desktop session and all apps are stopped. If you restart Remote Desktop Connection with the host computer and no one else has logged on locally, you will begin a new session.

   ■ Select **Close** in the upper-right area of a reduced Remote Desktop Connection window, select the **Shut Down** right arrow | **Disconnect**. This is the same as selecting the Close button on the Connection Bar.

SET UP AND USE A WIRELESS NETWORK

Wireless networks have become a popular way to create small networks in homes and small businesses for the simple reason that you don't have to run cables everywhere. Even more enticing are the wireless ("Wi-Fi") hotspots in coffee shops, airports, and other public gathering areas. With a wireless access point connected to the Internet, any wireless-enabled computer within approximately 150 feet (46 m) of the access point indoors can connect to the Internet and communicate with any other network-connected or wireless-enabled computer. If the access point is also connected to a wired network, all the members of the wired network are available to the wireless computers. Chapter 9 talked about the hardware requirements needed to do this. Here we will talk about what is needed to set up and use a wireless network in Windows 8 and make it secure.

Note The effective range of a wireless access point is highly dependent on which protocol (802.11b, 802.11g, or 802.11n) you are using ("n" is better than "b" or "g"), the types of walls you have to go through (wood and plaster are better than concrete or metal), and your device—see reviews.cnet.com and search on "wireless access points reviews."

Set Up a Wireless Connection

The first task is to make a connection with a wireless access point and then set it up so its use is secure. If you have a recent computer with wireless capability that is turned on (there may be a small switch on your computer to do that) and is near a wireless access point, your computer will try to automatically connect. In most public Wi-Fi areas you need to enter a network security key to actually connect. If, on the desktop, you select the network connection in the notification area, you will see a message that you are not connected, but a connection is available. Continue from here to set up and secure the connection.

1. If you are within a Wi-Fi hotspot and have a wireless-enabled computer, notice that the wireless icon in the notification area of the desktop's taskbar is dark with a white asterisk in it. If you don't see the wireless icon, skip to step 5.

2. Move the mouse pointer to the taskbar's wireless icon, and you will get the message that you are not connected, but that connections are available. If you don't see this message, skip to step 5.

3. Select the wireless icon to open a panel listing the wireless networks that are locally available. Select the network you want to use. If you want to connect automatically to that network in the future, select that option | **Connect**. If you don't see one or more local networks, skip to step 5.

4. If you have never connected to this network before and it's a protected Wi-Fi network, you'll be asked to enter a network security key. Do that and press **ENTER**. You should see the message "Connected" in the Networks panel. If you don't see the "Connected" message, go to step 5. Otherwise, select any area outside the panel to close it and skip to the next section, "Manage Wireless Network Sharing."

5. If you did not get a connection in the previous steps, open the **System** menu and select **Control Panel | Network And Internet | Network And Sharing Center**. If you are already connected, you will see your connection both graphically and textually. If so, skip to the next section, "Manage Wireless Network Sharing."

Access type:	Internet
HomeGroup:	Joined
Connections:	Wi-Fi (Matthews)

6. If you don't see a wireless connection available, make sure you are within a reasonable distance of a wireless hotspot, that it is turned on, and that it is available for you to use. Private hotspots may not be visible to you.

Manage Wireless Network Sharing

When you use a wireless connection, you most likely do not want other network users to access your computer. That is the default setting, but check and make sure that is the way your connection is set up.

1. If the Network And Sharing Center is not already on your screen, open the **System** menu and select **Control Panel | Network And Internet | Network And Sharing Center | Change Adapter Settings** on the left of the window. The Network Connections window opens, displaying the connections available on the computer.

2. Open **Wi-Fi** to see the Wi-Fi Status dialog box, shown in Figure 10-14.

3. Select **Properties |** the **Sharing** tab, and look at your connection-sharing settings. In most circumstances where you are using a public Wi-Fi hotspot, you do *not* want these check boxes selected, which is the default in a public network. In a home network, the setup shown on the right is the default. The primary instance in which you would want this enabled would be in a secure organizational setting.

Figure 10-14: A wireless network is particularly susceptible to intrusion and needs to be protected.

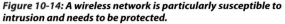

4. When you have assured yourself that the settings are the way you want them, select **OK | Close** in the Status dialog box, and close the Network Connections and the Network And Sharing Center windows.

▷▷ Use a Wireless Network

Once you have a wireless network up and running the way you want, you can use it in the same way you use a wired network.

1. Select the **Internet Explorer** icon on the desktop's taskbar to open this browser, and explore the Web in the same way you would with a wired network, as shown in Figure 10-15.

2. Close Internet Explorer and open your email app, which you can use in the same way as with a wired network connection.

3. Close your mail app, and try any other networking app you use.

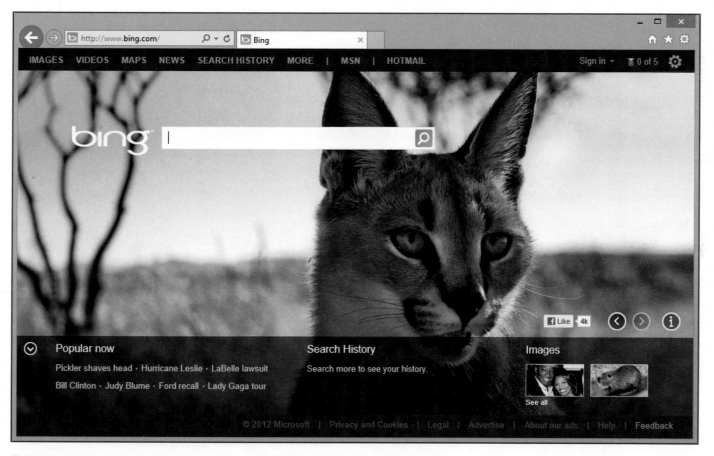

Figure 10-15: You can use a wireless network connection in the same way you used a wired one.

Understand Windows Defender

Windows Defender guards your computer against malware, spyware, and other unwanted apps and replaces third-party antivirus programs. It watches what is happening on your computer and looks for viruses, spyware, and apps that are trying to install themselves or change important Windows settings, both without your approval. Windows Defender does this on a real-time basis, as well as letting you manually start a scan of your computer. It uses a virus and spyware database that tracks, with the user's approval, what apps it thinks might be dangerous.

Review Windows Defender Settings

By default, Windows Defender is running on your computer and you must take some action to turn it off, if that is what you want, although that is not recommended. To open, review, and possibly change the Windows Defender setting:

1. Open the **System** menu and select **Control Panel** | the **Category** down arrow | **Large Icons**, scroll to the bottom, and select **Windows Defender**. Windows Defender appears, as shown in Figure 10-16.

2. Select the **Settings** tab to display the settings you can change to have Defender run the way you want.

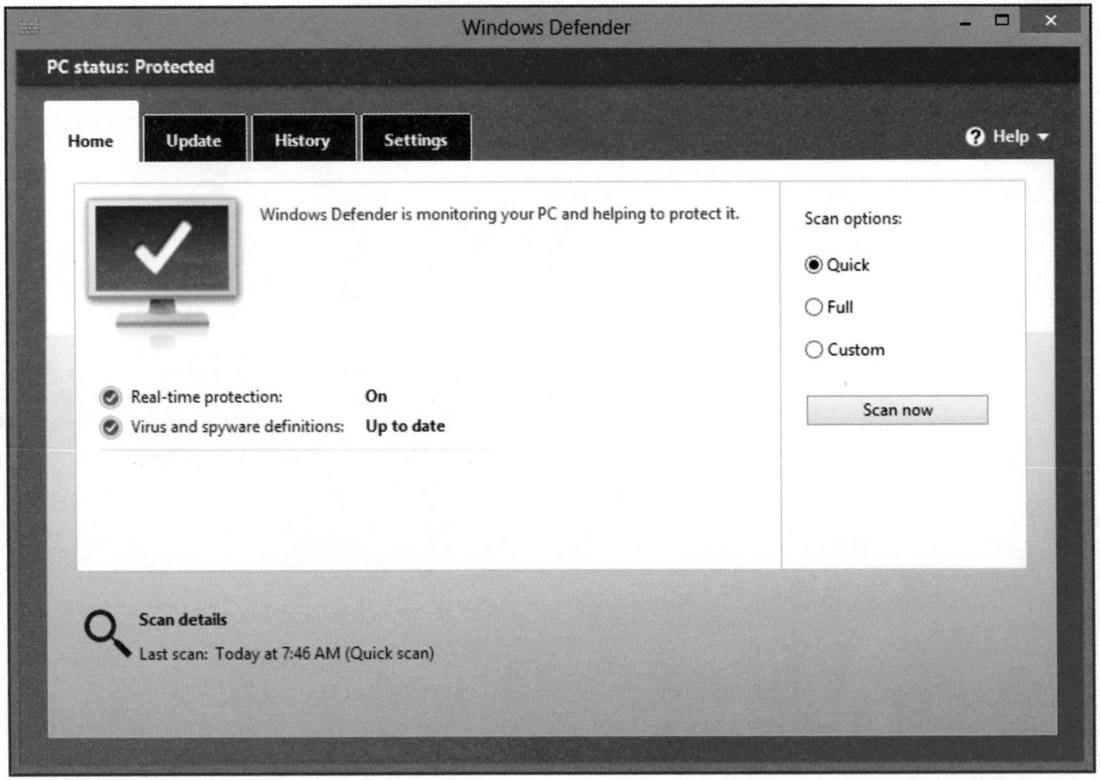

Figure 10-16: Windows Defender provides built-in protection against a number of possible attacks on your computer.

3. Select each of the options on the left, and for each, scroll through the settings and make any changes that meet your needs.

4. One setting that is not set by default, but I that recommend, is in the Advanced options. Select **Scan Removable Drives**. This prevents your bringing a virus or spyware into the computer on a Universal Serial Bus (USB) flash drive.

Real-time protection	☑ Scan archive files
Excluded files and locations	Include any archive files, such as .zip or .cab files.
Excluded file types	
Excluded processes	☑ Scan removable drives
Advanced	Include removable drives, such as USB flash drives, when running a full scan.
MAPS	
Administrator	☐ Create a system restore point
	Create a system restore point before removing, running, or quarantining detected items.

5. When you have finished, select **Save Changes**.

Do a Manual Scan

If you suspect that software you don't want has gotten on your computer, you can run a manual scan to see what Windows Defender finds.

 Note Windows Defender is watching what is happening on your computer all the time to try and prevent viruses, malware, and spyware from being installed. If it sees something, it will stop the process and alert you.

1. Select the Windows Defender's **Home** tab. Select the Scan option you want to use:

   ■ **Quick** scan checks the most likely areas in your computer where a virus or malware could reside.

   ■ **Full** scan checks your entire computer, including running programs, for a virus or malware. This can take an hour or more.

   ■ **Custom** scan lets you choose the drives and folders you want scanned.

2. Select **Scan Now**. The scanning will immediately start (except in the case of a Custom scan). As the scan runs, you will see the progress and be told if anything is found. If a virus or malware is found, follow the prompts to deal with it.

Q **Windows Defender is scanning your PC**

This might take some time, depending on the type of scan selected.

[Cancel scan]

Scan type:	Quick scan
Start time:	12:50 PM
Time elapsed:	00:00:08
Items scanned:	4546

3. When you have finished, select **Close** to close Windows Defender and then close the Control Panel.

Index

Numbers

3G and 4G connections
  availability, 88
  cost per month, 88
  down/up speed, 88
  establishing, 89
  plans, 88
  reliability, 88

Symbol

| (pipe) character, use of, 9

A

A: drive, explained, 67
accessibility options. *See* ease-of-access settings
accessory apps. *See also* apps
  Calculator, 145
  Character Map, 145
  displaying, 144
  Notepad, 145
  Paint, 145–146
Action Center
  changing settings, 121–122
  described, 121
  opening, 121
action terms
  Move, 9
  Open, 9
  Point, 9
  Select, 9
  Start, 9
  Switch, 9
address bar, 70
  described, 18
  identifying, 17
Aero Peek, 23–25. *See also* desktop
  hiding open windows, 25
  returning to desktop after peeking, 24
  turning on, 24
  using, 44–45
Aero Shake, 23, 25

Aero Snaps, 23
  left-aligning floating windows, 26
  maximizing floating windows, 25
  restoring maximized windows, 25
  restoring vertically maximized windows, 26
  restoring windows, 26
  right-aligning floating windows, 26
  vertically maximizing windows, 25–26
Alt key. *See* keyboard shortcuts
antivirus programs. *See* Windows Defender
APIPA (Automatic Private IP Addressing), 235
App bar
  controls on, 20
  displaying in style window, 8
  hiding, 20
  opening, 33
app icons, adding to desktop, 41. *See also* icons
app images, using, 18–20
apps. *See also* accessory apps; desktop apps; hidden apps
  closing, 7, 17–18
  controlling with Task Manager, 141–143
  creating documents with, 148
  downloading and installing, 127–129
  pinning to Start screen, 33
  scheduling, 136–137
  searching, 8
  searching for, 75–77
  seeing options for, 23
  snapping, 8
  starting, 16
  starting in Run dialog box, 143
  starting older, 143–144
  starting on desktop, 10
  stopping, 140–141
  switching, 138–139
  switching among, 8
  switching on desktop, 139
  switching on task list, 139
  switching on taskbar, 139
  taskbar previews, 23
  terminology, 4
archiving attribute, described, 80
attaching files to email, 111–112
audio. *See also* sounds
  controlling volume, 176–177

  playing CDs, 173–176
  Windows Media Player, 174–175
audio files, playing on Internet, 105
Automatic Updates, turning on, 120
autorotate, turning on and off, 8

B

background, changing for Start screen, 36–37
backing up
  encryption key, 211–212
  files, 81–82
  folders, 81–82
  to Internet, 213–214
  with SkyDrive from desktop, 216–219
  with SkyDrive from Start screen, 214–216
broadband connection, explained, 89
browser navigation. *See also* Internet browsing
  Back and Forward buttons, 93–94
  opening context menus, 93
  Pages recently entered button, 93
browsers
  Desktop IE 10, 90
  Internet Explorer (IE) 10, 90
Burn Files to Disc option, choosing, 83
burning
  music CDs, 183–184
  music DVDs, 183–184

C

C: drive, explained, 67
cable TV Internet connection
  availability, 88
  cost per month, 88
  down/up speed, 88
  reliability, 88
Calculator app, 145
Calendar
  adding events, 115–116
  opening, 115
  saving events, 116
  using, 115
camcorder, importing video from, 187–190

camera images, importing, 152–153
cameras, installing, 150–151
capturing screen images, 156–157
CD drive, identifying, 67
CDs. *See also* media
    copyright law, 182
    versus DVDs, 190
    playing, 173–176
    ripping with Media Player, 180–182
    writing files to, 83–85
    writing folders to, 83–85
cellular Internet connections
    availability, 88
    cost per month, 88
    down/up speed, 88
    reliability, 88
Character Map app, 145
Charms
    Devices, 15
    opening, 8, 14
    Search, 15
    Settings, 14
    Share, 15
    Start, 15
chatting in Messaging, 116–118
check boxes, using in dialog boxes, 21
classic window, opening, 18
client-server LANs, 222–223
Clipboard, saving images to, 8
Close button
    described, 18
    identifying, 17
cloud, saving information to, 213–214
colors, changing for desktop, 37–38
Command buttons, using in dialog boxes, 21
command prompt, typing DOS commands at, 143–144
compressing files and folders, 79–81
compression attribute, described, 80
computer
    locking, 8
    terminology, 4
Computer tile, 16–17
connection types. *See* Internet connections
context menus
    jump lists, 26
    opening with keyboard, 7
    opening with mouse, 4
    opening with touch, 6

control keys, 7
Control Panel
    Category view, 49
    Large Icons view, 49
    opening, 48–49, 120
    opening categories, 49–50
    opening components, 49
    reviewing settings in, 192–193
    Small Icons view, 49
controls
    accessing from Settings pane, 20
    opening, 6
    PC Settings, 56
    System menu, 56
    using in dialog boxes, 21
cookies, handling in desktop IE, 103
Copy command, 73–74
copying
    Internet information, 104–105
    network files, 245–246
    network information, 245–246
    pictures from Internet, 105
    text from Internet, 105
Ctrl key. *See* keyboard shortcuts
Cut command, 73–74

D

D: drive, explained, 67
date and time
    requiring administrator permission, 51
    setting, 13, 50–51
defragmentation, 86
deleting
    files, 71
    folders, 71
    fonts, 170
    threads from Messaging program, 118
    Web History in desktop IE, 101–102
desktop. *See also* Aero Peek
    adding app icons to, 41
    Aero Peek, 23–25
    Aero Shake, 23, 25
    Aero Snaps, 23, 25–26
    altering appearance of objects, 40–41
    changing resolution, 38–40
    changing text size, 38–40
    described, 13

displaying, 37
    icons, 13
    interface, 12
    jump lists, 23, 26
    mouse pointer, 13
    navigating, 23–27
    opening from Start screen, 12
    peeking at temporarily, 24
    returning to Start screen from, 13
    seeing hidden parts of, 24–25
    showing and hiding open windows, 8
    showing from notification area, 13
    switching Start screen from, 8
    switching to, 8
    taskbar, 13
    taskbar previews, 23, 27–28
desktop apps. *See also* apps
    closing from keyboard, 141
    closing from taskbar, 141
    displaying thumbnails of, 139
    using Close button with, 141
    using Close command with, 141
    using Exit command with, 141
desktop colors, changing, 37–38
desktop icons
    aligning, 42
    arranging, 42
    renaming, 42
    resizing, 42
desktop IE (Internet Explorer) 10, 90. *See also* IE (Internet Explorer) 10 browser; Internet security in desktop IE
    accessing Web History, 101–102
    adding favorite sites, 96–97
    adding sites to Favorites bar, 101
    changing home page in, 98
    controlling content, 103–104
    controlling Internet security, 102–104
    copying Internet info from, 104–105
    InPrivate feature, 104
    opening favorite sites, 97
    opening menus in, 97
    organizing favorite sites, 100–101
    saving favorite sites, 97
    searching webpages in, 105
    viewing pages in, 105
desktop themes, changing, 37–38
device drivers, finding, 131
devices, sharing, 200
Devices charm, 15

Internet searching
   from Internet Explorer, 94–95
   from sites, 95–96
Internet security in desktop IE. *See also* desktop
   IE (Internet Explorer) 10
   categorizing websites, 102–103
   handling cookies, 103
   Protected Mode, 102
IP addresses
   APNIC (Asia Pacific Network Information Centre), 237
   ARIN (American Registry for Internet Numbers), 236
   entering, 235
   getting block of, 236–237
   obtaining automatically, 235
   private, 236–237
   public, 236–237
   RIPE (Réseaux IP Européens), 236
ipconfig, testing networks with, 237

J

jump lists, 23, 26

K

keyboard. *See also* touch keyboard
   closing desktop apps from, 141
   copying with, 74
   customizing, 54
   displaying Log On screen with, 2
   entering password, 2
   hiding App bar and controls, 20
   moving with, 74
   multiple users on screen, 2
   opening App bar, 33
   opening charms, 14
   opening context menus, 7
   opening objects, 7
   opening tiles, 11
   reordering groups, 35
   selecting objects, 7
   style screen, 19
   switching apps, 138
   using, 6–10
Keyboard icon, 14
keyboard shortcuts, 7. *See also* shortcuts
   closing windows and apps, 7
   Copy command, 73–74

Cut command, 73–74
Ease of Access settings, 51
moving objects, 7
opening system options, 7
Paste Command, 73–74
shutting down, 7
System menu, 61
Windows key combinations, 8
zooming in, 7
zooming out, 7
keyboards
   On-Screen, 8
   split, 8

L

landscape mode, rotating between portrait, 8
Language setting, changing, 55
LANs (local area networks). *See also* WLANs (wireless LANs)
   client-server, 222–223
   peer-to-peer, 222
   in Remote Desktop Connection, 251
   versus WLANs (wireless LANs), 225
Libraries folder, 61
   navigating, 69
   sharing items in, 248
links, using to browse Internet, 93
list box, using in dialog boxes, 21
Lock screen, displaying, 8
locking computer, 8
Log On screen, displaying, 2
logging onto domain, 3

M

Mail program. *See also* email; Web mail
   applying formatting, 110–111
   attaching files to email, 111–112
   color options, 110
   copying addressees, 109
   creating email, 108–109
   editing addressees, 109
   effects options, 110
   establishing email account, 106
   font options, 110
   Forward option, 109
   initiating, 107
   receiving email, 109

removing addressees, 109
Reply options, 109
responding to email, 109–110
sending email, 108–109
size options, 110
style options, 110
malware, protecting computers from, 258–259
mapped network drives
   connecting to, 243–244
   disconnecting, 243–244
maximized windows, restoring, 25
Maximize/Restore button
   described, 18
   identifying, 17
maximizing windows, 8
media. *See also* CDs; DVDs
   accessing online, 177
   buying online, 178–180
Media Player. *See* Windows Media Player
menus
   using, 21–22
   using to browse Internet, 93
messages. *See* Mail program
Messaging program
   chatting, 116–118
   deleting threads, 118
   setting options, 118
   starting, 116–118
Microsoft account, creating for passwords, 195–196
Minimize button
   described, 18
   identifying, 17
minimizing
   current window, 8
   open windows, 25
   windows, 23
mouse
   copying files and folders, 73
   displaying Log On screen with, 2
   entering password, 2
   features, 4
   hiding App bar and controls, 20
   mirror touch, 4–5
   moving files and folders, 73
   moving to corners, 5
   multiple users on screen, 2
   opening App bar, 33
   opening charms, 14

W

Web. *See* Internet
Web History in desktop IE
  deleting, 101–102
  setting, 101–102
  using, 101
Web mail. *See also* Mail program
  Outlook.com, 112–113
  using, 112–113
webpages
  copying from Internet, 105
  copying text from, 105
  indicating, 93
  printing, 164
websites. *See* sites
Wi-Fi connection
  establishing, 89
  explained, 88
window border
  described, 18
  identifying, 17
windows. *See also* floating windows; open windows
  closing, 7–8
  versus dialog boxes, 21–22
  filling part of desktop with, 8
  hiding with Aero Peek, 25
  maximizing, 8
  maximizing vertically, 25–26
  minimizing, 8, 23, 25
  purpose of, 21
  resizing, 23
  restoring, 26
  restoring vertically maximized, 26
  switching to, 4–5
  unhiding windows, 25
  unhiding with Aero Peek, 24–25
Windows 8
  controlling use of, 200
  keyboard, 2
  mouse, 2
  opening, 6
  restoring, 122–124
  starting, 2–3
  touch, 2
  ways of using, 2

Windows 8 IE 10 browser. *See* IE (Internet Explorer) 10 browser
Windows 8 style interface, 10–11. *See also* style screens
Windows Defender
  doing manual scans, 259
  using, 258–259
Windows Firewall, setting up, 201–203, 239
Windows Help, opening, 8. *See also* Help feature
Windows key combinations, 8
Windows Mail. *See* Mail program
Windows Media Player
  Burn feature, 183–184
  controls, 175
  Details pane, 176
  displaying visualizations, 185
  importing video from camcorder, 187–190
  list options, 176
  list pane, 176
  menu options, 175
  navigation pane, 176
  Now Playing, 175
  organizing music, 182–183
  Play To button, 176
  playback controls, 175
  Previous/Next playlist, 176
  randomizing music, 182
  ripping CDs, 180–182
  shop for CD/DVD, 176
Windows sessions, ending, 28
Windows Update, automating, 120–121
Windows views
  desktop, 10
  selecting, 10–13
  Start screen, 11
  Windows 8 style interface, 10–11
wired Ethernet
  cabling, 227
  connecting devices, 226–227
  crossover cables, 227
  hardware, 226–227
  hub, 224
  NIC (network interface card), 224, 226
  router, 224
  switch, 224
  using, 223–224
  UTP (unshielded twisted-pair), 224

wireless 3G and 4G connections
  availability, 88
  cost per month, 88
  down/up speed, 88
  reliability, 88
wireless hardware for networks
  adapters, 228
  selecting, 227–229
  speed, 228
  wireless access points, 229
Wireless icon, identifying, 14
wireless networks
  managing sharing, 256–257
  setting up, 254–259
  using, 257
  Windows Defender, 258–259
WLANs (wireless LANs). *See also* LANs (local area networks)
  802.11* standards, 224–225
  access points, 225
  adapters, 225
  downsides, 225
  versus LANs, 225
Word, copying Internet text from, 105. *See also* documents
workstations, role in client-server LANs, 222
World Wide Web. *See* Internet

X

Xbox Music app
  buying songs, 178
  using, 177–178
  using points, 180

Z

zipping
  files, 80
  folders, 80
zooming in and out
  with keyboard, 7
  with touch, 6

Quick Reference

Actions Taken with Various WINDOWS Key Combinations

Key(s)	Description
WINDOWS	Switches to the Start screen from the desktop and to the desktop from the Start screen once the desktop has been otherwise opened.
WINDOWS+ 1, 2...	Switches to the desktop and opens the first, second, etc., application on the taskbar.
WINDOWS+B	Switches to the desktop and selects the notification area.
WINDOWS+C	Opens Charms.
WINDOWS+D	Shows the desktop, hiding open windows.
WINDOWS+E	Switches to the desktop and opens File Explorer.
WINDOWS+F	Searches files.
WINDOWS+H	Opens the Share pane.
WINDOWS+I	Opens the Settings pane.
WINDOWS+K	Opens the Devices pane.
WINDOWS+L	Locks the computer and displays the Lock screen.
WINDOWS+M	Switches to the desktop and minimizes the current window.
WINDOWS+O	Turns a tablet's autorotate between portrait and landscape on or off.
WINDOWS+P	Opens the settings for a projector.
WINDOWS+Q	Searches apps.
WINDOWS+R	Switches to the desktop and opens Run.
WINDOWS+U	Switches to the desktop and opens the Ease of Access Center.
WINDOWS+W	Searches settings.
WINDOWS+X	Opens the System menu.
WINDOWS+Z	In a Windows 8 style window, displays the App bar.

WINDOWS+.	Snaps an app first to the right side of the screen and then to the left.
WINDOWS+TAB	Switches among apps.
WINDOWS+ HOME	Closes all but the selected window on the desktop. When pressed a second time it reopens all windows originally open.
WINDOWS+F1	Opens Windows Help.
WINDOWS+ PRT SCN	Saves an image of the screen to the Clipboard; **+ALT** saves just the open window.
WINDOWS+ UP ARROW	Maximizes the selected window. If this is followed by **WINDOWS+ DOWN ARROW** the window is restored to its original size.
WINDOWS+ DOWN ARROW	Minimizes the selected window, unless the window was originally maximized, in which case the window is restored to its original size.
WINDOWS+ LEFT ARROW	The selected window fills the left 50 percent of the desktop. If this is followed by **WINDOWS+RIGHT ARROW** the window is restored to its original size.
WINDOWS+ RIGHT ARROW	The selected window fills the right 50 percent of the desktop. If this is followed by **WINDOWS+LEFT ARROW** the window is restored to its original size.
WINDOWS+ SHIFT+ UP ARROW	The selected window fills the desktop vertically, but maintains its previous width. If this is followed by **WINDOWS+SHIFT+DOWN ARROW** the window is restored to its original size.

Special Control Keys

Key(s)	Description
ALT+F4	Close a window or an app
ALT+SHIFT+ARROW KEYS	Move the selected object on the screen in the direction of the arrow keys
CTRL+plus sign key (+)	Zoom in
CTRL+minus sign key (−)	Zoom out
CTRL+ALT+DEL	Open system options, including ones for shutting down

Quick Reference

Implementing Common Terms with a Mouse, Touch, and a Keyboard

Action Term	With a Mouse	With Touch	With a Keyboard
Select an object on the desktop, in a window or dialog box, or on a menu	**Click** the object	**Tap** the object	Use **TAB** or the **ARROW KEYS** to highlight the object
Start an app in the Start screen	**Click** the tile	**Tap** the tile	Select the object and press **ENTER**
Open an object on the desktop such as a window or folder	**Double-click** the object	**Double-tap** the object	Select the object and press **ENTER**
Start an app on the desktop	**Double-click** the app	**Double-tap** the app	Select the object and press **ENTER**
Open an object's context menu	**Right-click** the object	**Touch** and hold for a moment, then release	Select the object and press the **CONTEXT-MENU** key
Open the app bar for an app	**Right-click** the app	**Swipe down** the app	Select the object and press the **CONTEXT-MENU** key
Move an object on the screen	**Drag** the object with the mouse	**Drag** the object with your finger	Select the object and press **ALT+SHIFT+ARROW KEYS**
Point on an object such as a title bar or border	Move the mouse so it is on the object	Move your finger so it is over the object but not touching it	Use **TAB** and **ARROW KEYS** to select the object
Switch to the desktop from the Start screen	**Click** the desktop tile	**Tap** the desktop tile	Press **WINDOWS+D**
Switch to the Start screen	**Point** to the lower-left corner of the screen and click	**Swipe** from the right edge and tap the **Start** icon	Press **WINDOWS**
Switch to another running app	**Point** to the upper-left corner, move down, and click the app	**Swipe** from the left edge until the app opens	Press **WINDOWS+TAB**
Open Charms	**Point** to the lower-right corner and move up	**Swipe** from the right	Press **WINDOWS+C**